James T. Rapier and Reconstruction

Negro American Biographies
and Autobiographies

John Hope Franklin, Series Editor

Loren Schweninger

James T. Rapier and Reconstruction

The University of Chicago Press

Chicago and London

The University of Chicago Press, Chicago 60637
The University of Chicago Press, Ltd., London

Printed in the United States of America
82 81 80 79 78   9 8 7 6 5 4 3 2 1

Library of Congress Cataloging in Publication Data

Schweninger, Loren.
  James T. Rapier and Reconstruction.

  (Negro American Biographies and autobiographies)
  Bibliography: p.
  Includes index.
  1. Rapier, James T., 1837–1883.   2. Reconstruc-
tion—Alabama.   3. Politicians—Alabama—Biography.
I. Title.   II. Series.
E185.R3S38   328.73′092′4 [B]   77–81734
ISBN 0–226–74240–7

Unrevised parts of chapter 1 appeared in *Journal of Negro History* 60 (Jan. 1975): 29–44. © 1975 by The Association for the Study of Negro Life and History, Inc., and in *Civil War History* 22 (Dec. 1976): 293–307. ©1976 by Kent State University Press. An unrevised part of chapter 2 appeared in *Civil War History* 20 (March 1974): 23–34. © 1974 by Kent State University Press. An unrevised part of chapter 3 appeared in *Ontario History* 67 (June 1975): 91–194. © 1975 by The Ontario Historical Society. Unrevised parts of chapter 7 appeared in *The Alabama Review* 28 (July 1975): 185–201. © 1975 by The University of Alabama Press, and in *The Alabama Historical Quarterly* 32 (Fall and Winter 1970): 129–56. An unrevised part of chapter 8 appeared in *The Alabama Review* 29 (April 1976): 83–103. © 1976 by The University of Alabama Press.

LOREN SCHWENINGER is assistant professor of history at the University of North Carolina—Greensboro.

For Patricia

Fight on in the noble cause, and we will anchor by and by. It is the old war over again, of right against the lie, but on our side is right and truth. Who can doubt the result? If all classes of us will only drop our political animosities, stop our bickerings, and work with a will for the good of a common country, ever holding fast to the great truths of liberty, a wide, deep sea of prosperity awaits our beloved State and nation.

Contents

Contents

Series Editor's Foreword

Despite revisionist writings on reconstruction, the distortions, misconceptions, misrepresentations, and passionate advocacy continue to blur our understanding of the era following the Civil War. Central to that misunderstanding have been the contemporary and later portrayals of those Negro Americans who played leading roles in the reconstruction drama. At the turn of the century a prominent historian described them as "penniless black dupes" under the control of unscrupulous carpetbaggers and treacherous scalawags. More recently a distinguished historian depicted them as harmless, for the most part, but suffering from a bad reputation made by those among them who were loud-talking, "unscrupulous troublemakers or innane ninnies." As long as such views prevail, it is virtually impossible to obtain a clear picture of what actually happened and what was the real character of the blacks who participated in reconstruction.

One must not underestimate the difficulty that one encounters in attempting to draw an accurate picture of reconstruction. The general difficulties are compounded when one attempts to write about blacks during that period. As Professor Loren Schweninger points out in a most illuminating discussion of the materials used in this work, the scarcity of the sources in Negro American biography is matched only by the biases and inadequacies of white testimony, which has usually been the principal and, at times, the only source for such biography. Happily, in this biography of James T. Rapier, Professor Schweninger did not rely on white testimony not merely because there were letters and other primary materials left by Rapier and other Negro Americans that refuted or blunted the white testimony, but also because he was convinced that in order to get a full understanding of the views and activities of Rapier and his

associates, a different perspective—he calls it a black perspective—
was called for. The materials were relatively sparse and quite
scattered, but the author pursued them relentlessly—in Ottawa,
Washington, St. Louis, Montgomery, New Orleans, and numerous
other places.

In the pages of this book James T. Rapier—teacher, member of
Congress, astute farmer and businessman, and widely traveled
observer of the human condition—comes to life in a unique way.
Here is a Negro American who is both articulate and visible. There
is a full account of the Rapier family, of the parents' aspirations for
their children, of the son's education and teaching career in
Canada, and of his decision to return to his native Alabama. In
dealing with Rapier's entry into politics and his leadership, it was
not necessary for Professor Schweninger to rely on Rapier's white
critics to discover what he was up to. There were times when the
white press greeted his vigorous campaigning with complete
silence. But Rapier told his side of every important event, from his
role in the Alabama constitutional convention, to why he ran for
Congress, to how he felt when his life was threatened by his
enemies.

There is in this work yet another important revelation. In his
account of reconstruction in Alabama, the author brings to light
several matters that have hitherto been explored inadequately if at
all. He makes it clear that in Alabama the bitter rivalries among
Republican factions weakened the party about as much as anything
the Democrats ever did and were on several occasions responsible
for Republican defeat. There were not only rivalries between
conservative and Radical Republicans but also between black and
white Republicans and even among black factions. The picture that
emerges is no less complex but remarkably different from most
accounts of either white Reconstruction or black Reconstruction.
And because new perspectives are provided, the picture is in much
better focus.

JOHN HOPE FRANKLIN

Acknowledgments

This study began in John Hope Franklin's 1969 seminar on Alabama reconstruction at the University of Chicago. Over the years Professor Franklin has made suggestions, offered constructive criticism, read and reread various drafts. His example of rigorous scholarship and genuine concern has been a continual source of strength and inspiration. I am also very grateful to Arthur Mann of the University of Chicago; Joseph Logsdon of Louisiana State University, New Orleans; William Cohen of Hope College, Michigan; Richard Fuke of Wilfrid Laurier University, Ontario, Canada; and Eugene Pieter Feldman of the DeSable Museum of African-American history. At one time or another they have all either offered rigorous criticism or made valuable suggestions.

It has been my good fortune to have four colleagues at the University of North Carolina at Greensboro who have taken a deep interest in my research and writing. Richard Current read the entire manuscript twice and made numerous suggestions for its improvement. The questions raised by Allen Trelease provided a basis for rethinking several aspects of the problem. Richard Bardolph offered numerous substantive and stylistic suggestions. And Robert Calhoon, a major source of gentle encouragement, read and criticized several chapters. This generous assistance, as well as two grants from the Faculty Research Council, an Excellence Fund Faculty Summer Fellowship, and the congenial atmosphere at the University of North Carolina at Greensboro have greatly facilitated the research and writing of this study.

Having visited some one hundred libraries, archives, and courthouses in the course of my research, I have accumulated more debts than I can properly acknowledge. Several librarians and archivists went far beyond the call of duty. Among them were James Walker and his staff at the National Archives; Milo Howard and his assistants at the Department of Archives and History in Montgomery; Dorothy Porter at the Moorland-Spingarn Research Center, Howard University; as well as the staffs at Fisk University and the Tennessee State Library in Nashville. I would also like to express a special note of gratitude to Margaret Fitzsimmons, who typed this study as a dissertation as a warm expression of friendship, and to my father, Ivan Schweninger, who spent a good deal of time going over the manuscript in its various stages, and suggested ways of improving the prose. Sara Tillery and Nancy Berg efficiently typed later drafts. Patricia Eames Schweninger spent a summer doing research in Alabama, listened to stories ad nauseam about the Rapier family, and typed two early drafts while keeping things going at home. None of those who provided assistance, however, should be held accountable for any errors contained herein.

Prologue

On April 26, 1870, the morning stillness on capitol hill in Montgomery, Alabama, was broken by the sound of cannon fire. Only nine years before, on the same hill, a cannon salute had celebrated the formation of the Confederate States of America; but now, after four years of Civil War, the emancipation of three and a half million slaves, and the beginning of congressional reconstruction, the firing signaled a different kind of celebration. Through the streets of the capital, on horseback, astride mules, walking, in wagons and carriages, came five hundred recently emancipated slaves, assembling at the very spot where Jefferson Davis had announced the bombardment of Fort Sumter and near a fading sign that read "Negro Brokers." Forming a two-block-long procession, complete with bandwagon, military company, banners of President Grant, and national flags, the freedmen and freedwomen began wending their way, two abreast, through the streets of Montgomery—down Market to Perry, and out Perry to a field near the West Point railroad station. Numbering nearly a thousand, they clustered around a temporary rostrum, awaiting a speech from one of their brethren.

As the gathering quieted, a tall, fully-bearded, well-dressed black man rose from a chair on the stage, and with an air of dignity and confidence, stepped forward to address the audience. "Fellow Citizens, It affords me much pleasure to meet and participate with you in celebrating the ratification of the Fifteenth Amendment to the Constitution of the United States," Alabama-born James Rapier began. "I shed no tears at the breaking up of the Federal Government, for so far as the negro was concerned, it had been a cheat and a sham, and its flag, the sacred emblem of liberty, was 'a flauntin' lie.' "[1] But now, according to the law of the land, the right of a

xiv   Prologue

citizen to vote would not be denied because of race, color, or
previous condition of servitude. The future held great promise,
Rapier explained with undisguised optimism. Half a million black
children had already learned to read and write; as many black
adults had acquired land; and politically, blacks had progressed
from nominal freedom in 1866, to become voters, officeholders,
and now United States senators. Fight on with this noble cause, he
commanded, in a deep, powerful voice. Who could doubt the
result? If Americans—black and white—would only drop their
political animosities, stop their bickering, and work for the common good, a wide, deep sea of prosperity would await the state and
nation. That blacks in the cradle of the old Confederacy, under the
protection of the Constitution of the United States, could now cast
their ballots beside their former masters was indeed reason for
sanguinity. The Montgomery celebration, and others like it across
the South, marked the apogee of the nineteenth-century black
struggle for full citizenship.

Yet such events, so vital to understanding black participation in
reconstruction, have received little attention from historians. The
first chroniclers of the period, imbued with turn-of-the-century
"scientific" racism, ignored the serious intentions of blacks.
Authors like John W. Burgess, James Ford Rhodes, and William
Archibald Dunning asked How could uncivilized, semi-barbaric
Negroes have contributed anything worthwhile to southern civilization? Inherently simpleminded, indolent, and subservient, blacks
had no pride in their race, no control over their sex urges, no
aspirations or ideals. "During Reconstruction, they left no mark on
the legislation of their time," proclaimed Rhodes, the most influential American historian of his day. "None of them, in comparison with their white associates, attained the least distinction."[2]
    The first historian of Alabama reconstruction, Walter Lynwood
Fleming, also viewed the activities of Negroes with disdain. The
penniless black dupes, he said, under the control of impecunious
Northern intruders, or carpetbaggers, and traitorous Southern
villains, or scalawags, organized a secret oath-bound society, the
Union League, as well as a powerful, unified, political organization, the Republican party. They then murdered innnocent whites,
raped white women, corrupted an honest government, and pressed
for complete "social equality."[3] Negro rule was the nadir in
Alabama history.

At the same time, Fleming contended that Conservative white Alabamians, magnanimous and honor-bound, attempted to work in behalf of freedmen, but after six years of failure, these whites finally fused into a single homogeneous party and peacefully overthrew their oppressors. Before the war, in 1865, and during the early period after the war, he wrote, political divisions among whites had been sharply drawn; there had been no "Solid South"; and within the White Man's Party there had been extreme differences. But the incubus of Negro domination had forced whites to unite. Like Burgess, Rhodes, and Dunning, Fleming sterotyped Negroes as mindless and uncivilized, and, enlisting his sympathies squarely on the side of white southern Conservatives, looked upon their participation in reconstruction as a tragedy.

Such sterotypes did not go unchallenged. Early in the twentieth century, authors W. E. B. DuBois and John Roy Lynch, and later, historians Alrutheus A. Taylor and Horace Mann Bond offered alternatives to the traditional or conservative (so-called because of their identification with the Southern Conservative political party) interpretation of reconstruction. They told of glittering Negro civilizations in Africa; the desire of freedmen to maintain amicable relations with whites; and the intelligence, moderation, and honesty of most black reconstruction leaders. "There was one thing that the white South feared more than Negro dishonesty," DuBois asserted, in an oft-repeated statement, "and that was Negro honesty, knowledge, and efficiency."[4] In addition, historian Vernon Lane Wharton described many black politicians as men of integrity and substance. In Mississippi, he said, Negroes who became United States congressmen, senators, and state officials were all men of outstanding ability. Despite this challenge, called revisionism, as late as 1950 most historians uncritically accepted the turn-of-the-century interpretation.

Since then, however, there has been a general reappraisal of almost every aspect of reconstruction. Historians have investigated in some detail the motives and backgrounds of so-called carpetbaggers and scalawags; the origins of the Fourteenth and Fifteenth Amendments; the constitutional and economic problems of the period; the politics of Lincoln, Johnson, and Grant; the principles of congressional leaders, and the questions of amnesty, disfranchisement, and impeachment; the rise of the Ku Klux Klan and the Southern Democracy; "redemption"; and many other subjects.

Revisionists (as evidenced by recent revisionist studies of the period) emphasize the complexity of the era, suggest the biracial, bipartisan, and bisectional (words used by DuBois) nature of ignorance, corruption, and greed, and sympathetically examine the behavior of blacks. The recent outpouring of scholarship (and perhaps, with the exception of Negro slavery, no aspect of American history has received more attention) has been so exhaustive that revisionism is now the new orthodoxy.

But with few exceptions, the revisionists have not asked the basic questions of how blacks functioned in reconstruction, how they viewed reconstruction, and what changes took place in the black community during reconstruction? And if little is known about the role (rather than the behavior) of freedmen, even less is known about Negro leaders—the black reconstructionists. For many, the simplest biographical information (place of birth, status at birth, color of parents, amount of education, and family background) is shrouded in mystery. And for most, important questions remain unanswered: How did these leaders gain political power? Did they represent the wishes of the black masses? Did they work to improve the educational and economic conditions of their race? Did they resist violence and intimidation? Could they have taken any effective measures to prevent the overthrow of reconstruction? Did they cooperate with white politicians: natives (so-called scalawags), Northerners (so-called carpetbaggers), and national party leaders? Did they attach any significance to the black convention movement? Despite the fact that historians, both traditionalist and revisionist, readily admit that the Negro is the central figure of reconstruction, they have failed to examine the postwar era through the eyes of blacks.

The few attempts to fill this void have obscured rather than illuminated the role of blacks in reconstruction. Relying on conjecture and myth, recent studies of black reconstructionists are replete with factual errors, misrepresentations, and vague speculations. Biographies of P. B. S. Pinchback (Louisiana), Josiah Walls (Florida), and Robert Brown Elliott (South Carolina) neglect basic inquiries: Who were Elliott's parents? Where was he born? Where did he receive his education? Even works which might be considered more scholarly are marred by fundamental weaknesses. A thin biography of Robert Smalls (South Carolina) ignores such indispensable primary sources as the *New National Era* (the most important black reconstruction newspaper), local probate records, and statements of blacks before congressional committees. And a volume titled *First Freedom: The Responses of Alabama's Blacks to Emancipation and Reconstruction* relies almost entirely on the testimony of white planters, white newspaper editors, and white Freedmen's Bureau officials. The *actual* responses of blacks, in their own words, appear only thirty-two times in over two hundred pages. In a similar manner, a sketchy account of Negro political leader Jack Turner (Choctaw County, Alabama) is merely a summary of white newspaper editorials and white court testimony, telling us more about what others thought of Turner than about Turner himself.

The most serious deficiency of these studies, however, is that they lack information about the antebellum period. Not only are the most basic inquiries unanswered, but a host of essential questions about prewar black enterprise, family relations, mobility (both vertical and horizontal), education, values, lifestyles, and day-to-day activities are simply ignored. Although recent scholarship has greatly expanded our knowledge of slaves and slavery as well as of free Negroes, the same initiative and imagination have not been brought to an investigation of the prewar backgrounds of the black reconstructionists. In most cases the same errors are repeated in sketch after sketch and book after book. In short, recent writings, based on inadequate research, relying on mythology, lacking a black perspective, and ignoring the antebellum era, have done little to deepen our understanding of the black reconstructionists.

In this study of James T. Rapier, I hope to show that it is possible to examine in detail the role of blacks in reconstruction, to see events through the eyes of an intelligent and ambitious Negro leader, and from that perspective to view the seemingly familiar events of reconstruction in fresh detail and intricacy. Born of free black parents in Florence, Alabama, a quarter-century before the Civil War (1837) and educated in Canada (1856–1864), Rapier emerged during reconstruction as one of the South's outstanding black political leaders. Idealistic, yet tough-minded, only four months after Appomattox (in a keynote address to the Tennessee Negro Suffrage Convention) he told Southern whites: "We know the

burdens of citizenship and are ready to perform them."[5] He later
(1867) served as chairman of the Platform Committee at the first
Alabama Republican state convention, helping to draft a document, which, among other proposals, called for free speech, free
press, free schools, and equal rights for all—white and black. He
served both as Assessor (1871–1873) and Collector (1878–1883) of
Internal Revenue, representative to the International Exposition in
Vienna (1873), and was editor and publisher of the Montgomery
Republican Sentinel. A leading figure in the black labor movement, he attended three national conventions (1869–72), organized
the first state affiliate of the National Negro Labor Union (the
Alabama Negro Labor Union), and constantly spoke out against
the deplorable condition of black tenant farmers. He was the first
black candidate for state office in Alabama (1870), and, though
defeated, he later (1872) won a seat in the United States Congress,
where he pushed through legislation making Montgomery a port of
delivery, proposed a bill to improve the public education systems
of the South, and delivered a powerful speech in support of the
1875 Civil Rights Act. After reconstruction, though defeated in two
races for Congress (1874, 1876), he continued his struggle to assist
freedmen in the quest for political rights, economic opportunity,
and social dignity.

Contemporary observers compared Rapier (in stature, influence,
and intelligence) to Frederick Douglass; and historians have placed
him among the most effective of the black reconstructionists. Yet,
like other nineteenth-century Negro leaders, much of his life is
veiled in mystery. Various secondary sources (both specific and
general) have incorrectly stated that he was the son of a wealthy
white planter and a slave; that he attended Franklin College
(Nashville), Montreal College (Quebec), and the University of
Glasgow (Scotland); that he studied law, passed the bar, and
entered the legal profession; that he served in the Forty-second
Congress (1871–1873) as a senator, and at the Tennessee constitutional convention (1865); that he represented the United States at
the Paris International Exposition and received an appointment as
voter registrar (1867); and that he ran against Nicholas Davis for
Alabama secretary of state. Other studies have maintained, falsely,
that he urged black workers to revolt against white property
owners, attempted to force "social equality" on the white race, and
entered politics for his own personal aggrandizement. One author-

ity asserted, with no supporting evidence, that he lacked influence
among blacks, especially when compared with Alabama's Jeremiah
(Jere) Haralson, who was "a better natural politician."[6] Another
pictured the stately, reserved, and erudite Rapier, who usually
traveled by train, mounted on a swift steed, riding at a gallop
across the Alabama Black Belt distributing subversive leaflets, "his
full black coat flapping in the breeze."[7] Still another, examining
Republican activists during reconstruction, failed to mention
Rapier in a chapter concerning party leadership.

It is perhaps a significant comment on the present status of
mid-nineteenth-century black biography that no source indicates
the correct occupation of Rapier's father (a free black barber), the
precise location of his schooling (Buxton and Toronto, Ontario), or
the transformation of his political philosophy (from moderate to
radical), much less the significance of his multisided career as a
teacher, newspaperman, plantation manager, labor leader, editor,
publisher, public speaker, internal revenue officer, congressman,
emigrationist, and leader of his race.

It is not surprising that so little is known about Rapier. Even
sympathetic white contemporaries (on whose testimony much of
the present literature is based) had vague notions about his
background, influence, and character. Three days after he spoke at
the voting rights celebration in Montgomery, for instance, the
Alabama State Journal, one of the South's leading Republican
newspapers, ran a half-column article on Rapier, a fellow Montgomerian and the state's most prominent black reconstructionist. It
said that he had been born a slave. In bondage he had been
obedient, respectful, and patient, seeking no special privileges at
the cost of another's injury. Knowing that justice would triumph,
he had foreseen, from the gloom and discouragement of slavery,
the coming of a glorious day. If contemporaries, even those
supportive of black aspirations, could be so misinformed, it is little
wonder that historians have been misled.

But the major purpose of this study is not to correct factual
errors. It seeks rather to examine the sweeping social, economic,
and political developments during the nineteenth century through
the mind of an intelligent, sensitive, dedicated, and astute black
leader. Such an investigation, by nature, is not without certain
limitations: an emphasis on the importance of one man's life; a
reliance on little-known and, at times, seemingly inconsequential

facts; the necessity (especially considering the present state of black biography in the middle period) of examining Rapier's family and educational background in some detail; and the need (again in light of recent studies) to document primary source material as accurately as possible. At the same time, an in-depth study of the life and times of James Rapier, including his slave and free black antecedents, his schooling in Canada, and his accomplishments and failures after the Civil War, offers a new perspective on a period of far-reaching change—change of greatest significance perhaps for those whose skin marked them apart from the majority of their countrymen. Seen in this light the gathering of Montgomery blacks to solemnize the passage of the Fifteenth Amendment was an historic event, one of many in the long struggle of blacks to achieve full equality.

1

Slave Antecedents

Equality was only an illusion when blacks were sold on the auction block, forced to work on white-owned plantations, brutalized because of their color, denied legal recourse, and looked upon as ignorant, immoral, and uncivilized. Even the most talented, resourceful, and energetic could aspire to little more than economic self-sufficiency—a "quasi-freedom." In spite of this, Negroes confronted their condition with an enormous resiliency. Although an examination of a single black family (the antecedents of James Rapier) and black community (Nashville) is, in a limited sense, only an analysis of one small group of slaves, in broader perspective, it reflects the unconquerable spirit of other blacks, who struggled so courageously under the burdens of bondage.

Born in Albemarle County, Virginia, about 1790, the black slave Sally grew up on the 1540-acre tobacco plantation of Charles S. Thomas, a friend and neighbor of Thomas Jefferson. At a young age she was sent to the fields. She, along with forty-one other slaves on the big gang, prepared beds, planted seeds, transplanted shoots, wormed and topped young plants, and hung, stripped, sorted, and bundled the final product. When she was about eighteen, Sally suffered (or accepted) the sexual advances of a white man, probably John Thomas, the owner's eldest son; and in September 1808, she gave birth to a mulatto boy, John. Some years later, in 1817, she gave birth to a second mulatto child, Henry. As Virginia law required that progeny take the status of the mother, both children were born in bondage, but because they were part of a trust estate, as outlined in the elder Thomas's will, they were protected against sale or separation. Consequently, when one of the heirs (again probably John) joined the westward migration of slaveowners across the Appalachians into the Cumberland River

Valley, Sally, John, and Henry were transported as a family to Nashville, Tennessee.

Though relatively small and leisurely, even by Southern standards (with a population of only 3500 in 1820), Nashville's urban environment offered many new opportunities. With her master's permission, Sally hired out as a cleaning woman, a practice common among female city slaves, and secured an agreement to retain a portion of her earnings. She then rented a two-story frame house on the corner of Deaderick and Cherry streets in the central business district. Converting the front room into a laundry, and manufacturing her own soap (blending fats, oils, alkali, and salt in a small vat in the front yard), she established a cleaning business. Sally also arranged for her eldest son, John, to work as a waiter and pole boy for river barge captain Richard Rapier, who was plying the Cumberland-Mississippi river trade between Nashville and New Orleans.

As early as 1800, the powerfully built, two-hundred-pound Rapier, along with several of his hired slaves, transported a load of Tennessee tobacco down the Cumberland, Ohio, and Mississippi rivers, twelve hundred miles to the Crescent City, returning with a bargeload of sugar, tea, bread, coffee, molasses, brandy, Spanish cigars, and other supplies for the settlers along the Cumberland. Later he established two retail stores, one with Nashville businessman Lemuel T. Turner, and the other with James Jackson, an Irish immigrant who had helped lay out the town of Huntsville. In 1818, after purchasing a tract of land for four thousand dollars at Florence in the Alabama Territory, at the lower end of the Muscle Shoals rapids in the Tennessee River, he organized a third business venture, this one with Alabama merchant John Simpson. Then, after hiring John and eight other Tennessee slaves, he left for Alabama.

When Rapier, John, and the other bondsmen arrived at Florence in May 1819, they found dense forests of oak and cedar, which stretched as far as the eye could see, thickets of bushes and vines crowding the riverbank, and herds of deer bounding through the woods. The deep rumble of the fifteen-mile rapids could be heard in the distance like continuous thunder, and only a few crude cabins marked the spot. Nevertheless, Rapier supervised the construction of a two-story frame building and soon opened the first retail store in the region, Rapier and Simpson Company.

Despite the severe economic depression (1819–22), the new company grew and prospered by bringing supplies for the local planters up the river from New Orleans. John and the other hired bondsmen skillfully maneuvered huge barges upstream (one, the *General Jackson*, equipped with sails, carried a cargo of 110 tons) at a time when 90 percent of the river traffic terminated in Louisiana with the selling of barges as lumber. As time passed a close bond developed between the rugged barge master and his hired mulatto slave.

Meanwhile, Sally, who had been able to see her son periodically when Rapier visited Nashville, had also built a thriving trade. Rising before dawn, she set out on rounds to pick up dirty clothes and linens, bringing them back to the house on Deaderick to begin a fourteen-hour day washing, cleaning, and drying. Toward dusk she made her rounds again, delivering the cleaned items to her customers. "Fine linen and wearing apparel for both sexes were given in her charge for careful treatment," one of her children later recalled. "All the best people of the community gave her credit."[1] Though her income was small (three dollars a week), and though part of it went for food and clothing and part to the master, she soon had saved nearly three hundred fifty dollars. She hid the money in a tea cannister in the attic, in the hope that someday she would be able to purchase "free papers" for her sons. To that end, she also arranged for Henry to hire out running errands and saved the money he earned in the hidden cannister. But in October 1827, the tall, buxom, and still attractive Sally (then in her mid-thirties), gave birth to a third mulatto son, James, and though the father was the famous antebellum judge John Catron (who presided over the Tennessee Supreme Court and later served as a justice on the United States Supreme Court), Sally despaired that with three slave children (Tennessee law, like Virginia's, assigned progeny the status of the mother), she might never be able to save enough to free her family.

But her despair soon turned to joy. She received word from Florence that her eldest son had been emancipated. "I bequeath one thousand dollars to my executors for the purpose of purchasing the freedom of the mulatto boy, John, who now waits on me, and belongs to the Estate of Thomas," Richard Rapier stipulated in his will, and the Alabama General Assembly, the only legal emanci-pator of slaves in the state, passed a law in 1829 freeing "a certain male slave by the name of John H. Rapier."[2] A short time later, with the final disposition of the Thomas estate, Sally saw an opportunity to help Henry gain his freedom. According to the settlement, she and "the two mulatto boys" were to be turned over to one John Martin, an affable young man who wanted to sell part of his inheritance for a quick profit. Fearing that her children might be sold down the river to Mississippi, she urged Henry to escape. Heeding his mother's advice, the seventeen-year-old slave fled and eventually settled in Buffalo, New York.

Shortly after Henry's escape, Sally went to Ephraim Foster, a prominent Tennessee lawyer, and asked for assistance in putting James out of Martin's reach. "Will you talk with him [Martin] and see what he will take for the boy?" she asked. "Very well, Aunt Sally," Foster replied, "I will see him and let you know what can be done." After a few days Foster told her that Martin wanted four hundred dollars. "I have saved only three hundred fifty dollars," Sally explained, but quickly offered a proposition: If Col. Foster would pay the extra fifty dollars, have the bill of sale made to himself, and hold James in trust—be his protector—for a few months, she promised to pay the fifty dollars with interest.[3] Foster agreed and the bargain was sealed. Soon she paid off the debt and received a bill of sale, "free papers," for six-year-old James. "Many persons congratulated Mother," James wrote, but others said she had acted strangely, purchasing her child before she had bought herself.[4] Even then, however, he was not completely free. The law required emancipated blacks to secure a document of manumission from the local court, and then to leave Tennessee immediately. So despite having "free papers," James was still legally a slave.

But neither the law nor slavery seemed to curtail his activities. As a young boy, he performed a variety of chores for his mother. He ran errands for her and for the white gentlemen around the place, kept salt in the hopper for making soap, cut wood for the fireplace, and delivered cleaned clothes to various parts of the city. He also attended a school for blacks, which remained open a few months each year. But often, he recalled, there was no school because there was no teacher. About 1835, he said, a free black instructor, described as "a fine scholar," was nearly whipped to death by whites.[5] There was a general opposition to educating slaves for fear that they might forge their own freedom papers. Despite these difficulties, under the tutorage of free Negroes Daniel Watkins,

Rufus Conrad, and Samuel Lowery, who conducted classes from
time to time, Thomas secured an education. Though he had neither
paper nor books nor even proper clothing and though his school
was a drafty, one-room building with rickety benches, James had
an intense desire to learn and quickly mastered the basics of
mathematics, reading, and writing.

About 1841 James hired out as an apprentice barber. Working
for bondsman Frank Parrish, who had earlier established a barbershop in the public square, he quickly learned the trade. "James [is]
still with Frank Parish [sic] and has the character of a good barber,
So a Gentleman toald me," his brother John H. Rapier, who had
taught himself to write by using a system of phonics, observed in
1843. "He is well thought of by the Gentleman's. James has
manners to please almost anyone who do not let their prejudice go
far on account of color."[6] Two years later James was still with
Parrish, earned twelve dollars a month, and had begun violin
lessons with Negro musician Gordon McGowan. "James will make
a man of musick I think. He seems to be very fond of it."[7]

Having served a five-year apprenticeship, the nineteen-year-old
slave opened his own barbershop in 1846. He established the shop
in the house where he had grown up (and where his mother still
operated her cleaning business). The location proved ideal. Within
a few steps of several banking houses, newspapers, and law firms,
as well as the county courthouse, Market Square, and the capitol,
the place on Deaderick, he explained, was convenient to bankers,
merchants, lawyers, politicians, and professional men. He counted
among his customers a number of famous Tennesseans, including
one-time governor William Carroll; businessman E. S. (Squire)
Hall; plantation owner William Giles Harding; Whig political
leader Ephraim Foster; preacher William G. Brownlow, who
became governor during the Civil War; and Francis Fogg, the
well-known Davidson County lawyer, who visited the Thomas
shop daily. "He returns to us in the evening," noted Mrs. Fogg
approvingly, "with face smooth and curls nicely arranged."[8]

While attending to his duties as a barber, James listened attentively to conversations that took place among his customers.
"They had time to talk in the barber shop. Nobody seemed in a
great hurry. Everything was discussed—social, commercial, political, and financial."[9] He remembered conversations about the
abolitionists, the advancement of cotton on the Liverpool market,

the magnetism and sporting proclivities of Andrew Jackson, plantation acreage along the Mississippi, and runaway blacks. Once he recalled being sharply questioned about fugitive slaves. General Harding, having traveled all the way to Buffalo in search of one of his bondsmen, recounted that he had chanced to meet James's brother Henry, who had treated him in a very cold and indifferent manner. James could do little but apologize for his brother's "rudeness." Though he usually remained silent when the conversation turned to such controversial issues, sometimes he ventured an opinion on slavery. While shaving a young Virginia lawyer, for example, he defended the Wilmont Proviso, a proposal to prohibit "the peculiar institution" in the newly acquired Mexican territories. "The set back I got caused me to be careful in the future. Among other things he told me I had no right to listen to a gentleman's conversation."[10] Despite such "set backs," James built a flourishing business. Charging twenty cents for a haircut, fifteen cents for a shave, and a dollar for a tooth extraction, he operated one of the most prosperous "tonsorial establishments" in Nashville. And in the city's first business directory (published in 1853), he advertised in large, boldface type: "Jas. Thomas, Barber Shop, 10 Deaderick St."[11]

Because it offered an opportunity for economic independence, the barbering trade was an attractive one to Nashville blacks. In fact, of the eight barbers advertising in the 1853 directory, six were Negroes. Perhaps the best known of these was Thomas's friend and mentor, Frank Parrish, a tall, handsome, well-dressed slave, who had traveled (with his master, Edwin H. Ewing) to England, Scotland, the Germanies, Persia, and Egypt. "Frank was an elegant dresser, by nature polite and gentlemanly, and [a] most conspicuous character," wrote Thomas, who greatly admired Parrish. "Everywhere in Europe and the Orient [he] was taken for the principal man of the party. All rushed to take care of him. It kept Frank busy trying to explain that 'I am not the one,' but the people thought he was modest and heaped more attention on him."[12] As early as 1836, Parrish had established a bathhouse-barbershop in Nashville, and by 1853 had enough money to purchase his freedom. By the time of his death in the early reconstruction period, Parrish owned his own home, ran a good business, had entered politics as a delegate to the first statewide black convention, and had accumulated a few thousand dollars in real and personal property.

Though most blacks in the community were unable to save thousands of dollars, quite a few became economically independent. Such black enterprise seems all the more remarkable considering the extensive legal codes specifically designed to curtail the activities of Negroes. Slaves were not legally allowed to own personal property, purchase real estate, buy liquor, sell garden vegetables, or earn money. But many were able to evade these restrictions. Sally hired out, earned money, rented a house, and operated a business. She lived so long at the corner of Deaderick and Cherry that whites in Nashville thought she was free and owned the property. She moved about the city with little hindrance, even boarded her grandchildren (see chap. 2) as they attended school, and secretly advised Henry to escape to the North. In a similar manner, James Thomas hired out, earned money, and established a business. He eventually accumulated a large amount of personal property—furniture, mirrors, clothes, and about a thousand dollars in cash—and while still a slave became the manager of one of the largest barbering establishments in the city. He traveled to various parts of Nashville without a pass, entertained free blacks in his home, and attended Negro church meetings. He recalled that at one such gathering a black congregation, made up mostly of slaves, sang until twelve o'clock at night. The owners not only failed to curtail such activities, he wrote, "but seemed to encourage them."[13] Though separated by hundreds of miles, forbidden to travel, and denied postal privileges, the Thomas family remained very close. As a slave and free Negro, John Rapier (who settled in Alabama) visited Nashville frequently, and eventually sent his children to live with their slave grandmother. "Mother, James and my two Sons that are with Mother are all well when I Last heard from them," Rapier explained to his fugitive brother Henry in a long letter. "I entend to go up to Nashville in the course of ten days and See them all."[14] In April 1845, after visiting the Tennessee capital, he reported that his mother looked as young as she had eight years before, worked just as hard as ever, and hardly took time to talk with him as she waited on a long line of customers.

Nor were other blacks constrained by the codes. Frank Parrish accumulated a large amount of personal property (paintings, books, china, silver, furniture, and clothes), and Solomon Porter, a close friend of Thomas, wore a gold-buttoned, gold-trimmed topcoat to flaunt his wealth. Hundreds of slaves hired out as barbers, hackmen, rivermen, shoemakers, laborers, blacksmiths, stewards, cooks, porters, hostlers, coopers, laundrywomen, and some, like Sally and James Thomas, achieved a degree of economic independence. Blacks also congregated in their own churches, moved about the city without passes, and, despite anti-immigration laws, continued to enter the state. Many bondsmen, acquiring the means to buy "free papers" but denied legal emancipation, purchased their freedom anyway and lived in a state of "quasi-freedom."

Perhaps part of the reason for the failure of the codes was that whites did not take a hard-line position in enforcing them. A number of Tennesseans, both slaveholders and non-slaveholders, entertained genuinely liberal sentiments toward blacks. The most conspicuous in Nashville was Ephraim Foster, a lawyer, plantation owner, and United States senator. Praising Negroes as "remarkably steady and industrious workers," Foster assisted many bondsmen in securing their freedom.[15] Other Tennessee whites condoned gradual emancipation, among them state legislator James Alexander, who proposed a law for the eventual manumission of slaves. Echoing the philosophy of Thomas Jefferson, he said that according to the laws of nature all men were equal and ought to be free. A few went even further. Alfred Alfred asked the state legislature to seek the immediate emancipation of all bondsmen in the South. "Loose the bands of wickedness. Undo the heavy burdens. Let the oppressed go free."[16] Praising free blacks as peaceable, quiet, industrious, and trustworthy, Francis Brown said that their habits were the best guarantee that all Negroes, once free, would become good citizens. And Alexander Donalson, the brother-in-law of the most famous of all Tennesseans, Andrew Jackson, claimed that it was the duty of good Christians to deal justly and humanely with their chattel. As happiness in the hereafter depended on this, he directed that all his slaves be emancipated.

Despite such sentiments, which were most prevalent before 1830, the vast majority of Tennesseans, as well as other Southerners, held quite different views. "Now my own father [John Catron] had no time to give me a thought," Thomas admitted. "He gave me twenty-five cents once. If I was correctly informed that is all he ever did for me."[17] Despite having fathered a Negro child, Catron, like most whites, looked upon blacks as despicable human beings, who were degraded by their color, given to vice and licentiousness, and without motive for virtuous conduct. He saw free Negroes as indolent, thieving, ungovernable, worthless, lazy, and depraved humans—the lowest caste.

Thomas not only rejected these characterizations but asserted that poor whites constituted the lowest group in southern society. Without land, slaves, or even a trade, they were something of an anomaly in the South. If a poor white man attempted to wait on a gentleman, Thomas explained, or measured him for a pair of shoes or a suit of clothes, the gentleman would not stand for it. On the other hand, Thomas was accepted on the plantation as a barber, fiddler, and even as a friend. "It was not in the white man's place," he observed, "to play the part of servant."[18]

Perhaps tiring of "the part of servant," Thomas asked Ephraim Foster to present a petition to the Davidson County Court for a deed of emancipation. Appearing in the Nashville courtroom on March 6, 1851, the twenty-three-year-old bondsman stood silently as Foster explained to the nine-judge panel: "James has always maintained an exemplary character." He was industrious, honest, moral, humble, polite; and his conduct warranted the respect of whites. "He is a man of worth in his place."[19] The testimony of such an eminent Tennessean swayed the magistrates (as it had previously), and after a short deliberation they ordered "the slave James, otherwise called James Thomas, emancipated and forever set free."[20]

Now able to address the court himself, Thomas quickly asked for immunity from the 1831 law requiring freed blacks to leave the state. He argued that he had led a moral and productive life, had conducted himself in an honorable manner, and had always earned a good living. Having acquired many faithful customers, he would be greatly damaged having to start anew in some strange country. Boasting that he could easily post the five-hundred-dollar good behavior bond, he received the immunity, becoming the first Negro in the county (and perhaps in the state), under the 1831 law, to gain legally both freedom and residency.

Two years before, Sally had died of cholera. A woman of enormous drive and dedication, she had devoted her life to freeing her children. Due in large measure to her indefatigable efforts, the three slave children—John H. Rapier, Henry K. Thomas, and James P. Thomas—had all secured their freedom before the Civil War. Sexual exploitation, miscegenation, separation, and legal restrictions—the very forces designed, in part, to destroy the black family—did not lead to disintegration and disunity in Sally's family, but to an extraordinary feeling of loyalty, unity, and love. This, coupled with the vitality of a black community where hundreds of Negroes learned trades, maintained their families, and acquired wealth was an enduring legacy for later generations of blacks, especially for one of Sally's twenty-six grandchildren, James Thomas Rapier, who not only came to live with Sally and James (after whom he was named) in the capital city, but who attended the Negro school for nearly six years. Rapier's slave antecedents as well as Nashville's flourishing black community would prove to be enduring sources of strength and sustenance during the troublesome years of reconstruction.

2   Free Black Antecedents

Equality was illusory for free blacks in nineteenth-century America. They were circumscribed and castigated because of their color, denied due process of the law, compelled to labor on white-controlled plantations, and regarded as inferior. And, like slaves, even the most talented and ambitious could aspire to little better than economic self-sufficiency, while most were victims of grinding poverty. Struggling for full acceptance in a white-dominated society, acquiring the values of hard work, frugality, and individual initiative, free blacks faced a dilemma: though yearning to become part of America, they would always remain separate. Yet much as bondsmen challenged "the pecular institution," free Negroes also confronted their condition—and did so with an enormous inner strength. Though, again, an investigation of the free black antecedents of James Rapier, like an analysis of a single slave family, is only the study of a small group of blacks, it does reflect the remarkable ability of some free Negroes to thrive within the lowest caste.

As a freedman James Thomas continued to operate his highly successful barbershop much as he had done as a slave. Within a few years, he had managed to save two thousand dollars, and put most of the money into city real estate.[1] As a man of some means, he decided to take a pleasure trip to New Orleans, a city he had first visited as a bondsman as early as 1842. Arriving in the Crescent City, he learned that a boyhood friend, William Walker, had recently organized a confederation of states (Nicaragua, Honduras, San Salvador, Costa Rica) in Central America and that mulattoes had received high office in the new confederation. Consequently, Thomas decided to leave the United States. "It was necessary in those days," he later wrote, "when about to travel, particularly in the direction of free Territory, on any Railroad, steamship or stage, to have some reputable [white] person [vouch for] you."² Identified as a trustworthy free Negro by a Louisiana merchant, one Mr. Dyas, and joined by his nephew John H. Rapier, Jr., he booked passage (February 23, 1856) for Nicaragua on the steamer *Daniel Webster*.

After having been at sea only three days he was accosted by the ship's captain, who demanded to see his papers. As the crew and passangers looked on, Thomas fumbled through his pockets for the documents. He had been the center of attention many times, but to have a crowd of forty people gawking at him as though he had stolen a horse was extremely annoying; he finally produced his deed of manumission.

Porting first at Belize (Honduras), then Greytown (Nicaragua), he went by land to Granada, where he met with Walker. "I delivered a letter that his father had written to him. He read and looked as though in deep thought several minutes. That was the first news from home in a long time."³ Learning that a quadroon had been appointed secretary of state in Nicaragua, Thomas was optimistic about the prospects for blacks in the new government, but his hopes were soon dashed when he ascertained that Walker not only planned to proclaim a dictatorship but to reestablish Negro slavery. After a short stay, Thomas and Rapier returned to the United States. Years later Thomas recalled sitting in a plaza in Granada, looking at the marketplace, and being asked by an American: "Why did you come?" "I don't know," he replied, and in a voice close to a whisper, repeated, "I don't know."⁴

Returning to Tennessee via Missouri, Iowa, and Illinois, he wrote in October 1856 that he had visited Chicago, inquired about the country in the Northwest, and had come home with the intention of raising several thousand dollars and returning to Wisconsin. "I have been dreaming of that country for some time."⁵ To raise the money, he set about collecting some old debts, putting his property up for sale, and permanently closing out his barbering business, despite the supplications of many old customers. "The people of Nashville are anxious that I should commence business again," he admitted with indifferent satisfaction, "but I do not like the idea much, not at all if I can do better."⁶ But before he could wind up his various personal affairs, Thomas abruptly left Nashville, pushed quickly through Kentucky, and crossed the Ohio River into free territory.

He had left suddenly "as a consequence of a rumor (false I have
no doubt) that the Negroes had an Insurrection on foot, to be
carried into effect Christmas."[7] Though traveling with a wealthy
white physician named Scott, Thomas was still fearful, as twenty
Negroes had been executed (by hanging, bludgeoning, and de-
capitation) in Tennessee alone, ten of them at the nearby Cumberland Ironworks.[8] With only a few dollars in his pocket, he
continued his journey northward into Wisconsin. Though genuinely impressed with the rugged, snow-covered terrain, he decided
that perhaps some town along the Mississippi, or out West, would
be more suitable. He therefore turned southward, traveling
through Iowa to Kansas. "I am going towards Pike's Peak. I may
stop at Leavenworth to pick up the money sprinkled along the
road," he later exclaimed, noting that he had joined the Colorado
gold rush.[9] Better judgment prevailed, however; concluding that
"Getting gold is too much of a wild goose chase," he found
employment as a barber and companion to Colonel Benjamin
Clark, a Kentucky plantation owner.[10]

In the company of such a well-know white man, he returned to
the South for the first time since the slave insurrection panic.
"During the winter I have spent several weeks in this city of fires,"
he wrote from a suite in Louisville's elegant Galt House, admitting
that Clark was a young, well-bred, gentleman, who had a great
deal of money.[11] What was the nature of his newfound employment? In the absence of opera, he took in the theater—Eliza Logan
being the chief attraction, but most of the time he simply lounged
around one room or another, watching the chambermaids "beating
in with dusting brushes."[12] Despite such easy living, he soon
"earned" fifteen hundred dollars. By early March he was ready to
start out on his own. "I can not break off from him all at once, but
with the aid of Kind Providence," he said with tongue-in-cheek,
having probably flimflammed the colonel out of the money, "we
will leave tomorrow for [Chicago]. There I think I will Jump the
game and begin to make investigations."[13]

He was referring to investigations about real estate prices in the
Midwest. In April 1857, he succeeded in "jumping the game,"
traveled to Keokuk, Iowa, and after several discussions with fellow
Tennessean Jerome S. Ridley (who had acquired a small fortune—
seventy-five thousand dollars—speculating in land along the Mississippi), he purchased a downtown lot for six hundred fifty
dollars, boasting that it was sure to turn a 100 percent profit within

six months. "If I exercise my wits a little I will make big money." But further investigations revealed that even better opportunities for profit existed in the Kansas Territory. Once again he was on the move, journeying to Topeka and Tecumseh, purchasing thirty one lots for eight hundred ninety-one dollars, and bragging for a second time that the property would quickly appreciate in value. Though planning to settle in Kansas, he changed his mind after being assaulted by a group of proslavery ruffians, and in July he continued his odyssey across Missouri. Arriving in St. Louis, he found a thriving black community and, with a sigh of relief, he concluded: "I expect to be here for some time."[14]

Within a short time he had acquired considerable wealth. As early as 1858 *The Colored Aristocracy of St. Louis*, a directory of the forty-three wealthiest Negroes in the city, estimated his worth at fifteen thousand dollars.[15] Only a decade later, under the headline "Rich Nigs Wed," the St. Louis *Dispatch* reported that Thomas and Antoinette Rutgers, both free blacks, had been married at St. Vincent's church. "The ceremony was an imposing affair. Many of the elite of the city were present. The husband is worth nearly $400,000."[16] Though at this time, such an estimate was excessive, through some spectacular real estate transactions (in one he bought thirteen acres for seven thousand dollars and sold them two years later in 1872 for twenty-eight thousand dollars), marriage to the beautiful and wealthy Antoinette (whose father, Louis, had been among the early slaves in Missouri), and large profits from two businesses (a ten-chair barbershop and a real estate brokerage house), Thomas amassed by 1882 a fortune equal to that amount. At the height of his financial career, he owned two entire blocks of downtown property, rented forty-eight apartments in various parts of the city, lived (with Antoinette and their five children) in a mansion overlooking the Mississippi River, and owned a three-story summer house in nearby Alton, Illinois. The disastrous tornado of 1896, however, leveled most of his apartments, killing twenty-five of his tenants, and this, coupled with the serious economic depression (1893–1896), forced him to take out a slew of mortgages. He never recovered from the two calamities, and in 1913, when Thomas died, little remained of his once great wealth.[17]

Also making various sojourns through Ohio, Indiana, Illinois, and Wisconsin during the antebellum period was James's brother,

Henry Thomas, who finally settled in Buffalo, New York. In 1842, he, too, opened a barbershop, locating in the basement of Buffalo's fashionable hotel Niagara. He quickly built a thriving trade and began purchasing real estate. He bought a lot in the city (for one hundred dollars) and a tract of several acres near the Seneca Indian Reservation (also one hundred dollars). About 1844, he married a black woman, Maria, who bore him eleven children, ten boys and a girl, Sarah. Despite a lucrative business, in 1852, to avoid apprehension by slave catchers (encouraged by the passage of the Fugitive Slave Law), he moved his family to the Negro community of Buxton, Canada West. With resources he had saved as a barber and with profits of 400 percent from the sale of his Buffalo property, he purchased a hundred acres of wilderness land, and set about clearing the trees, building a log house, and putting in a crop of corn, wheat, and barley. "The settlement improves slowly, but prospects are good for its success," he noted in 1856. "The lumber mill is making improvements for the neighborhood. Soon the railroad will pass through. The school is flourishing. I have six acres in wheat and 2 in barley."[18]

Besides farming, Thomas took an active part in community affairs, serving on the board of directors for the first black-owned, black-operated business venture in Canada—the Canada Mill and Mercantile Company—and helping to establish a Negro sawmill, gristmill, and country store. He also joined St. Andrew's Presbyterian Church, devoting as much as one work day a week to church affairs. During the Civil War he joined the local militia, expanded his property holdings to two hundred acres (valued at two thousand dollars), and following the war he continued his involvement in various business enterprises and community affairs until his death.[19]

Although John H. Rapier, Sr., also became a barber, married, started a family, and acquired real and personal property, unlike his two brothers, he settled only two hundred miles from Nashville, in Florence, Alabama.[20] Shortly after his emancipation, Rapier married Susan, a nineteen-year-old free black from Baltimore, Maryland, and started a family. Between 1831 and 1837, the couple had four children: Richard (born December 13, 1831), John, Jr. (July 28, 1835), Henry (1836), and James Thomas (November 13, 1837)—all born free according to the Alabama law which (like the Virginia and Tennessee statutes) gave black children the status of their mother (see fig. 1). But before the eldest had reached his tenth birthday, Rapier's wife died in childbirth at the age of twenty-nine. Only the etching on her tombstone, located in the white section of the Florence cemetery, told of her birth, on Christmas Day 1811; death, along with her two infant children, Jackson and Alexander; and solitude, "depart my friends and dry up your tears, for I must lie hear [sic] till Christ appears."[21]

To care for the four boys, Rapier acquired a young slave, Lucretia, and in 1848, though not formally married (as the law forbade free blacks from marrying or even gathering with slaves), he began a second family. During the next decade he and Lucretia had five children: Rebecca, Joseph, Thomas, Charles, and Susan, who, according to the law, were born in bondage. "Such a life as is led by Lucretia and Father, I do not believe that God sanctions," one of Rapier's free sons said, expressing his repugnance to family bondage, "nor do I sanction it."[22] Rapier made repeated attempts to free his enslaved wife and children, but he had little success. In 1860, for instance, despite a statute forbidding emancipation entirely, he made application to the Lauderdale County Court seeking their emancipation. Though a hearing was set for May 12, 1862, the case never came before the court. His second family remained in bondage until the end of the Civil War.

To provide for his children, Rapier, like his brothers in Nashville (later St. Louis) and Buffalo, opened a barbershop. Charging twenty cents for a haircut, fifteen cents for a shave, and ten cents for massaging scalps and trimming beards, he soon built up a prosperous trade, taking in as much as one hundred dollars a month. Even at the low point of the 1857 depression, he maintained a monthly income of fifty dollars, bragging in June of that year: "In the last Six months my work was good for upwards of three Hundred dollars."[23] Earning about one thousand dollars a year during the antebellum period (a sum which was ten times the national per capita average), Rapier became a comparatively wealthy man.

Nevertheless, he continually complained about his chosen occupation. "I am tyrad of the business," he said on more than one occasion, "but I must content My Self as best I can."[24] During the early forties, he found fault with the depressed price of cotton (four and a-half cents a pound), the sharp decline in the value of slaves (from four hundred fifty to three hundred fifty dollars), and a

Figure 1 GENEALOGY OF THE RAPIER-THOMAS FAMILY

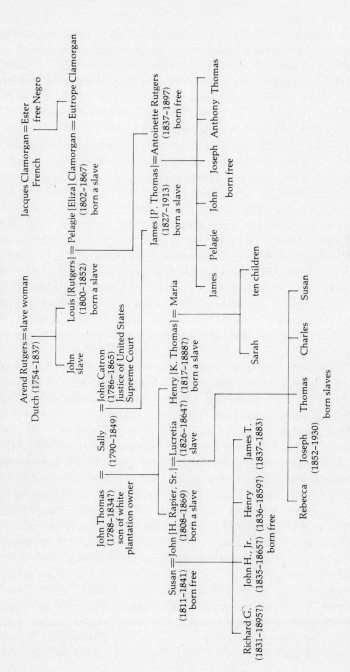

special capitation tax levied on free blacks—four times the amount imposed on whites—but expressed greatest dissatisfaction with the barbering business.[25] Later he grumbled that John Goins, a young, affable free Negro, had opened a barbershop in the area and had attracted many customers because he was a younger man. "To tell the truth, I hate the name Barber," he closed one letter; "I look upon many occupations as Superior to a Barber."[26]

Despite this bitter confession, he remained at the barbering trade for forty years (1829–69). During that time he not only made a good living, but set aside a portion of his earnings for the education of his children. He sent John and James to school in Nashville and provided a few dollars each month for their board, room, and tuition, despite the fact that they stayed with Sally. "My two sons are with mother," he noted in February 1843. "John and James are well pleased with their grandmother and [school] and Do not want to come home, So James writes."[27] A short time later, Rapier expressed satisfaction at the progress of the two boys: John, at age ten, had begun to write poetry; James, at eight, had already become competent in arithmetic, handwriting, and reading. He was so pleased with their achievements that he continued to pay for their schooling in Nashville for six years.

The school was also popular among other blacks. At the fall session in 1850, thirty-three Negro scholars crowded into the small classroom, and enrollment later jumped to nearly fifty. Black youngsters, slave and free, walked miles through the dense woods of the Cumberland River Valley "to get some learnin' "; and free black Harriet P. Young stipulated in her will that a niece, Mary Jane, should receive an education there. By 1850, the literacy rate among slaves in the city (including James Thomas, who had earlier attended the school) was perhaps 25 percent, while the federal census takers reported that 158 of 264 adult free Negroes—60 percent—could read and write. But the school was responsible for more than a high literacy rate. A number of black reconstruction lawyers, doctors, government officials, politicians, and church leaders received their first training at the Nashville school. Treasury department official and Negro banker James Carroll Napier, for instance, took his early training there; as did reconstruction lawyer Samuel Lowery, who was admitted to argue a case before the United States Supreme Court, and Nelson Walker, who served as president of the 1865 Tennessee Negro suffrage con-

vention. Daniel Watkins, the pastor of the Colored Christian
Church, who was described as "one of the most eminently pro-
gressively and [well] educated colored men in the State," not only
attended, but taught at the school. The Rapier brothers also later
gained distinction. In all, two generations of blacks received a
rudimentary education at the Nashville school.

Rapier sent his eldest son, Richard, to live with his brother
Henry K. Thomas and attend school in Buffalo, New York. Posting
a monthly check of ten dollars to help defray the expenses of board,
room, and tuition, he expressed satisfaction at Richard's advancement: his penmanship, ciphering, and verse writing had improved
markedly since he had been in the North. "Study your books well
and try to give your father satisfaction," he directed, pointing out
that Richard was fortunate to have kind relatives who were anxious
to assist him in every way possible. If he refused to study hard, it
would surely have a negative effect on the younger boys. "I am in
hopes your will Show me you have not been in Buffalo all this time
for nothing and that I can hold you up as an example to your lettle
Brothers."[28] Rapier kept the somewhat defiant Henry in Florence,
but he soon elicited a promise from his fourth son, who said he
would settle down and try to apply himself if he could attend
school. Some time later Rapier proudly admitted that all of his
boys were in school and doing quite well.[29] He deserved to be
proud of the educational accomplishments of his children; all could
read and write at an early age; one excelled in arithmetic, another
in writing, another in composition—and all this at a time when
Alabama law denied free colored children the right to an education.

Besides the statute which forbade teaching free Negroes to spell,
read, or write, under a five-hundred-dollar fine, other laws restricted the activities of free blacks, who were prohibited from
buying liquor, playing cards, or visiting slaves. Any free person of
color found in a slave quarters without written permission from the
master could receive thirty-nine lashes. State codes required free
men of color to pay a two-dollar capitation tax, women a
one-dollar fee, and each child one dollar, and prescribed a seven-
year prison sentence for free Negroes who offered assistance to an
escaping bondsman. After the Nat Turner revolt in 1831, a statute
prohibited free Negroes from entering the state, under penalty of
being sold into slavery. According to the law, all blacks were slaves
unless they could prove otherwise, and, as free persons had to

satisfy white magistrates, they lived in constant fear of being sold into slavery.

But, like his mother and brothers, Rapier circumvented the law, first by educating his children, and then, in 1855, by helping a slave escape. During a trip to Canada, he heard about the death of Sam Ragland, a fugitive slave from Alabama who had acquired a home and several acres of land in Toronto. Ragland had died intestate, and the authorities had put his property, valued at five thousand dollars, in escrow until a legal heir could be found. Rapier knew Sam's brother, Milton, a slave belonging to Franklin County plantation owner Colonel Sam Ragland, and upon his return to Alabama, he informed the slave owner of the five thousand dollars worth of property. Colonel Ragland decided to claim the property, and subsequently he, Rapier, and Milton traveled to Buffalo. Fearing that Canadian authorities might not relinquish the property to a slave owner, Ragland remained in Buffalo, while Rapier and Milton traveled to Toronto, proved kinship, and acquired a deed to the property. After their return to Buffalo, Rapier left for Alabama, but when the master went with Milton back to Toronto to have the property transferred in his name, the slave declared his freedom.

Although Rapier, who had secretly urged Milton to remain in Canada, had committed the most serious crime of the antebellum period, he incurred no reprisals. On the contrary, he was highly esteemed by whites in the community. "He is unquestionably a good Selection," a white judge, S. C. Posey, wrote in 1867, noting that Rapier had been selected as voter registrar for the Forty-third District, "the best that could be made here or anywhere else."[30] The staunchly conservative Florence *Journal* said that he was familiarly known as "Uncle John" to everyone in the area and, as one of Lauderdale county's oldest residents, was respected by all classes.[31]

Whites esteemed Rapier partly because he was a man of wealth and property. As early as 1831 he had paid three hundred dollars for a small lot in the main business section of Florence, fronting twenty-two feet on Court Street; nine years later he purchased an adjacent lot, together with a two-story white frame house at a public auction. Like his brother in Nashville, Rapier used his house as a place of business as well as a residence. He later bought two more parcels of land in the city (1844) and during the 1850s purchased four lots near the outskirts of Florence, one hundred acres in the Minnesota Territory, three city lots in Toronto, and made a down payment on one hundred acres of wilderness land in Buxton, Canada West.

Visiting the Negro community (see chap. 3) in the fall of 1856, he advanced William King, the founder-director, one hundred seventeen dollars, and then paid Robert Harris, a Negro laborer, an additional seventy dollars to clear the trees, burn the logs, and build a fence on his land. After returning to Florence, via Chicago (the fastest place, he said, that he had ever visited), he posted a second payment, secured the promise of financial assistance from his son John, Jr. (who was then living in the Minnesota Territory), and employed a fugitive slave, Isaac Riley, to build a house on the cleared land. Construction had been going on for some months when his son asked him to abandon the house-building scheme. Why build a house in the Canadian wilderness? It was best to complete it for two reasons, Rapier said: first, the deed required the construction of a residence, and if King could show that they had not complied with the conditions of the contract, they might lose the land. And second, King was in financial difficulty. If he were to go bankrupt, the government might favor those who had complied over those who had not. Eventually he completed the house, paid off the mortgage, and received a deed to the property. The value of his Buxton holdings increased as the population of the black community grew from eight hundred in 1856 to nearly two thousand during the Civil War, and, similarly, the worth of his real estate in Florence appreciated as that community expanded from a few hundred residents in 1840 to eight hundred in 1850 (making it the fifth largest community in Alabama), and to fourteen hundred in 1860. Rapier also acquired stock in the Memphis and Charleston Railroad and saved two thousand dollars in cash—a total wealth on the eve of the Civil War of nearly ten thousand dollars, twelfth largest of any free black in the state.

He attributed his financial success to the maintenance of certain values. "Settle debts," "Save money," "Stay away from liquor," "Stick the closer to work," "Say you will do well," "Say nothing but what is right," "Keep out of debt," he told his sons, explaining that young men, of both colors, should save their money, buy real estate, use steady industry, and stay away from cigars, liquor, and disreputable women. The way to become rich was to purchase land in the West, near some growing town with natural advantages, and then settle down, keep sober, and mind your own business. Life was filled with disappointments, especially for the young, but "a man must be disopoynted in life when younge to make him Smart when old."[32] Conquer adversity by working diligently, rather than by falling back on the bottle.

If Rapier preached industry, frugality, sobriety, and honesty, he also filled his correspondence with personal matters. He bemoaned his son Henry's falling out with his brothers, but expressed pleasure at the loyalty of Richard, James, and John, who corresponded frequently and returned to Florence for occasional visits. Shortly after the firing on Fort Sumter, John, Jr., articulating the concern of James and Richard, wrote that he felt it his solemn duty to render some assistance to his father, even if that meant returning to the South. "He must be in an unhappy condition surrounded, as he is, by infuriated soldiers, and all those poor children to look after. I hope he saw the coming storm and sought safety in flight."[33]

Although the elder Rapier had not fled from Alabama, he had often contemplated leaving the South. During the 1850s, for example, he had been a faithful subscriber to the *African Repository*, the publication of the American Colonization Society. Though he considered emigrating to Africa, he finally decided against it. The object of colonization, as he explained in a blistering letter to the president of the society, was not to promote the welfare of Negroes, but rather to rid the nation of them. He was satisfied that a large majority of the society's members would not care "if all the free negros in the United States was at the Botom of the Sea, [just] So they was out of the United States."[34] On another occasion he asked John, Jr., to send him a newspaper from Minnesota containing material about the treatment of blacks in the North, as he was then considering a move to a free state. And he was urged to leave: "Move out West, Father, Give Lucretia and the children some kind of a chance for Justice and yourself peace of mind."[35]

But he remained in the South. He had acquired considerable real estate, built up a profitable business, and raised two families along the Tennessee River. Further, he had made a number of friends—both black and white—in that region. It seems paradoxical that Rapier had so many white friends and yet had so openly flouted the laws of Alabama. But there were many such paradoxes in his life. Separated from his mother during most of his youth, he became a devoted and loving father. Barred from the professions by law, he became a highly successful barber, earning enough to make real

estate purchases in Alabama, Minnesota, and Canada. Denied a
formal education, he gave up half of his monthly earnings to send
his children to school. Known as "Uncle John" to whites, he
committed the most serious crime of the pre-Civil War period—
helping a slave to escape. And emerging from the degradation of
bondage, he preached hard work, frugality, temperance, and
honorable conduct. By valuing property, his family, and learning,
John H. Rapier, Sr., like his brothers James and Henry Thomas,
proved that, despite the caste system, free blacks could prosper,
even in the antebellum South. This, too, was a heritage that would
serve James Rapier well in the years ahead.

3

The Rapier Brothers

It seems paradoxical, then, that John H. Rapier, who considered himself an Alabamian and remained in Florence for fifty years, should urge his four boys to settle outside the South. But there was no paradox in Rapier's advising his sons to leave Alabama. Acutely aware that they could never enter a profession, secure a higher education, or receive equal justice in the region of their birth, he betrayed his own deep, though outwardly unexpressed frustrations and fundamental misgivings about the South by pressing his children to seek their fortune in the Promised Land.

Heeding their father's advice, Richard and Henry journeyed first to Buffalo, New York, where they attended school and lived with their uncle, Henry K. Thomas; then they crossed into Canada, where they continued their schooling. In 1855, the two brothers set out across the Rocky Mountains in search of gold, ending up along the Feather River in California. Finding it played out, they took up farming; they purchased three hundred acres of fertile land near Auburn, sowed one hundred forty acres of wheat and barley, and harvested (in the first year) nearly two thousand bushels of grain. After a short while, though, irreconcilable differences developed between them and Henry left, never to be heard from again. Richard, however, remained in California, cultivating the rich soil for nearly a quarter-century.

John, Jr., also left Alabama. "Having concluded to Emigrate to Liberia, I take this method, as the only available one, to acquire the necessary Knowledge incumbent upon such an intention," he explained to the president of the American Colonization Society, obviously attempting to flaunt his facility with words.[1] When would the next vessel sail for Africa? he asked. How could he secure passage? How much would the voyage cost? Two months

later he still had received no response, so he wrote again, requesting the same information and demanding a prompt reply. "Believe
me, Sir, that I am serious in my idea of Emigrating. In this Country
I can not live."[2] Receiving no facts after this second inquiry, he
decided to join his uncle James Thomas, who was making arrange-
ments to join the Walker filibuster in Central America.

But Rapier became disenchanted with the poverty and misery of
that region, and after a few months he returned to the United
States, following the Mississippi northward to the Minnesota
Territory. Working at first as the personal secretary of Parker H.
French, a coadventurer in Nicaragua, he soon left French (in a
dispute over wages) and began a career as a free-lance journalist.
During the next four years, he contributed more than a hundred
articles to five different newspapers, including the Little Falls
Pioneer and Democrat and the St. Paul *Times*, writing on such
diverse themes as man's destruction of nature, the virtues of
Minnesota, snuff and snuff dippers, the Republican party, Henry
Ward Beecher, and reminiscences of the Walker filibuster.

Besides writing on various topics of the day, he also penned a
number of poems during the course of his stay in Minnesota. His
verse meditated on death, heaven, love, and solitude. Death was
rest. "With happiness to the tomb I turn . . . and I be at rest." Yet
there was also an affirmation of immortality; for example: "wearing God's eternal crown," "Heaven's Eternal Throne," and

> Come sweet sister with us to Heaven
> And sing sweet songs with us above.

Even his more lyric love poems iterated this faith. To Louise,
he concluded:

> May the storms blow lightly on Thee
> May the rains softly descend
> Peace and rest forever bide thee,
> Heaven and glory thy final end.[3]

He also voiced, along with the nature poets of the day, an
attraction for solitude and night—where he could be alone with his
thoughts. In "Death" the twenty-one-year-old Rapier wrote,

> Let me die Young, while the heart's free and light
> While the genial Sun glows—ere the shades of night

Fall o'er my soul, and darken the day
  When happily Death, shall steal life away

Bury me in Springtime when nature is gay
  Bury me in Springtime when bright is the day
Bury me deep, near some murmuring stream
  Where sweetly I'll sleep, and in quiet dream

Let roses bloom o'er me, let violets blow
  Unostentacious, without pomp or show
Rear no tablets to mark my lonely grave,
  And be, my funeral dirge, a willows wave

Let officious mourners dare not come near
  With meaningless wailings and sorrowless tear
For I would have none, at my death repine
  Care not for my fate, but oh! weep for thine.[4]

Though such trite poeticisms as cherry lips, murmuring stream,
pearly tear, bleeding heart were characteristic of most of Rapier's
verse, he was often capable of felicity in phrase and line. He spoke
of the mazes of the morrow, the lengthy stride of time, the pangs of
earth, the vales of living green drenched in light. And at times he
approached good verse, as in "Peace and rest forever bide thee."
Evidently he had read the poetry of the time, for some of his lines
echoed William Wordsworth and William Cullen Bryant. Another
indication that Rapier was an avid reader was his considerable
vocabulary. But more important than his versification, which was,
to be sure, painfully conventional in form and theme, was his
humanitarian philosophy—"God's invitation to all the human
family"—and a genuine sympathy for people that pervaded even
the crudest verse.[5]
Rapier also wrote tracts contending for the rights of black
people. In one, entitled "Have Colored Children Rights?" he
reprimanded the St. Paul Board of Education for failing to provide
school facilities for Negroes. Demanding that some provision be
made for black children, he asked: Why were blacks required to
pay a school tax if they could not secure a public education?[6] In a
second, "Can Colored Citizens Pre-empt?" he chided local federal
land officials for failing to honor homestead applications of blacks,

declaring such action illegal.[7] And in a third, an address to Negroes concerning emigration, he admitted his growing disgust with the United States, a land of inexorable prejudice, degradation, and alienation. He invited his brethren to seek a homeland "more congenial, more liberal, and more willing to provide the blessings of liberty and equality."[8]

As if following his own advice, Rapier left Minnesota in December 1860 and journeyed to Port-au-Prince, Haiti, the capital of the first Negro republic in the Americas. After a short time in the Caribbean, however, he wrote his uncle James Thomas that, though he had arrived there imbued with sentiments of abolition-ism and universal freedom, he now felt that a man who believed in such sophistry was insane. Based on his witnessing firsthand the poverty of blacks in Haiti after fifty-seven years of freedom there, he proclaimed himself in favor of slavery. He was satisfied that no greater curse could be imposed upon the United States or any other country than emancipation. Once free, he said, Negroes take up the fiddle, banjo, or tambour and devote themselves to dancing, drinking, and playing. "This is sharp language for a negro to use, but it is [as] true as it is strange. If ever I make my permanent home in a country where negroes live in any considerable quantities, it will be where they are slave."[9]

In Port-au-Prince he secured lodging with a wealthy Cuban named Errie (a distant relative of Toussaint L' Ouverture) and found a position teaching English to mulatto children. In his spare time, as he had done in Minnesota, he contributed a number of articles to local newspapers, but now he focused his attention on the class structure. Describing the upper class, mostly mulattoes, as highly educated, refined, and cultured—and the lower class, mostly blacks, as densely ignorant, uncivil, and boorish—he said a deep hatred existed between the two groups, a hatred that often resulted in violence and bloodshed. Ironically, mulattoes fled from white oppression in the United States because they had inherited the Negro blood of their mothers, only to find death in Haiti because they had inherited the white blood of their fathers. He advised his brethren: "Be wise, Learn from the past. Turn your eyes not hither, but to the British West Indies."[10]

He himself journeyed (in February 1861) to Kingston, the capital of British Jamaica. There he lived with a government official in a large villa and began a course of study in dentistry and anatomy under the famed Canadian doctor William Beckett. In the United States, he recalled with great irritation, he was nothing but a "damn nigger," ostracized because his skin was olive by a mixture of Negro and white blood; but in Jamaica, he mingled with the wealthiest class, expressed his opinions on a variety of subjects, and lived in comparative luxury. "To tell the truth a very different kind of idea pervades one's heart and head," he admitted shortly after his arrival, "when one can meet every man on equal terms."[11]

Despite his enthusiasm for the British West Indies, he eventually left Jamaica, and, after having lived almost two years in the Caribbean, he returned to the United States. He settled first in Ohio but soon enrolled in the department of medicine and surgery at the University of Michigan, the first Negro to gain admittance. Though he impressed the faculty with his knowledge of Latin, the natural sciences, mathematics, including algebra and geometry, as well as of current medical prescriptions, he wrote that the university had been thrown into an uproar because an American of African descent had dared to present himself as a candidate for admission. "Whoever heard of such impudence," he remarked sarcastically. "They say I am nothing but a 'nigger.' "[12]

It was perhaps because of such hostility that he withdrew from the university after only a few months. In the autumn of 1863, however, he enrolled in the medical school of Iowa University at Keokuk; and the following June, Rapier received an M.D. He then applied for a commission as a surgeon in the United States Army. Detailing his experiences as a dentist in Kingston, his work at the University of Michigan, and his medical courses at Iowa University, he immodestly presented himself as a man of superior talent and accomplishment, though he admitted that he was a quadroon from the state of Alabama. Accepted as an assistant surgeon in the federal army, he reported to the Freedmen's Contraband Hospital in Washington, D.C., in June to attend to sick and wounded Negroes. Almost at once he found himself pleasantly surprised by the cordial treatment accorded black army officers, even by white enlisted men: in visiting the various departments, he received a military salute from the guards as promptly as if he were Oliver O. Howard. He also discovered there were few respites from the exhausting sixteen-hour days, the continuous stream of wounded and dying Negro soldiers, and the pressures of surgery. "I never worked so hard," he divulged shortly after his arrival, "had so little rest, and felt so tired as I do now."[13] Despite such a demanding schedule, he found time for some social activities, such as establishing a friendship with the well-known Canadian physician Dr. Anderson Abbott, who, like Rapier, had attended school at Buxton, and on at least one occasion—the legal emancipation of Negroes in Maryland—drinking with his friend late into the night.

Along with attending to the sick and wounded, Rapier expressed his concern for freedmen in a number of other ways. Dining with Frederick Douglass (who had only the day before met privately with President Lincoln), Rapier discussed the course of the war as well as the condition of Negroes in the South. He also asked George Whipple of the American Missionary Association (a philanthropic organization founded to assist blacks) to grant his cousin Sarah Thomas, who had taught several years in Canada, a teaching position at a freedmen's school. And he urged Tennessee governor Andrew Johnson to commission black officers in their own regiments. "I am emboldened to [make] this suggestion by a knowledge of the liberality that has ever distinguished your political career, with which, as a Tennessean, I am familiar."[14] Thus, between 1863 and 1865, John Rapier, Jr., despite his earlier misgivings about the wisdom of freeing blacks in the Caribbean, devoted himself unselfishly to serving Negroes in the United States.

While Rapier was traveling in Canada, Central America, the Minnesota Territory, from island to island in the West Indies, and to different parts of the United States, his younger brother, James Thomas Rapier, was also making various sojourns in the United States and Canada. "James is on the Steamer Chocktaw," John Rapier, Sr., wrote in 1856. "She run from this place to new orleans." The elder Rapier lamented that he had not seen his son in several months. "James is getting out of harness very much, drinking and gambling. I would very much like to see him settle down."[15] He was not in favor of boys running the river to make money, preferring to see them working for two shillings a day. Yet Rapier, then nineteen, spent more than a year steamboating on the Cumberland, Tennessee, and Mississippi rivers, stopping in Nashville, Natchez, and New Orleans only to gamble, drink hard whiskey, and assert his manhood by fighting and by frequenting the brothels. But in the fall of 1856, Rapier, Sr., ended a letter with a sigh of relief: James had finally promised to continue his education and would enter the Buxton School in Canada.

Located 170 miles southwest of Toronto, in Kent County, Buxton was the most successful black utopian experiment in the Americas. Founded by William King, a Scotch Presbyterian minister, the community began (1848) with only sixteen settlers (King and fifteen emancipated Louisiana slaves he had once owned) and fifty acres of cleared farmland. The number of residents increased rapidly, however, and King, who at first had doubted the practicality of settling Southern slaves in the North, soon praised Buxton Negroes for showing themselves just as capable as unpropertied white Europeans in making a new life in America. By 1856 the settlement boasted a black population of eight hundred, as well as two sawmills, a shingle factory, a brick factory, a potash factory, a two-story brick temperance hotel, two churches, two hundred homes, and a thousand acres cleared, planted, and fenced. Buxtonites were especially proud of their non-tuition school, where some one hundred forty students, both black and white, were enrolled. The King school, observed fugitive slave Samuel Ringgold Ward, was so much more efficient than the local public schools that whites as far as twenty miles away gladly availed themselves of its advantages. Thus, children of both races read, recited, and played together, without distinction.

Enrolling at the King school in October 1856, Rapier launched into a study of geography, grammar, writing, and mathematics. He also read the Bible and studied several languages. After four months in Buxton, he expressed appreciation that his father had advised him to continue his schooling. "I am getting along at school very well, but you will perceive that at once from my writing, grammar and spelling."[16]

But young Rapier soon lost interest in getting along well at school and turned his attention to a variety of moneymaking schemes. In a letter to his brother John Rapier, who was living in the Minnesota Territory, he explained his desire to start a business producing potash, a silvery white substance used in glassmaking. He also investigated other business possibilities which included starting a retail store, building a sawmill, investing in real estate, and renting some farmland. In short, during his first months in Canada, Rapier experimented in a number of business adventures and seemed preoccupied with material things. "Money is devilish scarce," he wrote. "If I could make $200 in one year I would be satisfied."[17]

Along with his business schemes, Rapier also became involved in politics. In another letter to his brother, he asked John to join him in seeking the postmastership of Buxton—an important political patronage job that carried a good salary. Some of the most influential men in the area had agreed to sign a petition in their behalf, but the Tories were in power, and even though Reverend King was a Reformer, a Tory stood the best chance of getting the office. "Will [you] turn Tory as I am? The government will [probably] give the office to a Tory."[18] He justified his position by asserting that the Negro settlers were not concerned with politics anyway; they were leaving it to King to fight the Loyalists. Evidently, at this time, Rapier saw no contradiction in supporting a strongly antiblack political party in order to secure a lucrative patronage position.

It would appear also that he saw no inconsistency in living in a communal society and disregarding the rules against drinking, fighting, and entertaining loose women, as he admitted having had altercations with several settlers, drinking hard liquor (despite King's strict rule against alcohol), and entertaining "women in the business." He had also fallen out of the habit of attending church. In April 1857, however, all was changed when he was overtaken by a religious conversion. "There has been a great [Methodist] Revival here," he said excitedly, "and it is still going on—Some 70 odd have professed Religion." With a better heart than ever before and with the help of God, he had made peace with his Savior, which everyone must do, he said, if they want to see His face. "I am delivered," he concluded triumphantly.[19]

After his deliverance Rapier repented his youthful indiscretions. As a result of his spiritual transformation, his old materialism was replaced with a determination to continue his education and eventually to enter the ministry. "I have not a red cent in my pocket, nor can I lay my hands on one," he added, admitting the failure of his business ventures.[20] But now he cared very little about material things. By the grace of God, he would seek a higher education, even if he had to scrub floors to earn enough money for tuition.

Not only did James make his peace in the spring of 1857; he also attempted to make a convert of his brother. In one letter to John, Jr., he quoted the thirty-third chapter of John: "If a man is not born again he cannot see the Kingdom of God"; the fifty-sixth

chapter of Isaiah: "There is no peace for the wicked"; Paul's letter
to Timothy: "Christ came to this world for sinners"; Romans eight:
"Without holiness no man shall see the Lord"; Corinthians two:
"Behold all old things pass away and new things appear"; and the
fifty-sixth chapter of Isaiah again: "There is no peace save by God."
He even added a little homily of his own: John, Christ died on the
cross for you as much as He did for the Queen of England or the
Czar of Russia. "When I hear from you again let me hear that you
are trying to get Religion."[21] As if to reinforce the hope of reward
with the threat of punishment, he gave his appeal an additional
emphasis: "God will be strict in marking your sins against you. You
will die [in] damnation if you don't seek the Lord."[22]

Unimpressed with his brother's joyous surrender to piety, John
recorded in his diary, "Letter from James. Buxton, Professed
Religion. Damn Fool."[23] Complaining further, he wrote James a
sarcastic query: Now would it not be advisable, whenever he
corresponded, to select a tract, such as are published by the various
Sunday schools, especially one that might assist an inconvincible
sinner, and mail it? The scoffer wrote the zealot several times
urging him to drop religion entirely from his letters, threatening
that if he did not cease sermonizing "I will be compelled to drop *all*
correspondence with him."[24]

Shortly after his religious conversion James Rapier began to
study in earnest. In another letter to his brother he gave a report of
his progress: "You will think it strange probably to hear that
someone so Ignorant as I, am in Latin and Greek, but I am doing
well."[25] Rapier also studied Spanish, history, shorthand, and
phrenology, a science based on the notion that the character is
revealed in the contours of the cranium. He soon advanced to
reading Old Testament scriptures, classical literature, and higher
mathematics. After submitting to his year-end examinations,
despite a fever, headache, and boots that pinched his toes, he said
that the Lord God of Hosts had changed his heart, and that now he
wanted to attend college. Adding with a note of concern that it
might be difficult to gain admittance, he put his faith in the Lord
Jesus Christ.

Despite his intense desire for a higher education, Rapier remained at Buxton during the 1857–58 school year, working diligently at his school assignments. "I study very hard now," he
wrote, "and I am getting along very well at school. We have a
Splendid teacher."[26] In one letter he recounted that, although he

had read *Caesar* for only two months, had studied the rudiments of
Latin for only six, no one in the class, with the possible exception of
Henry Gracy and George Morris, whites, and John Riley, a Negro,
had done as well reading the ancient Roman language. "I can knock
off a chapter of *Caesar* as slick as any of them."[27] The record
suggests that Rapier recited grammar lessons with ease, had an
excellent grasp of his mathematics course, and helped teach the
younger children to read and write. Outside the classroom he spent
a good deal of time reading the Bible, an assortment of newspapers,
including the Florence *Gazette*, Chatham *Planet*, and *Provincial
Freeman*, a Spanish book, and biographies of famous men. Midway through the school year, the young student proudly admitted
that King had urged him to go on to college and that he planned to
attend a normal school in Toronto for the next four years. "For 2
things I have in view only," he confided, "to serve my God and get
an education."[28]

Rapier had, in fact, a third object in view: the improvement of
the lot of Negroes in the Southern states. In a two-thousand-word
missive written on the last day of February 1858, he enthusiastically proclaimed that he had been cutting wood in the frosty
afternoon air to enliven his spirits and to brighten his ideas for a
debate that night. The question was an old one: Who had suffered
the most at the hands of the white man, the Indians or the Negroes?
He, Julius Rector, and William Harris planned to defend the Indian,
as not all could be on one side; William Scott, Peter King, and
Reverend Moore were prepared to defend the colored man. As if
anticipating the arguments of the opposition, he wrote that bondage deadened the mind, keeping it in a refrangible state; blacks
therefore had little opportunity to improve their condition. He
complained that whites had all the power; problems had always
been solved by whites; and the answer had always been, "Niggers
cannot and never will be anything." That was easy to understand;
blacks were behind the times two thousand years; "the farther we
run, the worse they beat us."[29] When a Negro would attempt to
elevate himself, other Negroes would say, "You will never be a
great lawyer, or doctor, or political leader." Rejecting these
counsels of despair, he vowed to make something of himself and
promised to do his part to solve the problems facing blacks. He
vowed that if he lived and God were willing, he would return to the
South some day and assist his brethren.

During these years in Buxton, Rapier lived with his aunt and uncle, Maria and Henry Thomas, and their family. He had a deep admiration for the Thomases, affectionately calling his cousin Sarah "sister," referring to his aunt as a devoted and loving mother, and describing his uncle as an intelligent, sensible, hard-working father. When his uncle planned a trip to Buffalo, New York, in 1857, Rapier expressed concern that Henry might be sold back into slavery, but explained that his uncle was not afraid, as he did not think they would recognize him after so many years. At the same time he told how his uncle had planted eleven acres in corn and wheat. "I should like to see him do well, for I believe he is a Clever Man, but he is poor. I think, if he were able, he would help me on to College."[30] Still, Rapier credited Henry, more than anyone else, with having set him an example that would lead him on to the summit.

Despite his fondness for the Thomases, he missed his own family. "My thoughts turn back to the home of our boyhood," he wrote nostalgically to his brother John, one bitterly cold winter day in late January 1857. Then, he and his brothers had been together; they had "breathed as one";[31] but now they were scattered across the face of the earth—in Minnesota, California, Alabama, Canada. "Do you ever expect to see us all together again?" He himself felt, sadly, that they would never be reunited. "Did you ever think how small our family is?"[32] He had guessed correctly that the Rapiers would never be together again: Henry and Richard, after their unsuccessful search for gold, remained in the West, and John, Jr., who would soon depart for the Caribbean, never returned to the South.

Perhaps the high point of Rapier's stay in Canada occurred in 1860, when he was chosen to address the Prince of Wales, who had stopped in Buxton during a tour of the United States and Canada. "We hail the visit of your Royal Highness, Albert Edward, heir apparent to the British Crown [the future Edward VII], with unmingled satisfaction," Rapier told a large audience of blacks and whites who had gathered to see the royal entourage.[33] In Buxton, he explained, blacks had found a refuge from the cruel oppression of slavery as well as an opportunity for education, social standing, property ownership, and a full religious life. More than a thousand settlers, including many fugitive slaves, now lived in Buxton, where they maintained their families in comfort. "Here we enjoy true freedom, a blessing denied us in the land of our birth."[34]

Other observers, however, viewed the black community in quite a different light. A special reporter for the New York *Tribune*, for example, visited the settlement in the summer of 1857, and said that it was certainly no realization of a utopia. The cabins did not resemble the neat, whitewashed houses of a New England village; eveything was new, rude, and rough. To a city-bred man the timber seemed terribly crude, and the road merely a wide lane cut through the forest, with roots everywhere. John Rapier, Sr., admitted that he had never thought much of the place, as Buxton residents could not produce as much as they needed. To outsiders, the settlement seemed to offer little, but to James Rapier, who secured an education there, and to Henry Thomas, who toiled on his own land, it proffered hope and independence.

To continue his schooling, Rapier left the black community in 1860 and enrolled in a Toronto normal school. Poring over his lessons in Latin, Greek, geometry, and ancient history, he studied sixteen hours a day, despite some burdensome financial problems. In the fall of 1861, for instance, he was forced to borrow money to pay for his accommodations, but during the winter, he was thrown out of his lodging because he could not pay the rent. Left with only four dollars with which to continue the academic year, he never wavered from his avowed purpose to obtain a higher education, and he finally secured an additional loan. Despite such pecuniary hardships, he again expressed a disdain for the materialism that had once been so paramount in his thoughts. Others might have more money, he wrote, but he was nearly out of debt, had studied very hard, and had gained a good education. "I will work hard, hire out, and stay in school," he promised. "In six months more I can graduate."[35]

Besides studying so diligently, he found time to follow military events in the South, rejoicing as federal armies swept into Alabama. "The Federals are making good headway down south," he said in 1862; they had already been to Florence, where the freed slaves had cheered their arrival.[36] Early in 1863, he received a teaching diploma, returned to Buxton, and found employment as a schoolteacher at one of the King schools. He then enlisted, along with his uncle, for first-class service in the local militia, and purchased fifty acres of farmland for one hundred eighty dollars. "Buxton has improved a great deal Since you were here," he explained to his brother. "I find some very clever people here."[37]

Buxton had indeed prospered. With a population that had grown to over two thousand, the black community boasted two large sawmills, several shingle, stave, brick, and potash factories, four schools (with a combined enrollment of over three hundred), four churches (Methodist, Baptist, and two Presbyterian), over two thousand acres under cultivation, twenty-five miles of road, as well as two hundred fifty frame houses, comfortably furnished and whitewashed. "To-day the thermometer stands at five degrees below zero, with snow a foot deep," one observer said, "yet there is not an able bodied man in the settlement who is not in the woods with an axe and crosscut saw, making staves for the foreign market and taking saw logs to the mill."[38] Such a thriving community stood as a symbol of black enterprise and achievement.

Rapier had not only witnessed firsthand the enterprise of former slaves in freedom during his stay in the North, he had also engaged in some business ventures, become involved in politics, secured a superior education, entered the teaching profession, experienced a religious awakening, and made the decision to dedicate his life to the uplifting of blacks in his native land. Yet he had always considered himself a Southerner. "You can imagine my feelings when I heard that Gen. Beauregard had ordered the firing on Fort Sumter. I listened to the sounds, and though many miles away, I fancied I heard the cannon, in thunder tones, say, 'The year of jubilee has come, return, you exiles, home.' "[39] Then, late in 1864, his formal education completed, determined to devote his future to improving conditions among Southern Negroes, he returned to the town where he had spent much of his youth, Nashville, Tennessee, to begin his life's work.

4

The Beginnings of Reconstruction

The Tennessee capital had changed a great deal in eight years. The unhurried town of Rapier's youth had been transformed into a lively, bustling city, with drays and express wagons crowding the narrow streets, fruit peddlers thronging the sidewalks, dock workers scurrying about the wharves, and regiments of blue-coated soldiers marching up and down Front Street. Unlike other areas of the urban South (Richmond, Charleston, Atlanta), Nashville had experienced a wartime boom. The population, only twenty thousand before the war, had exploded to nearly eighty thousand; and even in the midst of a Rebel counterattack (the Battle of Franklin), the city's busy commercial life continued without interruption. Nashville, one resident proclaimed in 1865, was one of the most thriving and prosperous cities in the South. Yet the city's prosperity was not shared by Negroes. The vast majority of the twelve thousand freedmen and freedwomen, called contrabands of war, who had flocked to the capital between 1862 (the date of the Confederate evacuation) and 1865, suffered from inadequate housing, improper medical care, and even malnutrition. "Huddled together, in rickety tenements and government houses," one observer noted, "they are deteriorating both physically and morally."[1]

Though deeply distressed by the condition of these blacks, which contrasted so greatly with the flourishing Negro community he had just left, Rapier could do little to assist his brethren. The exigencies and dislocations of the war forced him to find temporary employment as a reporter for a Northern newspaper covering the Union war effort. In the spring of 1865, he moved to Maury County, Tennessee (sixty miles south of the capital), rented about two hundred acres of land, and set about planting some cotton. In that year he not only raised a large crop of the staple in Tennessee, but he also launched his career in reconstruction politics, entering the debate over the question Shall three and a half million recently emancipated slaves be granted the elective franchise?

White public opinion, in both the North and the South, was opposed to extending the vote to Negroes. Even civil rights leader Charles Sumner, radical Republican Thaddeus Stevens, and abolitionist William Lloyd Garrison, who had sworn to be as harsh as truth, as uncompromising as justice, stood in opposition. Garrison rhetorically asked the nation in 1864: When in the history of mankind had emancipation from bondage ever been followed by the granting of political privileges? The Chicago *Times* contended that the nation in even discussing such a question, had been affected by some disease; and the New York *Times*, though admitting the infeasibility of the plan, suggested getting rid of the problem by sending the Negro race back to Africa. Illustrative of numerous journals in the old Confederate states, the Nashville *Dispatch* maintained that, without the protection of their masters, more than a million Negroes had died during the war. Freedmen should learn to practice habits of health care, steady industry, self-control, and self-denial, and "not be stuffed with confused notions of parties and politics."[2] Blacks were ignorant, landless, and would, if extended the vote, not only dominate the politics of the South, but demand social equality. "For the present we have done enough for the negro," Tennessee governor W. G. Brownlow, who had earlier frequented James Thomas's barbershop, said, summarizing the sentiments of his contemporaries. "Negro voting cannot fit my natural prejudices of caste."[3]

It was therefore up to blacks to speak out, and they were anything but reticent in doing so. Gathering in conventions across the South, they discussed a wide range of questions, including wages, literacy, schools, discrimination, the family, land ownership, and so-called social equality. But they emphasized the necessity for political involvement. Refusing to dwell on the oppressions of the past, disclaiming any desire for social mixing, they demanded their rights as citizens, rights guaranteed by the Declaration of Independence, rights, as one black spokesman put it, which were the legitimate result of the Civil War. And at one of these conventions, in Nashville, Tennessee, August 7, 1865, James Rapier added his voice to the movement for black political equality.

It was only mid-morning and already sultry when one hundred
forty southern black leaders gathered in the small chapel of the
African Methodist church near the capitol to answer the opponents
of Negro suffrage. The roster of delegates included businessman
J. C. Napier; the locally famous pastor, Daniel Watkins; lawyer
Samuel Lowery; and barbershop owner Frank Parrish, all of whom
Rapier had known since the 1840s. As the third speaker to address
the convention, Rapier made his way confidently among many of
his old friends to the speaker's rostrum. He declared that Negroes
had been denied equal rights too long; they fully understood the
burdens of citizenship; they realized, perhaps better than white
Americans, that voting was both a privilege and a responsibility,
without which there would be no true freedom. Rapier then
advanced a far-reaching plan. He charged the membership to
establish a statewide franchise commission, which would include
ninety-five subcommissions, one for every county in Tennessee.
What would be their function? To compile a book of statistics
concerning the advancement of blacks since emancipation. How
many schools had been established? Where were they located?
How many churches had been erected? How many Negroes
owned their own farms, equipment, real estate, businesses? What
occupations were being pursued by blacks? Rapier asked for
statistics on every conceivable aspect of Negro life. "Let us gather
all information showing our progress and fitness for the franchise."[4] The proposal—brief, specific, informative—was adopted
by acclamation.

Emerging as one of the most active and effective delegates at the
convention, Rapier not only served on four committees, Rules,
Permanent Organization, Business, and Agriculture (the latter two
ex-officio), but submitted a number of other proposals and resolutions. Though he continued to seek equal rights for blacks, he also
sought to harmonize relations between the races. In this vein he
opened the proceedings to members of the conservative press,
complimented a group of reporters from the Democratic New York
Herald, arranged for the distribution of the convention minutes to
members of the state legislature, and expressed appreciation to the
white community in Nashville for its hospitality.

It seemed proper, then, that he should be asked to deliver the
concluding address. Late in the afternoon of the second day, amid
the profound attention of the convention, Rapier spoke to the loyal

white citizens of Tennessee on behalf of his race. Why should Negroes be denied the franchise? he asked. It was not because only a few blacks could read or write, as literacy was not a test in Tennessee—and if it had been many whites would have been disfranchised. It was not because only a few ex-slaves owned property, as land ownership was not a qualification—and, again, many whites would have been stricken from the rolls if it had been. It was not because bondsmen had caused the late war, "which, in its march, trampled down your cherished institutions, devastated your fields, and burned your cities."[5] The Negro, though deeply involved in the Southern tragedy, had not been the cause of it. Enfranchising blacks, Rapier said, would not result in social equality, nor the Africanization of the state, as Negroes constituted only 20 percent of the voting-age population. Appealing to an American sense of justice and fair play, he said that Negro voting could not be long deferred. Other states had granted the same request; why not the Volunteer State? "It is only a question of time," he predicted with emotion and conviction as he articulated the sentiments of the black assemblage, "and [you too] must join the great march of events."[6]

But neither the Volunteer State, nor any other Southern commonwealth, joined the "great march of events" in the months following the war. Despite Rapier's appeal, white political leaders, occupying office under Andrew Johnson's plan of restoration, refused to recognize blacks as citizens. New state constitutions, written in 1865–66, not only excluded Negroes from the electorate, but explicitly insured social, political, and economic supremacy to whites. At the same time state legislatures enacted laws that restricted the testimony of blacks in certain court cases, punished Negroes for marrying whites, apprenticed black children to their ex-masters, and hired out freedmen convicted of vagrancy. Southerners also elected ex-Confederates to high office: the vice-president of the Confederacy, four ex-Confederate generals, five colonels, six cabinet officers, and fifty-eight former representatives, for example, journeyed to Washington to take seats in the thirty-ninth Congress. It seemed to Rapier that whites had drafted state charters, enacted state laws, and elected high officials, all with the clear purpose of keeping Negroes "in their place."

Discouraged by the direction of this Confederate reconstruction, he decided he would return to Alabama. Traveling along the

Tennessee River, he witnessed some of the destruction wrought by
the first modern war: the gutted buildings, twisted railroad tracks,
burned gin houses, neglected fields, collapsed bridges, bomb-
damaged factories, and ruined plantations. But even in this region,
where the fighting had been almost continuous, large areas remained
essentially unchanged from antebellum times. Among them was a
cucumber-shaped island in the Tennessee River only a short distance
below the spot where Rapier's father had first set foot on Alabama
soil as an eleven-year-old slave.

It was on this island that Rapier rented five hundred fifty acres of
farmland from plantation owner William Coffee, the son of John
Coffee, an old acquaintance of Rapier's father. He then set about
hiring twenty-one black tenant farmers, and in the space of two
years purchased four mules, two wagons, several plows, a boat,
and personally supervised the planting of two cotton crops. He also
hired another group of freedmen to begin clearing new land, both
to increase his acreage and to establish a steamboat woodyard
business. For the next two years he farmed the rich alluvial soil on
what was known as Seven Mile Island so successfully that an 1867
biographical sketch of Rapier ranked him among the most prosperous planters in the Tennessee Valley. "When at home, he works
every day in the field," the *Daily State Sentinel* beamed, "setting an
excellent example to whites as well as the colored race."[7]

But economic success was not enough to satisfy him while the
condition of freedmen went substantially unimproved. With neither
citizenship nor voting rights, he had to content himself with
criticizing Confederate reconstruction, especially the leadership
qualities of Andrew Johnson. Though a man of powerful intellect,
unusual firmness, and great combative power, Johnson, as leader
of the Conservative Republicans, had stood against every measure
designed to benefit those released from bondage: he had vetoed the
Freedmen's Bureau Bill, designed to assist Negroes in adjusting to
freedom, as well as the 1866 Civil Rights Act. Joined by ex-
Confederates, he had not only refused to acknowledge Negroes as
citizens, but even rejected them as human beings. Based on his
assessment of the President's record—Johnson's support for the
black codes, his refusal to allow Negro testimony in the courts, his
opposition to homestead legislation—Rapier concluded that he was
destitute of all political understanding. What do Negroes want? he
asked, and then answered his own question: protection, justice and

equality. "Any man who is too politically blind to see that political equality is the legitimate fruit of the war, or if he sees it, is too weak morally to tell his followers, is not worthy of the name statesman."[8] There were a few Republicans whom he thought deserved that appellation: Thaddeus Stevens, the great apostle of liberty, and Charles Sumner, the protector of Negro rights. They had both made a determined effort to assist blacks in their quest for equality. But freedmen were still slaves, he concluded, only now without masters.

Such a harsh judgment was certainly true for Negroes in Alabama. No sooner had the war ended than the state's general assembly enacted a series of laws reminiscent of the old slave codes. Freedmen, free Negroes, and mulattoes were forbidden to own guns, carry weapons, intermarry with whites, or testify in the various courts of the state, except in cases involving blacks. The assembly also passed a state vagrancy law that subjected any person without visible means of support to a fine of not less than fifty nor more than one hundred dollars and to imprisonment in the county jail, or to hard labor for the county, for not more than six months. Conceding that the vagrancy law nominally applied to whites as well as blacks, the Mobile *Nationalist* asserted that in practice it was applied almost exclusively to persons of color. "If a policeman gets mad at a colored person, he immediately arrests him on a charge of vagrancy. These arrests are generally made without warrants and with malice toward the whole race."[9] The assembly soon added to the foregoing legislation an apprenticeship law, requiring sheriffs to round up all minors (defined as those under 18 years of age) without visible means of support, and to deliver them to a local probate judge. The judge was then to apprentice the children to some suitable and competent person. "If said minor shall be the child of a freedman," the law read, "the former owner shall have preference."[10] Except for the latter section, the phrasing again made no reference to blacks, "but that this class is contemplated," said one observer, "is obvious to every mind familiar with the affairs of the state."[11]

Local ordinances also discriminated against freedmen. Considering the state codes, Rapier was not the least surprised when the Florence Board of Aldermen virtually reenacted the prewar slave patrol code, apportioning all whites between the ages of 18 and 50 into ten police companies, instructing them to patrol the streets during the evening hours, and granting them the authority to arrest all persons violating the law—especially a statute forbidding blacks from entering the town at night. "If by any pretext of their freedom negroes assume the right to attempt a violation of the law, or arrogate a pretension to become the equal of whites," an editorial in the Florence *Journal* threatened, "such conduct will bring upon them such a visitation of punishment as will make them forever regret the unsoundness of their reasoning."[12] Speaking as a friend of the freedman, and from a true knowledge of his character, as well as from memories of ownership, the *Journal* concluded: "We utter the sentiment of the Southern mind."[13]

Blacks found little relief from the discriminatory laws in the Alabama courts. In southern Alabama, George D. Robinson, a superintendent for the Freedmen's Bureau, wrote in 1866 that the civil courts were a source of cruel oppression to freedmen. Negroes were arrested on the most frivolous pretexts, and after a mockery of a trial, they were incarcerated. "In our courts the prejudice against the unfortunate black man is so strong as to excite the most marked attention of even obtuse minds," contended another bureau official in a different section of the state, adding that blacks arrested upon precisely the same charge as whites received vastly different punishments.[14]

Some cases never reached the courts. While attending to the routine of the plantation, Rapier heard disquieting rumors that freedmen in various sections of Alabama had been brutalized because of their color. Reports came to him that Negroes had been whipped, beaten, assaulted, discharged from employment, "not allowed to suckle child," not allowed to have a gun, searched without authority, and even sold.[15] But these lesser offenses paled beside the more sadistic crimes he heard had been perpetrated against freedmen. Negro farmer James Travick, who had shot a white man for forcibly violating his wife, for example, was brutally whipped and hanged by a group of whites. The same company later accosted Travick's wife, Edna, whipping her with a hickory stick "until her body was completely cut up," and captured his two children, Daniel and Jack, slashing off one child's arm, tearing out the other's eye, and lynching them beside their father, whose decaying body had not yet been cut down. About the same time, Rapier read several newspaper accounts concerning the violent activities of Horace King, an ex-Confederate soldier who had gone on a rampage murdering Negroes. "He is killing all the darkies," a resident of nearby Decatur (Morgan County) wrote. "He has already shot two freedmen through the head."[16] After the shootings, King had brandished his weapons, bragged about his accomplishments, and cursed and threatened the entire black race. "The civil authorities refuse to take any notice of King or his acts," an official lamented, *"except to quietly inform him to keep out of the way for a day or two!"*[17]

In the two years immediately following the Civil War, Alabama whites treated freedmen in much the same way they had treated their slaves in antebellum times. Under the presidential plan of reconstruction whites enacted state and local laws explicitly designed to keep blacks in a markedly subordinate status. They established a legal system based on caste, and frequently took the law into their own hands. But in March 1867, Congress took over the reins of reconstruction in Alabama and the South. The far-reaching laws were designed to provide a more efficient government in the rebel states and to insure political and legal equality for blacks by establishing military governments in the South, disfranchising certain "disloyal" persons, enfranchising blacks, detailing a procedure for voter registration, and specifying new conditions for the readmission of a state to the United States. With the advent of congressional reconstruction, James Rapier, along with other black leaders, looked hopefully to the future: at last the long-awaited opportunity for blacks to prove that they understood the burdens of citizenship had arrived.

But how did the new acts affect Alabama freedmen? What was meant by a more efficient government? And who would participate in the new regime? In the hope of answering these and other questions, Rapier called a meeting of Lauderdale County freedmen for April 24, 1867, at the Florence African Methodist Episcopal Church. It was dusk, the oil lamps already casting shadows in the small chapel, when Rapier rose from a chair facing the audience of one hundred fifty Negroes, walked to the altar, and called the meeting to order. Congress had passed two complex laws, he said in a brief introductory address, which not only divided the South into military districts, but disfranchised certain ex-Confederates, enfranchised freedmen, authorized the election of delegates, including former slaves, to a state constitutional convention, and charged that convention with the drafting of a new state charter. Once this charter had been ratified by a majority of the eligible and registered voters and approved by Congress, and once the state had accepted a newly proposed amendment to the federal Constitution (the Fourteenth), which granted Negroes citizenship rights, the state could reenter the Union. The initial step in this complicated process—the reason Rapier had called the meeting—was to select a Negro voter registrar (as directed by Alabama's military commandant), one of three persons in each district responsible for keeping records of voter registration, providing state officials with local election returns, and advising blacks as well as whites on their duties as electors. As the registrar would be the first black public official in Alabama history, Rapier entreated the gathering to select a man of exceptional intellect, outstanding ability, and unquestioned integrity. In concluding his remarks, he offered a word of caution: "In this our first act of participation in the politics of the State, [let us] proceed with calmness, moderation, and intelligence."[18]

Heeding the admonition, the freedmen began to organize under the congressional plan. They chose Oscar M. Waring as president of the meeting, James B. Goins as vice-president, selected a resolutions committee, and appointed a committee of five to nominate a Negro registrar for the Fortieth (later the Forty-third) Alabama Election District. After a brief recess, the Resolutions Committee returned with a statement expressing the sentiments of the freedmen in northwest Alabama: "We will endeavor to bring to the consideration of our new duties, a solemn sense of the great responsibilities now resting upon us as enfranchised citizens, and entertaining kindly feelings toward all men, regardless of antecedents, we will enter upon the discharge of our new obligations with a sincere desire to promote peace, harmony, and union."[19] A second resolution pledged support to the Republican party for its steadfast adherence to the cause of equal rights; a third arranged for the proceedings of the meeting to be published in the Florence *Journal*; and a final resolve called for freedmen to strive for economic betterment, educational improvement, and a well-ordered, dignified life. The committee of five then announced its selection for voter registrar: John H. Rapier, Sr. Though the fifty-nine-year-old Rapier was not as politically motivated as his son, he graciously thanked the gathering for such an honor and, in a short speech, expressed optimism about the future for blacks in Alabama. The delegates

unanimously approved both committee reports and, after several
more speeches, adjourned. Among the last to leave the church that
night were John and James Rapier, who walked slowly together
along Court Street toward the elder Rapier's barbershop and home.
The balmy night air seemed to enhance their general feeling of
satisfaction; they had been down that same street a thousand times
before, but never as citizens, voters, and acknowledged leaders of
their race.

Only a month after this first political gathering of blacks in
northwest Alabama, Rapier again issued a call for a meeting of
Negroes. The purpose, as he explained in the May 23 issue of the
Florence *Journal*, was to select a black representative to the state's
first Republican convention. Again a large group of freedmen,
conducting themselves, as a Conservative newspaper observed,
with notable propriety and decorum, gathered, but this time they
met at the Florence courthouse. As he had done previously, Rapier
began the proceedings with a brief speech. The Republican party,
the great party of Lincoln, had long been supportive of black
aspirations; it had existed in the North since 1854, but was now just
beginning in the South. Before he could conclude his remarks,
though, the black delegates interrupted, unanimously declaring
their choice for representative to the forthcoming convention. "The
freedmen send a delegate who I think will compare favorably with
any from the class in your convention," store owner John W.
McAlester, who operated the firm that succeeded Rapier and
Simpson, wrote Alabama governor Robert Patton the next day.
"James Rapier is a sensible man and disposed to do exactly right."[20]

Unlike McAlester, however, other northern Alabama whites,
especially those who had lived in the state prior to the Civil War,
entertained grave doubts about the desirability of black participation in politics. Sidney Cherry Posey, antebellum lawyer, circuit
judge, and member of the Alabama Secession Convention, believed
that the state should be saved from the humiliation of Negro
suffrage; and Neander Rice, a twenty-five-year resident of Florence
and a long-time spokesman for the hill-country farmers, the
common people, as he called them, also opposed the enfranchisement of blacks. Dr. James Steward, a faithful customer at Rapier's
barbershop, complained that the reconstruction acts made Negroes
equal to whites. "As a man born and reared in the South, I deplore
our present condition."[21] And the forty-year resident of Huntsville,

Joseph C. Bradley, said that appointing black registrars would greatly impede the growth of the state's Republican party, especially in the predominantly white counties. Despite such anti-Negro sentiments, these four, along with others who had similar feelings, cast their lot with the Party of Lincoln. How solidly they had become friends of the new party was illustrated by Posey's warning to whites that if they did not accept the participation of blacks in politics, the next step might well be confiscation, or complete disfranchisement.

Other white Republicans, newcomers to the state from the North, supported congressional reconstruction from the outset. Attempting to organize a league of black voters in Lauderdale County, for example, were two Ohioans, G. W. Street and one Dr. Yeiser, who spoke to a torchlight rally of several hundred Negroes near the Pisgah Church, some ten miles from Florence. A sea of burning torches and huge, shadowy images dancing against the pine forest greeted Yeiser as he explained the purpose of the conclave: to organize the Union League, a secret club with secret rituals. In a low voice, he asked each member of the audience to hold up his right hand, thumb and third finger touching, and to lower his arm slowly while softly chanting: "Liberty, Lincoln, Loyal, League."[22] Among those in the audience were John and James Rapier, who objected to the clandestine and ritualistic nature of the meeting. No sooner had it begun than they moved among the Negro audience, urging blacks to withdraw; and within a few minutes more than half of those in attendance, following the Rapiers, had moved silently away from the eerie scene. "The ostensible object of the meeting was to help the colored race," the Florence *Journal* noted in an editorial a few days later, but fortunately the gathering contained "elements of intelligence and honesty that could neither be hoodwinked, nor overcome, by the craft of their white brethren."[23]

Thus, at the outset of congressional reconstruction in northwest Alabama, three groups—natives, Northerners, and blacks—vied for political power. Though reluctant at first to accept Negroes as citizens, by late April 1867, native Republicans had become firm supporters of congressional reconstruction and had sought to lead freedmen. A few Northerners also attempted to guide blacks. Neither group was successful, however, due in large measure to the leadership of John and James Rapier, who quickly asserted their determination to reconstruct Alabama under the congressional plan.

Black political activity was widespread. When Rapier was calling and attending meetings in Lauderdale County, other blacks, from every section of Alabama, were holding meetings, making resolutions, speaking on the reconstruction bills, and selecting delegates to attend the Montgomery convention. Only two days after the first reconstruction measure passed Congress, Mobile blacks, including Lawrence Berry, E. C. Branch, and James Branch, held a meeting where they pledged themselves to the principles of equal political and civil rights to all citizens and recognized the right of every male citizen, without distinction of race or color, to vote in the forthcoming elections. While Mobile Negroes were among the first to respond to congressional reconstruction, freedmen in other parts of the state quickly began to organize. Under the leadership of Lafayette Robinson, later a member of the constitutional convention, the former slaves of Huntsville and vicinity formed an institute for local improvement, resolving to give their undivided support to unconditional Union men. In nearby Morgan County, Lewis Stibling, president of the local Union League, addressed league members at Decatur and solemnly promised "to vote only for the friends of the colored race."[24] In the Black Belt, Isaac Burt, J. Alexander, and John Cox, black residents of Kingston, resolved at a meeting some twenty miles from Montgomery to favor speedy restoration to the Union by conforming with the provisions of the military reconstruction bill. And in Montgomery, John Trainor and T. U. Barnard spoke to three thousand blacks on the voting responsibilities of freedmen.

Across the state Negroes discussed their new rights. "We deprecate any attempt to organize a 'White Man's Party' or a 'Black Man's Party.' The interest and destinies of both are the same and upon the sustaining of such relations depends the happiness and prosperity of the South."[25] So declared Wesley Cox, black chairman of a Party of Lincoln assemblage near the Georgia border at Bluffton in Chambers County. Miles away, five thousand freedmen listened to a Negro newspaper publisher in an open field adjoining the gasworks in Mobile. "We are here tonight to tell the world that after being enfranchised we are wise enough to know our rights," announced Lawrence Berry in much the same vein as Rapier's burdens of citizenship speech in Nashville, "and we are going to claim those rights."[26]

Most black leaders, like Rapier, sought political equality in a spirit of conciliation. When forty-two leading Negroes from southern Alabama assembled in Mobile to devise measures to advance the interest of black people, Charles Leveans sounded the keynote: "We should be moderate."[27] They had assembled as representatives of blacks; they should show themselves worthy by moving ahead cautiously. Such outstanding men as editor W. V. Turner of the *Elmore Republican*, Montgomery's Holland Thompson and Peyton Finley, and former Union soldier John Carraway, presented resolutions favoring the Stevens-Shaellabarger Bill, the abolition of legal distinctions between the races, and the establishment of a common school system. One resolution warned that widespread evils would follow a general confiscation of land, and another reemphasized a concern with the social and economic effects of freedom: "We sincerely desire a peaceable and happy relationship ... between us and our white neighbors and employers."[28]

The local, county, and district meetings culminated with the Republican state convention. One hundred Negro and fifty white delegates, drawn from every county in the state, assembled on June 4, 1867, in the House of Representatives in Montgomery to inaugurate the new party in Alabama. Convention president William H. Smith, a Southerner who had fled into Union lines in 1862, made a few brief opening remarks; then James Rapier, chosen a vice-president, spoke from the rostrum. With the same spirit of tolerance that had characterized his earlier efforts in behalf of the party, he asked that the proceedings be open to the press and proposed that journalists, no matter what their political persuasion, be given seats in the convention and extended the utmost courtesy. After his proposal had been accepted, he pressed upon the convention the importance of communicating the new party's principles to all Alabamians.

Although Rapier had not been inflammatory in presenting these resolutions, only moments after he left the podium a bitter dispute erupted. When the name of Richard Busteed, a federal district judge, was offered to the convention, a black representative from Mobile jumped to his feet. Straining not to lose control, Ovid Gregory, a free Negro who owned and operated a cigar store, resisted the motion. "A few weeks ago Judge Busteed opposed all the rights conferred on the colored man by the recent acts of Congress," he said, accusing Busteed of attempting to rob him of "all that was dear on earth."[29] But Gregory received a sharp

reprimand for the impropriety of his remarks from the aging Judge
S. C. Posey, who, like Busteed, had reservations about the
participation of blacks in politics. Remember that the work of
reconstruction had only just begun, Posey cautioned; the convention should accept anyone who promised allegiance to the party.
Alabama's first black lawyer, John Carraway, in a reply to Posey,
forcefully argued that Busteed, who seemed to think enfranchisement was a mistake, was an enemy of the black man. The
controversy raged until late into the night. Defending the judge
were General J. W. Burke, a former Union soldier from Ohio,
and David C. Humphries, a Douglas Democrat from Morgan
County; while, besides Gregory and Carraway, Albert Griffin, a
white Northerner who was editor of the Mobile *Nationalist*,
challenged Busteed's sincerity. It was not until late in the morning
of the second day that the dispute finally ended, with the delegates'
voting 148 to 25 against seating Busteed; but the bitter debate—
symbolic of the factionalism that would plague the party throughout reconstruction—had consumed more than half of the scheduled
two-day convention.

Rapier had not participated in the dispute. Instead, as a leading
member of the platform committee, he had spent the first day
drafting the party platform. Late in the afternoon of the second
day, he submitted to the gathering a series of resolutions endorsing
the congressional plan of reconstruction, supporting the proposed
constitutional amendments, and outlining several specific, if idealistic, aims of the party: free speech, free press, free schools, a
liberal contribution by the state for the purpose of public education,
and the outlawing of discrimination because of color or previous
condition. Adopting all of the resolutions unanimously, the delegates adjourned, but not before declaring: "We discountenance all
attempts to stir up strife."[30]

Despite the vote against Busteed and the unified support for the
platform, strong antagonisms had developed at the first statewide
Republican convention. Whites, especially those who had lived in
the northern and eastern sections of the state (Madison, Lauderdale,
and Randolph) before the war, left the convention disgruntled and
discouraged. Not only had they lost their fight over the Busteed resolution, but they had become fearful of the power of Gregory, Carraway, Griffin, and others they called extreme radicals. In an astute
analysis of the hostilities that had developed, a reporter noted that

"ex-rebels" had quarrelled with "untainted loyalists"; "ultra-Rad-
icals" had chafed at the slow pace of conservative Republicans; and
great diversity of sentiment had characterized the meeting, "however unanimous they may appear to have been in the adopting of
their platform."[31]

While freedmen and pro-Union white men convened to organize
in favor of the acts of Congress, the majority of Alabama whites
(perhaps 90 percent) was organizing against congressional reconstruction. At first white Democrats attempted to lure blacks
into the ranks of their party. The former Confederate colonel in the
Seventh Alabama Cavalry and editor of the Montgomery *Mail*,
Joseph Hodgson, recalled friendship and intimacy with freedmen.
"They have been the nurses of our children, the playfellows of our
childhood, and our faithful friends."[32] Another editor, John Forsyth
of the Mobile *Daily Register*, advised his fellow Democrats to
accept Negro suffrage as a fact and to "deal justly by the Negroes
and tell them kindly and honestly that they had better go with the
Southern white people."[33] And a spectacular debate on the white
marble steps of the capitol, May 14, 1867, pitted an unwavering
Yankee radical, Massachusetts Senator Henry Wilson, one-time
editor of the anti-slavery Boston *Republican*, against a staunch
Southern Conservative, James Clanton, chairman of the executive
committee of the Alabama Democratic party, both contending for
the vote of the newly enfranchised blacks. Standing where Jefferson
Davis had proclaimed the beginning of the Civil War, Wilson
promised hundreds of Negro listeners that the Republican party
offered them the best hope to secure their rights. In rebuttal,
Clanton appealed to a common heritage: "My colored friends, we
are Southern men, born upon the same soil, live in the same
country, and will sleep in the same graveyard."[34] The message was
that the destiny of the two races was the same; if blacks prospered,
the whites of the South would also prosper. It was therefore the
solemn duty of freedmen to cultivate the friendliest relations with
their former owners, who had always been their best friends.

Such rhetoric fell on deaf ears. When it became apparent that the
blacks had no intention of joining Clanton's party, Conservatives
abruptly changed their stance. During the summer (1867) they
began to insist (as Chief Justice Taney had argued in the Dred Scott
case) that innate black inferiority precluded Negroes from exercising
the rights of citizenship. An address prepared by a thirteen-county

Democratic convention protested that the white race, through the machinations of a political party, was about to forfeit its hereditary supremacy over the black race. With some machinations of his own, editor Joseph Hodgson set out to avert the forthcoming constitutional convention and thus thwart the efforts to codify the rights of freedmen, whom he had described in May as "the playfellows of our childhood, and our faithful friends." His scheme was simple: by invoking section three of the March 23 congressional act (which stipulated that only a majority of the registered voters could call a constitutional convention), and urging whites to register, but not vote, he could defeat the designs of Congress. As whites comprised about 45 percent (75,000) and blacks 55 percent (90,000) of the electorate, it would take a 90 percent pro-convention vote of all eligible freedmen to muster the necessary majority, something he viewed as highly unlikely, even given the anti-Negro proclamations of the Conservatives. "It is evident," he explained, "that the opponents of the Convention should see to it that a majority of all registered voters do not vote on the question."[35] Observing the gradual acceptance of Hodgson's plan among Alabama Conservatives, Freedmen's Bureau Commissioner Wager Swayne wrote from Montgomery: "What we have most to fear is 'No Convention.' "[36]

Rapier also took notice of the Democratic contrivances to halt reconstruction before it began, but, as he had done in the past, he continued to labor calmly in support of the reconstruction acts. A notice in the Florence *Journal* brought a substantial crowd to the Lauderdale County Courthouse on August 3 to hear him endorse the Republican platform, which he had helped draft, and exhort freedmen to register and vote both for the calling of a constitutional convention and for Republican candidates to attend it. One witness reported that the meeting was marked by good order and that Rapier's speech was as well received as it was effective. In the same month he wrote Governor Robert Patton, pressing him to fill the vacant county probate judgeship (caused by the death of V. M. Benham) with Neander Rice, a man who had the approbation of both races. As a representative of the interests of freedmen, he respectfully suggested that the governor appoint a successor to Judge Benham who would treat Negroes in a respectful and businesslike manner. Carefully choosing his words, Rapier continued by admonishing the governor to fill all such positions with men who supported the reconstruction policy of the government, "so that [our] work may not be retarded by influential officials!"[37] One such official, he believed, was Sidney Posey, who was also a candidate for the judgeship. If men like Posey came to the fore— men who had joined the party only to mark out a path for blacks, the whole concept of political equality would be nullified. But when Posey was selected over Rice, Rapier was forced to realize that despite his indefatigable efforts, he still lacked influence in the new party.

Antagonisms developed further between Rapier and Posey at the Florence courthouse meeting of September 9, 1867, a meeting held to nominate three candidates to represent Lauderdale and Limestone counties at the constitutional convention. Posey, the presiding officer at the assemblage, suggested that each county select one representative and then negotiate for the third. He passed over Rapier, and nominated Dr. James Stewart, but enthusiastic partisans of Florence-born Rapier pressed for his nomination, and after a spirited debate, the assembly nominated both men. The third representative, then, Daniel H. Bingham, was chosen for Limestone County. Most Republicans looked with favor on these choices. The nominations would receive the unanimous support of Republicans in the area, predicted E. G. Young, the secretary of the meeting, as the nominees were men of exceptional ability. Of Rapier, Neander Rice wrote a succinct and praise-filled description: "a colored man, was born in this town, is an educated man, a fine speaker, a man of good habits, very temperate, is much respected by all in our County."[38] Thus, despite Posey's antipathy, many white Republicans greatly esteemed Rapier.

Voter registration began immediately. The new laws allowed the registration of all male citizens twenty-one years and older who had not been disfranchised for participation in the rebellion, had not given aid or comfort to the enemies of the United States, and had not been members of any state or the national legislature, and had not held any executive or judicial office and then joined the Confederacy. But the laws had no provision against perjury, and at different times disfranchised former rebels signed the so-called ironclad oath and registered to vote. "Some of the most unrepentant secessionists in Limestone County are permitted to register," complained J. T. Tanner, a partner in the Athens banking house of Tanner and Newell. "Under the present arrangement those who opposed secession are excluded."[39] In the adjoining county of Lauderdale, H. W. McVay, a surgeon in William Sherman's army as it marched through Georgia, said that many old Confederates had perjured themselves, while Union men had little opportunity for political office. McVay had been imprisoned in the South, but now what thanks did he get? Such men as Robert Patton, who had lent financial support to the Confederacy, were considered better Union men than he. The exact number of perjurers was not tabulated, or indeed known, but a good deal of false swearing doubtless occurred in Limestone, Lauderdale, and other Alabama counties. Nevertheless, statewide black registration outnumbered white 90,350 to 74,450.

On October 1–3, 1867, Alabama blacks voted for the first time in the state's history. In Florence, the polling place for Lauderdale, the local press reported that Negroes waited to vote in a quiet and peaceful manner; and in Athens, the polling place for Limestone, blacks balloted without disturbance. By more than five to one, the voters in the district approved the holding of a convention in Montgomery to draft a new state constitution. Among the victorious candidates—Rapier, Steward, and Bingham—the balloting was close:

Lauderdale County		Limestone County	
Stewart	945	Rapier	1113
Rapier	916	Bingham	1111
Bingham	901	Stewart	1085
T. J. Spalding	110	T. J. Spalding	265
John Turentine	11	John Turentine	275

Though Rapier was the first and only Negro elected from the Forty-third Election District, and though the conduct of blacks during their first political experience was exemplary, success was less than complete.

Only two of every five registered voters in the area went to the polls. "We expected a large vote in this county," C. Wesson, the chairman of the registration board in Florence noted, "but we did not get it."[40] Fully two-thirds of the whites had not voted. "I found our white people did not like to vote for a Negro—it was the Negro that caused the apathy." Yet, he added in tribute to Rapier: "the Negro that ran has probably the best chance for a Negro in the state."[41] Wesson also observed that a large number of blacks did not vote because they had no means of getting to town—which, for some of them, was more than twenty miles away.

The election in other parts of Alabama went much the same as in the Forty-third District. Only 95,000 of the 165,000 registered voters in the state cast their ballots, and only one of every four whites. The Florence *Journal* felt that the election had elicited a feeling of indifference in the minds of Conservatives. Black voters, on the other hand, filed quietly into the polling places and cast their ballots. One observer in Montgomery believed that the colored men of Alabama had proved, by their orderly, well-behaved, and kindly manner, that they were capable of exercising the privilege of voting. Another election onlooker described Mobile as absolutely quiet. Though the streets had been filled with men from the country, not a drunken or boisterous person had been seen anywhere. "The colored people, some of whom had walked twenty miles with their pack, voted and went home."[42] In all, seventy-two thousand freedmen and eighteen thousand whites (54.7 percent of the registered voters) had cast their ballots in favor of the constitutional convention, thus complying with the stipulation in the reconstruction act requiring that a majority of registered voters determine that a convention should take place, and aborting, at least temporarily, the machinations of the Democrats.

The state had now officially approved the calling of a constitutional convention, and ninety-two of the ninety-six delegates sent to Montgomery to write a new state charter supported congressional reconstruction and professed allegiance to the Republican party. But perhaps most important, James Rapier had won a significant victory. Coming within a few votes of leading all candidates on a ticket that included two highly esteemed and long-established white residents of the area, he had shown that, proceeding with calmness, moderation, and intelligence, a black man could be elected to a position of great importance in a district where whites outnumbered blacks by more than two to one.

The 1868 Constitution

The Alabama constitutional convention, the first under the reconstruction acts, met at the capitol in Montgomery on November 5, 1867. Though the Conservative Montgomery Daily *Mail* warned that the convention planned to Africanize Alabama, most Democrats found comfort in the reflection that a majority of the delegates were white men of Southern birth. In attendance were fifty-one native white Southerners, twenty-seven Northerners, and only eighteen Negroes. White Southerners were thus in a position to make decisions on such vital questions as Who should be granted the franchise? Who should be allowed to hold office? and What provisions should be incorporated into the constitution concerning racial equality. To reassure its Conservative constituency, the Montgomery *Daily Advertiser* ran several editorials stating that the native white majority would never impose any disability on their fellow citizens.

Other whites were impressed by the high quality of Negro leadership, especially that of James Rapier, who, they said, possessed all the attributes of an influential and effective delegate: he was educated, intelligent, and dedicated; he had scored a decisive election victory in a predominately white district; and he had delivered an eloquent plea for black suffrage at the Nashville Negro Convention. "Few men in the South," the *Daily State Sentinel* asserted, "have done more to secure the rights of the colored people."[1] Even the Democratic editor of the Florence *Journal* praised his superior education, his fine speaking ability, his clarity of thought, and his "native talent." Recognizing his prestige, especially among the other Negro delegates, the *Journal* assured its readers that "from what we know of Rapier, we believe his influence will be exercised to secure the greatest good for the entire population—white and black."[2]

Rapier did, in fact, hope that the new constitution would benefit all the people, but he understood that to achieve such a goal, as well as to insure the success of reconstruction in general, whites and blacks had to work together with mutual understanding and tolerance. It was in this mood, at the convention's first business session, that he presented a conciliatory resolution. In a memorial to Congress, he proposed to remove the political disabilities of whites who had aided in the reconstruction of the state under the congressional plan. Requesting specifically that eight Republicans from his section of Alabama be granted voting and officeholding privileges, he included, among others, his protagonist Sidney Posey, who had earlier opposed both Negro suffrage and the condidacy of Negroes for seats in the convention. But such magnaminity was characteristic of Rapier. Like other black leaders: Hiram Revels (Mississippi), Joseph Rainey (South Carolina), Jefferson Long (Georgia), and P. B. S. Pinchback (Louisiana), who, at later conventions offered similar resolutions, he was willing to assist Southern whites as long as they remained loyal to the principles of reconstruction.

To balance the memorial that proposed to remove the disabilities of whites, Rapier (again like other black leaders) offered a resolution that would accord full citizenship to blacks. The implementation of the reconstruction laws, he said, rested solely upon the uninhibited franchise for Negroes. "Therefore, be it ordained by the people of Alabama in convention assembled that all colored male persons of the age of 21 years are hereby declared to be citizens of Alabama, and are entitled to all privileges and immunities of any citizen."[3] As at Buxton and Nashville, he had once again demanded that blacks be declared citizens as a first step toward political equality.

Other delegates were less concerned with citizenship rights for Negroes than with sweeping proscription of ex-rebels. Three spokesmen were typically vengeful. Albert Griffin, a vociferous opponent of the discriminatory legislation of 1865–66, who had come South at the end of the war, wanted a clause disfranchising all who had voluntarily taken part in the rebellion. If such a measure were not adopted, he predicted, the state would soon be in the hands of "those incarnate fiends" who had hunted down Union soldiers with bloodhounds. Striking at highly placed Conservatives, Andrew Applegate, an ex-Union soldier who had remained in the South after his discharge, demanded disfranchisement of all who had been officers in the provisional government (1865–67) of Alabama, and of editors of newspapers who had publicly opposed the reconstruction acts. Most severe in his criticism was Daniel Bingham, called another Thaddeus Stevens by Democrats because of his virulent attacks on the race provisions in the state's 1865 constitution. Caustically assailing a resolution pledging "charity toward all and malice toward none," he denounced ex-rebels as "those merciless wretches who ruined the country."[4]

In sharp contrast to such vindictiveness was the November 11 minority report of the committee on franchise. Headed by Thomas Lee, a black delegate from Perry County, and two prewar Whigs, Joseph Speed and Benjamin Whelan, who, like most members of their defunct party, had opposed secession, supported Stephen Douglass or John Bell in 1860, and had remained, to one degree or another (some while supporting the Confederacy) sympathic to the Union, the minority proposed to guarantee the vote to men of every race and color, except those convicted of treason or unwilling to take a loyalty oath to support, obey, and defend the Constitution and laws of the United States and Alabama. Defining a traitor as anyone who took an oath to support the Constitution and then engaged in rebellion, the minority report ignored explicit congressional instructions requiring a voter to swear he had not given aid or comfort to enemies of the United States.

A majority of the seven-member committee—John Keffer, a Pennsylvanian before the war and chairman of the Republican state executive committee, Joseph Davis, a member of the 1865 Alabama constitutional convention and a resident of the state before the war, Benjamin Norris, a Maine Free Soiler in 1850, and Griffin—rejected the mild minority proposal. Their report recommended instead the disfranchisement of all persons who had inflicted any cruel or unusual punishment upon any soldier, or who had been convicted of treason, bribery, embezzlement, malfeasance in office, or any crime punishable by a prison sentence, as well as persons who registered to vote in accordance with the reconstruction acts and refused to vote either for or against the proposed constitution. This recommendation, disfranchising most whites who opposed reconstruction, was, of course, highly proscriptive.

James Rapier rejected both reports, the majority's because it was too harsh and the minority's because it deviated from congressional guidelines. In an amendment proposed as a substitute for the entire

franchise section, he suggested that voting rights be extended to
every male citizen over twenty-one who had been a resident of the
state six months and of a county for three months. And, except for
persons disfranchised by the acts of Congress (until their disabilities
had been removed by Congress, at which time disfranchisement
would cease to be operative in Alabama), he offered political
amnesty. No person should be disfranchised merely for having
participated in the rebellion, he contended, or for a political offense,
such as refusing to vote in an election. By seeking to disfranchise
only those already denied the vote by Congress, Rapier had struck a
balance between the harsh proscription of the majority and the
lenient provisions of the minority. But the delegates were not ready
to compromise.

In a major convention debate radical and conservative Republicans fought bitterly to secure a franchise section compatible with
their own beliefs. John Carraway, the educated and cultured Negro
from Mobile, approved of the disfranchising clauses in the majority
report. As a Negro who had only recently been enfranchised
himself, he was not anxious to deny the vote to anyone, but the
loyal people of the South needed protection. Radical Andrew
Applegate, the ex-Union soldier, went even further. He proposed
extending the vote only to those who firmly supported reconstruction. On the other side, Northerner William Buckley argued that
the military bills disfranchised certain men for what they had done
in the past, but the majority report proposed to defranchise a large
number for what they might do in the future. Henry Semple, who
later became a strict states'-rights Democrat, now invoked the
authority of the federal government, pointing out that no state had
the power to disqualify a voter if Congress had not first granted
that power. Negro Thomas Lee maintained a benevolent (some
thought it obsequious) attitude toward ex-Confederates. He had no
desire to take away any rights of the white man. And to the far
right on the political spectrum was W. H. Black of Bullock County,
who proposed an amendment requiring all voters be able to read
the Constitution of the United States and write in a good hand, thus
disenfranchising most freedmen. The controversy over whose vote
should go into the ballot box illustrated the divisive forces working
at the Alabama convention, and indeed throughout the reconstruction South.

In general, Alabama Democrats supported Black's anti-Negro

amendment. At first optimistic about the possibility of a new state charter, the Montgomery *Daily Advertiser* soon became disenchanted with the discussions on capitol hill. Though accepting the results of emancipation, though guaranteeing the Negro all his civil rights, and though promising to aid him in every proper way and to improve his moral and mental condition, the *Advertiser* called for a means of limiting, if not excluding, the black vote. Speaking for the great majority of Conservative Alabamians, the *Advertiser* declared without reservation: "If the question were left for us to decide, we would certainly decide against Negro Suffrage, against Mulatto Suffrage, against Quadroon Suffrage, in short, we would have none of it."[5]

Rapier, of course, opposed such an extreme Conservative proposition, but he also stood against a number of the more radical Republican proposals. When Daniel Bingham moved to reject the majority franchise report and sought to insert an even stronger disqualification clause, for example, Rapier joined a coalition of 13 Negro members, 23 native Southerners, and 14 Northerners to defeat the motion 50 to 37. Only moments later, he resisted another effort toward greater proscription. When a Bingham supporter moved that the franchise report be resubmitted to a new committee, including Radicals Datus Coon of Dallas and Applegate, Rapier voted nay. Joining him were 13 blacks, 17 of the 35 Southerners present, and 20 Northerners; the proposal was rejected 51 to 38. Balloting the same day on a clause to disqualify electors who refused to vote either for or against the proposed constitution, 23 native Southerners, 17 Northerners, and a Rapier-led bloc of 13 Negroes again voted nay, rejecting the proposition 53 to 31.

After all the contentions for mild proscription, the article on elections in its final form denied voting rights to persons in five categories: those who had inflicted cruel or unusual punishment upon Union soldiers in wartime; those disqualified from holding office by the proposed Fourteenth Amendment to the Constitution; those disqualified from registration under the March 2, 1867, act; those not willing to subscribe to an oath disavowing secession and pledging to accept civil and political equality of all men; and finally, those convicted of treason or other crimes. The article went beyond the instructions of Congress in severity, although disfranchising neither all ex-Confederates per se, nor those electors who would abstain from voting when the constitution came up for ratification. By siding with moderate Southerners, Rapier and the other Negro delegates had at least succeeded in defeating the designs of the most radical members of the convention.

While laboring for a moderate disfranchisement clause, Rapier had also sponsored a section guaranteeing all citizens equal rights on common carriers. He proposed that the new constitution include an article forbidding discrimination because of color on the public conveyances in the state. On November 23, he delivered what the Conservative press dubbed "a violent and highly inflammatory harangue demanding entire social equality with the white race."[6] Rapier explained that he did not advocate social equality, only fair treatment. "It is past my comprehension the manner in which colored gentlemen and colored ladies [are] treated on railroads and common carriers," he said in reply to Henry Semple, a relentless proponent of racial separation. "I do not consider myself honored by sitting in a car beside a white man, simply because he [is] white," but every passenger should be accorded common courtesy.[7] Nevertheless, Semple maintained that proprietors of hotels, steamboats, railroads, and places of amusement had the right to demand reasonable regulations to separate the two races. With puzzling logic, he temporized that civil rights is not invaded so long as separation is demanded by the sentiment of the white race. As a member of the Committee on the Judicial Department, he and Joseph Speed, an ex-officer in the Twenty-Eighth Alabama Regiment, made proposals to separate the races by law in schools and other public places. Another article would prohibit intermarriage of white persons to persons of color to the fourth generation.

Negro delegates immediately expressed their dissatisfaction with the Semple-Speed articles and argued in favor of Rapier's proposal to prohibit discrimination. James Greene condemned the practice of putting black women in smoking cars with drunkards and poor whites; Ovid Gregory introduced a resolution to abolish all laws, regulations, and customs that contained distinctions based on color, caste, or previous condition; and John Carraway protested that a black man could not send his wife from one part of the state to another, for fear that she might be required to ride in a smoking car, and thus be exposed to insults from low and obscene white men. Carraway also delivered a fifteen-hundred-word condemnation of the proposal prohibiting intermarriage. He opposed marital mixing, but believed that the bill was offered only "to discriminate against, crush down, and brutalize a people on account of their color."[8] In contrast with Semple, who had betrayed his emotions with specious arguments, Carraway used clear and forceful reasoning to advance his case. If anti-Negro prejudices were so inculcated in whites that the convention did not dare allow blacks to ride in a decent car because whites objected, how could there be a danger that the two races would intermarry? The black members argued with equally persuasive logic against the separate school clause: though they did not want white-Negro schools, they believed the threat of mixed schools would force local school boards to provide equal educational facilities for Negroes. At the termination of the debate, Rapier, Greene, Carraway, Gregory, ten other Negro delegates, and forty white delegates successfully voted to table the Semple-Speed proposals. Their resistance had thwarted, at least temporarily, the effort to establish separation of the races by law in Alabama. But while the completed constitution did not expressly prohibit mixed education or intermarriage, neither did it forbid discrimination in public places.

Having opposed legal separation of blacks and whites in public places, and having claimed equal rights for Negroes under the law, Rapier also proposed plans to aid Negro laborers and tenant farmers. As a member of the Committee on Corporations, he suggested that the constitution include a family exemption clause to protect debtors from the public sale of their property. The amount of the exemption would be graduated in proportion to the number of persons in the family. His proposal was partially successful. Though it did not include a graduated property exemption clause, article fourteen of the constitution did exclude from execution for the collection of a debt one thousand dollars of personal and two thousand of real property. Rapier was less successful in his attempt to validate unpaid contracts made between black laborers and white planters during the Confederacy. He asked that the planters pay all outstanding contracts, in lawful money, at whatever the par value of depreciated Confederate currency was at the time of the agreement. On this matter the convention refused to act. Finally, four days before adjournment, he urged his fellow delegates to adopt a lenient oath of office that affirmed only obedience to the national and state constitutions and a pledge to discharge faithfully the duties of office. Daniel Bingham, who had earlier reviled ex-rebels as traitors, countered with a rigorous oath that required officeholders to swear that they had never been disfranchised. Only 11 voted with Rapier, and the Bingham amendment carried 72 to 12.

The convention members were eqully positive about who should take the new oath of office. Caucusing on December 2 as Republicans, they nominated an all-white state ticket which included six members of the convention (Applegate, Keffer, Charles Miller, Arthur Bingham, Robert Reynolds, Littleberry Strange) and two nonmembers: N. B. Cloud, the famous antebellum Southern agriculturist, and prewar resident William Hugh Smith, who was nominated for governor. The gubernatorial nominee greatly displeased Rapier, who, in a speech to the caucus, asserted that Smith had been unfaithful to the principles of the proposed Fourteenth Amendment. In addition, he held conservative racial views and "might back slide."[9] Refusing to sanction the ticket unless Smith's name were removed, Rapier explained that he could not support the list of proposed candidates unless all of them supported the aspirations of blacks. As a substitute, he nominated white moderate Robert Patton, who, though earlier having favored a white man's government in the South, had stood in opposition to the black codes and had supported the congressional plan of reconstruction from its inception. Rapier's suggestion had little effect, however, as the slate remained unchanged. Nevertheless, the overt enmity between Rapier and Smith symbolized the deep divisions within the party—differences, which, even at this early stage, seemed irreconcilable.

And Conservatives played upon these differences. "Negroes Bamboozled" read a headline in the Mobile *Register*. "We ask the colored man to look at the ticket and see how many of them are on it?" Not one was the answer. " 'Nary a Nigger' when the plunder is to be divided."[10] The paper pointed out that though blacks constituted 90 percent of the party's membership in the state, when it came time to nominate candidates for office, not a single Negro had been mentioned. "The niggers are only good to vote in the Radical party, but it is only the 'white trash' that is to be voted for."[11] There was no irony in a white man's party suggesting that blacks seek the prize of state office. Conservatives understood well, even at this beginning stage of reconstruction, that Alabama whites—Democrats and Republicans—were united in their antipathy to the idea of Negroes holding office.

On the day before the constitutional convention adjourned, Rapier and sixty-six other delegates voted in favor of the final draft. But nine native white Southerners protested against the adoption of the new state charter. A government framed by its provisions would, in their opinion, "entail upon the people of the State great evils."[12] One of the nine, James Stow, submitted a personal protest because the charter disfranchised and proscribed beyond the requirements of the military bills, omitted a separate school provision, and included a binding oath of office that forced a man to persevere in a particular course of conduct, though his opinions on the subject may have changed. Thirteen other whites repudiated the instrument because it did not separate blacks and whites on common cariers, nor prohibit intermarriage. Though dissension among Republicans, especially conservatives and moderates, was again apparent, a majority of the delegates approved the charter, and the newly drafted constitution went to the people.

The day the convention adjourned, Conservatives began a spirited campaign to prevent ratification. At a large and enthusiastic meeting in Montgomery on December 6, 1867, editors John Forsyth and Joseph Hodgson sounded the Democratic battle cry: "A White Man's Party." They refused to associate, directly or indirectly, with those who had "nigger on the brain."[13] The black man deserved every earthly and heavenly blessing, every civil right, security of life, property, education for his children, churches for his God, guidance, friendship, and protection, said Forsyth, but it was written in the decrees of nature that he could never govern. Hodgson agreed. It was not a question of loyalty or disloyalty, of rebellion or unionism, he exclaimed, but a question of race. If the proposed constitution were ratified, all the pent-up bitterness, revenge, and outrage of the white race would violently "sweep the race of Africans from existence." Hodgson bitterly opposed, as he put it, the atrocious system of universal suffrage, which subjugated the intelligence and property of white men to the ignorance and pauperism of blacks.

Leading Alabama Democrats, at various meetings throughout the state, used the same arguments. Former provisional governor Lewis E. Parsons, Democratic executive chairman James Clanton, and north Alabama Conservative James Irvin, charged that the constitution enfranchised ignorant blacks, disfranchised intelligent whites, prostrated the caucasian race, and elevated the semibarbaric

Negro to absolute supremacy. Clanton expressed kindness and friendship to the colored man, but opposed the enfranchisement of an ignorant, inferior race. Another Democrat asserted that by extending voting privileges to dumb, brutalized blacks, the constitution would convert Alabama, for the time being, into an African state; then Negroes like Rapier would disdain association with white men. Solidified behind the race issue, Conservatives across the state vowed opposition to the charter of the reconstruction convention and promised to use every effort to insure its defeat.

But how? We cannot reasonably hope to secure a majority against the constitution, James Clanton conceded in mid-January, but, he continued, a technicality in the terms for readmission could prove significant. Congress had required ratification by a majority of the registered voters. Recalling that 90,000 of the 164,000 registered voters had cast their ballots in the October election, Clanton, in a plan similar to Hodgson's earlier one, calculated that the abstention of only 9000 registrants would nullify the work of the convention. He therefore beseeched his fellow Democrats to register but to refrain from voting. "Non-voting for the present is not non-action. It is the most effective and powerful action."[14] It was to prove decisive on election day.

Conservatives, meanwhile, tried a different tack. "Turn Negro laborers into the streets if they belong to a Loyal League," the Mobile *Tribune* demanded, while a Montgomery newspaper published a list of men who were not to be hired because of their political affiliation. Reports circulated that hundreds of politically active blacks had been dismissed from their jobs, that Republican-owned businesses had been ostracized, and that Democrats who owned stores had refused to sell provisions to members of the opposition party. Using economic coercion to control the Negro vote, a tactic just beginning in 1868, was to become one of the most effective means of insuring white supremacy during the post-reconstruction era.

This kind of warfare, as well as the slate of white candidates, discouraged many blacks. "We wish to inform you that we have withdrawn from the Republican Party," Henry Thomas, Negro vice-president of Limestone County's Union League, announced in a local paper, "because we have been used as tools long enough."[15] Negro Republicans in many other counties followed suit, denouncing what they termed the nominating caucus and the all-white slate. Withdrawing from the Loyal League of Montgomery, ex-slave Caesar Shorter, who, like many whites, did not think freedmen qualified to vote, condemned the proposed constitution. Such disaffection played into the hands of the Democrats.

Paradoxically, in the midst of this campaign to defeat the proposed constitution and thereby save the white race from subjugation at the hands of blacks, the Union Springs *Times*, a Conservative paper, proposed Rapier as a candidate for lieutenant governor. The newspaper ranked him as among the most decent and intelligent members of the convention and added that he had traveled extensively, had received a creditable college education, and had conducted himself in a gentlemanly manner. He was, in every particular, except that of race, a superior man. Since the constitution granted eligibility for state office to Negroes, the *Times* challenged Rapier to test the sincerity of his white Republican cohorts by running for state office. Though he rejected this challenge, Rapier's dissatisfaction with the Republican candidate for governor prevented him from actively supporting the state ticket.

The election (February 1–5, 1868) reflected the discontent of Negro Republicans as well as the solidarity of the Democrats. Only 66,000 of the 170,000 registered Alabamians, or slightly more than a third, voted for the Republican state ticket; and only about 71,000, far less than half, favored the constitution. Clanton's scheme calling for voters to stay away from the polls had nullified the first reconstruction constitution. The Mobile *Nationalist* contended that the Democrats were only confessing their inability to defeat the constitution in a fair election, but General George G. Meade, commander of the Army of the Potomac at the battle of Gettysburg and now in charge of the Third Military District (which included Alabama), cited other causes for the Republican defeat: discharging black laborers, social ostracism through business relations, the lack of merit in the constitution itself, and a violent storm which had raged through the first two days of the election and kept voters away from the polls. But whatever the reasons, the Conservatives had scored a decisive victory.

It proved to be an ephemeral one, however, for now, to the consternation of thunderstruck Democrats, Congress rushed into law a fourth reconstruction act (March 11, 1868), which stipulated that a majority of votes actually cast should decide the election.

This act thwarted the plans of Alabama Conservatives and validated the February election returns. On June 25, 1868, with a new state charter, Alabama gained readmittance to the union of states.

Yet, the new constitution did not reflect the preferences of James Rapier, who had argued for a moderate disfranchisement clause, a lenient oath of office, a common carriers section in the bill of rights, and provisions for debtor relief, and who had striven to remove the disabilities of his adversaries and secure equal rights for Negroes. Rather, it reflected the views of Northerners and native whites, who had willingly sacrificed a section guaranteeing equal rights for blacks in order to codify a stringent oath and widespread disfranchisement. The convention had been called to extend full citizenship to freedmen, but the new state charter denied blacks one of the most basic rights of citizens, free access to public places. For Rapier, this was the tragic irony of the 1868 constitution.

6

A Negro on the State Ticket

Despite his refusal to stand behind the state ticket, Rapier mounted a determined campaign during the fall of 1868 in behalf of the Republican presidential nominee Ulysses S. Grant. In speeches in various towns and stations in northwest Alabama, he urged freedmen to vote for Grant, who, he said, supported equal rights for Negroes. At one stop, Mitchell's Junction, he was cheered again and again as he spoke from the pulpit in a small church. "Now, what do we want? We want a policy that will protect all men. We want a policy that will make the poorest man in the land the peer of the richest in the eyes of the law."[1] It was the Republican party, he said, that advocated such a policy. Among those in attendance was James P. Thomas, who had journeyed from St. Louis to Florence on a family visit. "Jim, in his black coat, looked dignified [and] wise. He occupied the chair. Called the house to order. He said, 'This is our day. We can't be denied.' "[2] But before Rapier could conclude his remarks, an alarm sounded. The entire assemblage, including Rapier and Thomas, fled into a nearby wooded area only a few minutes before a band of armed, white-hooded horsemen surrounded the church and began shooting through the windows. When Rapier returned to Florence, he was not surprised to find an anonymous note posted on his door; it instructed him to leave Alabama. "If you refuse to obey, your life will be worthless." Ignoring the threat, he continued his campaign in behalf of the Republican party.[3]

But early in September, the recently repaired Tuscumbia Female Academy (located seven miles from Florence in Colbert County) was gutted by fire. "Some miserable incendiary, with heart black with criminal intent," the editor of the *North Alabamian and Times* wailed, "placed a torch to the building."[4] Rumors quickly spread that a group of blacks, among them James Rapier, had conspired to burn the academy. Reacting swifty and violently, one hundred fifty outraged whites scoured the countryside searching for the Negro suspects. Forewarned by a friend, a freedman by the name of DePriest (the father of Illinois congressman Oscar DePriest), Rapier fled for his life, finding refuge to the south in Montgomery. But he had left behind everything he owned: sixty bales of cotton (worth thousands of dollars), two hundred fifty cords of wood, and his personal belongings. Recalling the incident some years later, he wrote that the Democracy had told him to quit politics or his life would be in danger. "I spurned the proposition and rallied the colored voters in my county as best I could. The result was, I lost my steamboat woodyard and my entire crop, and barely saved my life. One night four of us had been selected for hanging. By merest chance, I escaped."[5] It was small consolation, then, when only three weeks later, a Tuscumbia magistrate (John N. Green) cleared him of any involvement in the academy burning.

Why had he been accused? Because of his devotion to Republican principles, the *New National Era* surmised. As an enterprising black man, he was anathema to whites. Rapier agreed. "I was a very popular colored man at that time," he testified before a United States Senate committee, "and they wanted to give me a dose of their regulation tactics."[6]

But at least he had escaped. The other three Negroes sought that night: Jake Bell, Porter Simpson, and Benjamin Cooper, also active in politics, were captured and incarcerated in a guardhouse. The following morning, after Sunday church services, a group of one hundred disguised men overpowered the constable, dragged the three to a nearby bridge, tied ropes around their necks, and shoved them to their deaths. Left hanging for nearly a week, the corpses had cards pinned to them warning Negroes to behave themselves or they might suffer a similar fate.

Leading whites in the area not only condoned the lynchings but admitted the real impetus behind the mob action: black participation in politics. As long as freedmen listened to outsiders, read a follow-up editorial in a local newspaper, the gallows would be crowded with their race. Tuscumbia Democratic leader Robert Lindsey added: "The general sentiment of the community was that it was a very good thing. Those [three] negroes were the body and life of the Union League."[7]

To further disrupt the Union League, and more, to completely eliminate the Negro from politics, whites organized many such vigilante groups, calling themselves the Ku Klux Klan. "John Gracy was shot badly last Saturday and will probably die," Rapier's longtime friend Neander Rice wrote from Lauderdale during the campaign, "and we had a negro man killed in this county last week. [He was] shot in the nighttime."[8] Reporting a terrible state of affairs, he said that blacks were greatly intimidated by the roving Klan. The upcoming election would be a perfect farce; the Conservatives, who, according to Rice, were responsible for the violence, would carry every precinct. Disguised whites were "prowling about all parts of the country, intimidating and threatening the Negroes. . . . A mood of terrorism and anarchy reigns."[9]

Much the same could be said for nearly every region of Alabama. A group of hooded men, for example, lynched a black tenant farmer in Limestone County; and during a Grant rally in nearby Huntsville, one hundred masked horsemen galloped into the public square, wheeled into a battle line, and, according to one observer, "with the adroitness of veteran cavalry, commenced firing."[10] Up and down the Tennessee Valley, men wearing white hoods and robes rode, visiting Negro cabins, beating, whipping, robbing, and murdering innocent blacks. "These bands are having the effect of inspiring *nameless terror* among Negroes," wrote William B. Figures, the editor of the Huntsville *Advocate* and an official of the Freedmen's Bureau. "Nobody is found out, arrested, or punished."[11] In Mobile, Talladega, Tuscaloosa, and at least seven Black Belt counties, masked men burned buildings, including the Greene County Courthouse, raided Negro quarters "in regular old style," drove off shopkeepers, intimidated bureau officials, terrorized teachers at the freedmen's schools, and whipped innocent Negroes. Ryland Randolph, editor of the Tuscaloosa *Independent Monitor*, won a kind of national notoriety for his virulent attacks on "those great pests of Southern society—the carpetbagger and scalawag."[12] "White Man—Right or Wrong—Still the White Man!" read the masthead of the *Monitor*, and, as if to prove his sincerity, Randolph wrote an editorial wherein he rejoiced at the beating of Negro leader Allan A. Williams, who was "thrashed in regular ante-bellum style, until [his] unnatural nigger-pride had a tumble, and humbleness to the white man reigned supreme."[13]

Two Tennessee Valley newspapers reflected the attitude of

Conservatives toward the reign of terror. The *North Alabamian and Times* of Tuscumbia briefly recorded, without the slightest hint of disapprobation, the assassination by a group of disguised men of Henry Ellis, John Rapier's neighbor in Florence: "They forced open the door, took Ellis out, and shot him through the head."[14] The *Literary Index* also devoted a few lines to the murder, stating merely that Ellis, a very mean Negro, had come to his death from a pistol shot fired by persons unknown. Both papers all but ignored the fact that on November 21, some one hundred twenty-five mounted men, disguised in black sheets, rode into Florence, killed one black man by putting six shots through his head, and hanged three others.

And yet, in the very teeth of these chilling commotions, leading Democrats denied the existence of the Ku Klux Klan. The editor of the Florence *Journal* insisted that the Klan was a figment of the Republican imagination, and Robert Lindsay, who later became governor of Alabama, denied that the state had ever known an organization by the name of Ku Klux. Testifying before a Senate investigating committee during his incumbency, he went even further, saying, "I do not believe there has ever been a man whipped in the State of Alabama on account of his political principles—not a man, black or white."[15] Intimidation was all a myth.

But for James Rapier, who had fled to save his life, the Ku Klux Klan was very real, and, despite being cleared of any involvement in the academy burning, he remained in virtual seclusion for an entire year. It was a frustrating period. Lonely, depressed, and fearful of some outrage against him, he lived anonymously at a Montgomery boardinghouse (owned by James H. Hale, a mulatto carpenter) with transient Negro day laborers. He lived on the small amount of cash he had been able to take with him from Florence, some assistance provided by his father, who, despite the activities of the klan, had remained in Lauderdale County, and a small salary he earned as a census taker in the city's Negro Fourth Ward.

But Rapier spent most of the time pondering the future. Should he leave the South, return to Canada, move out West, or apply for a government position in Washington, D.C.? Once again, as in Buxton, his thoughts turned toward material things. "I have abandoned the idea of a clerkship in Washington," he confessed. "It would cost so much to live there and debar me from something that would pay me better."[16] Perhaps the one thing that kept him going during this trying period was the correspondence he received from members of the Rapier-Thomas family. But even this, in the end, proved to be disheartening: in August 1869, he received word that his father was seriously ill.

No longer a threat to the Conservative opposition, Rapier returned to Florence (exactly one year after he had fled) to render such assistance as he could to his bedridden father, who was suffering from convulsions, recurring nausea, and a steadily weakening condition. "Father keeps poorly. The Dr. has doubts as to his recovery. He has not eaten in five days," he said sadly, shortly after arriving. "He would like to be at your house to have Aunt Maria cook him Something he can eat," he continued in a letter to his uncle Henry Thomas, "but winds up with the unpleasant idea: 'I don't think I shall ever See them again.'"[17] Though Rapier tried to comfort his father, the older man's premonition proved to be correct, and on September 18, John Rapier, who had sacrificed so much for his children, died of stomach cancer.

In the agonizing months that followed, perhaps gaining strength from his father's purpose in life, Rapier reaffirmed his determination to remain in the South and assist blacks in their transition from slavery to freedom. "Our general elections come off next August. I may come forward on the State ticket," he announced, explaining that the new constitution, which he had helped draft, provided for the election of state officers by all the people, without regard to color. But in the meantime he remained busy as the executor of his father's will. In this capacity, he hired a housekeeper to care for the Rapier children, all of whom, except Rebecca, were still minors, then traveled to Canada, sold the family property in Toronto and Buxton, and, upon his return, secured admission for his fifteen-year-old half-brother, Thomas, to Fisk University in Nashville. "I especially request that you will not allow him to be frequently in the city," he explained to a university official, knowing from experience the temptations of urban life for a young man. "I would also like that you would confine him more to reading, writing & ciphering."[18] Posting sixteen dollars a month for Thomas's tuition, room, board, and expenses, Rapier kept in close touch with university officials concerning his brother's progress. "Thomas is well and seems more content and prosperous than [ever] before," came one reply from school administrator George L. White, who added, in deference to Rapier's growing political reputation, 'The interest in our school increases and the outlook was never more cheering. We hope, Sir, to have your sympathy and the support of your influence in our work."[19] Late in 1869, Rapier traveled to Washington, D.C., (see chap. 7) as a delegate to the first National Negro Labor Union Convention.

When he returned to Montgomery in the spring of 1870, he learned that the twenty-eighth state had ratified the Fifteenth Amendment, which made it illegal to abridge the right of suffrage because of race, color, or previous condition. To celebrate the occasion he and other Montgomery blacks (see Introduction) formed a procession on capitol hill and paraded to the grounds in the vicinity of the West Point depot. Addressing the celebrants, he discussed the abolitionist crusade, interpreted the meaning of the Civil War for blacks, and made a personal avowal. Recounting the conflict between the North and South over slavery, he told of the persecution of William Lloyd Garrison, the caning of Charles Sumner, and the murder of Elijah Lovejoy. "It was impossible," he said, "to eradicate the great curse of slavery by positive means."[20] So he had rejoiced at the coming of the Civil War. It meant that a slave father who had been taken from his little boy in Virginia could once again see his son; that a slave mother who had been torn from her little girl in Tennessee could once again see her daughter. Southern whites, he complained, had always followed a course in direct opposition to the interests of blacks. Instead of acknowledging Negroes as men and women, they said: "If you don't like things here, go back to Africa." "I was born in Alabama and do not know any other place," he exclaimed proudly. "My mother and father are buried in Alabama, on the banks of the beautiful Tennessee river. I have no home in Africa. I expect to stay here."[21]

After the Montgomery celebration, Rapier spoke at similar gatherings in a tour through the Black Belt. At Tuskegee in Macon County he addressed an enormous crowd of thousands of freedmen. "Our struggle began when the first black man set foot on Virginia soil," he said. "No one should be surprised at our rejoicing when he looks back on the road we have come"[22] Sharing the platform with Joshua Morse, state's attorney general, and former congressman Benjamin Norris, he explained that God had always intended America to be a land of equal opportunity. But during the speech, he became faint, suffering from what the press called a severe indisposition; as he was assisted from the platform, he received prolonged applause.

Several weeks later, apparently having recovered from his illness, he spoke at Wetumka in Elmore County on the injustices blacks had suffered at the hands of whites: the oppressions of bondage, the denial of family, the lack of citizenship. But now the government had finally decided that black people should have a chance in life. "This is all that we have ever asked."[23] Again sharing the occasion with leading Republicans—state auditor Robert Reynolds and Negro state legislator William V. Turner—his Wetumka speech was well received. "He's a good speaker, in fact the best colored speaker, if we may make one exception, we have ever heard," commented a white listener, while a black onlooker deemed the talk worth cherishing. "He is full of humor and all of his points and illustrations were quite apropos."[24] And again, he left the stand amid resounding applause.

Part of the motivation for Rapier's round of speeches derived from his wish to place himself before the electorate, even though he had never held an elective office, nor even a high official position (county or state committeeman), in the Republican party. There was a growing sentiment among Republicans, a sentiment that Rapier was well aware of, that a Negro should run for state office. The future success of the party depended on harmony in the ranks; there should be no jealousies, nor factional bickering, explained one Republican, expressing the views of many others. To unify the different elements it was necessary to recognize the just claims of blacks. "Let us elect such of their number as are worthy and competent, to places of honor, profit, and trust."[25]

And when a group of Montgomery Republicans, representing the Fourth Precinct, gathered at the courthouse in mid-August, they united behind Rapier to fill such a position of honor, calling upon him to take the chair and deliver the keynote address. Recovering from yet another illness, he respectfully declined at first, but after a standing ovation, he accepted and, in a brief speech, said that as Negroes comprised the bulk of the party's voting electorate in the state, they deserved a place on the ticket. Such a nomination would not only unify black Republicans but would indicate the sincerity of whites toward the principle of political equality. Yet no matter what the outcome of the forthcoming state convention in Selma, he concluded, all Republicans should work together for victory in the fall election. Shortly before the meeting adjourned, the delegates, by a voice declaration, selected him to represent the city at the Selma convention.

Despite Rapier's plea for harmony, shortly after the delegates took their seats in the Selma opera house, a dispute broke out. Judges Samuel Rice, Charles Pelham, and J. W. Haralson, all native Republicans, and John Keffer, a member of the 1867 constitutional convention, suggested that William Smith again head the ticket as the nominee for governor. United States Senator George Spencer and Rapier vociferously objected. The incumbent had appointed Democrats, including former secessionists, to high office, Rapier charged; in addition, he had failed to protect blacks against the ravages of the Klan, had made corrupt bargains with railroad interests, and had not appointed a single Negro to office. No doubt aggravated by the ninety-five degree temperatures (which, according to one Selma resident, had melted the wings off the mosquitoes), the ensuing vituperative factional fight continued unabated for two full days. Finally the delegates decided on a compromise: Smith would be acceptable if a black man were also put on the ticket. Then Nicholas Davis, of Madison, the staunch foe of the Smith faction despite his life-time residency in the state, placed in nomination James Rapier for secretary of state.

"I recognize him as a man of efficiency, practical ability, and good qualifications," white judge Joshua Morse told the convention.[26] J. T. Rapier was a man fully qualified and capable of filling such a position. Leaping to his feet, a white delegate from Hale vehemently interjected: "We are representatives of principle not of color. I tell you if a colored man is put upon the ticket, the same element you are trying to conciliate on the one hand, you will lose on the other." As a true friend of the African race in America, he besought the convention to present to the people of Alabama "a ticket we can all vote for."[27] Equally obstreperous was J. W. Haralson, who predicted that the nomination of Rapier, or any Negro, would seal the doom of the party. "It will be killed so dead that the hand of resurrection will never reach it."[28] And another white delegate amplified this prophecy: "We can't elect a negro. I beseech you, in the name of God, don't insist on this thing."[29] The battle surged back and forth for nearly two hours, but in the end, despite the vociferous opposition of the native white element, the nomination went to Rapier, who thanked the convention for the honor and promised to carry the campaign to every section of Alabama.

But even before he left Dallas County, Rapier was approached by wealthy industrialist John C. Stanton, who, as director of the Alabama and Chattanooga Railroad System, had received several million dollars in low-interest bonds from previous Republican administrations. Fearing that the nomination of a Negro might bring the party down to defeat and, in turn, jeopardize his profitable relationship with the state, Stanton offered Rapier ten thousand dollars to withdraw from the contest. Rumors soon spread that Rapier would accept the bribe. "The future may develop the fact that Rapier has betrayed his race—and that his nomination was arranged to prevent other negroes from taking a place in the picture," the Montgomery *Daily Mail* observed a day after the convention adjourned. "He is a fly in the ointment, which the white Radicals are about to remove with a silver spoon."[30] One editor claimed that he had uncovered indisputable proof that the Negro nominee would remove himself, making way for a white replacement. Another indicated that ten thousand dollars was just the beginning. "If he plays it smart, he can get much more."[31] Rapier not only rejected the offer, but reported the attempted bribe to the local district attorney, though no action was ever taken against Stanton.

Despite the rumors of withdrawal, three Republican newspapers immediately announced their support for the Negro candidate. He had integrity, intellect, education, and honesty, proclaimed the *Alabama State Journal* (edited by William Loftin); he would represent "the rights and interests of the *Whole People* of Alabama, without regard to race or party."[32] In addition, he was faithful to duty, politically astute, possessed of a natural kindness, and was both confident and genuinely modest. He was, in short, a man of great merit. The *Southern Republican* (edited by Pierce Burton) also acclaimed him as a "gentleman of great natural ability and finished education," and offered the suggestion that if no colored man could have been found in the state with the necessary qualifications to enable him to perform efficiently the duties of a high office, no colored man would have been nominated.[33] Though less eulogistic, the *Mobile Republican* (edited by Negro Philip Joseph) said that as a state official Rapier would represent the claims of black Republicans.

With the backing of these papers, Rapier mounted a vigorous campaign for state office. Speaking at dozens of Republican rallies, barbeques, and conventions, he urged Negroes to vote for the entire Republican ticket. Greeted almost everywhere by large and enthusiastic crowds, he crisscrossed the state from September until early November, delivering major campaign addresses in Montgomery, nearby Wetumka, and Union Springs (Bullock County), in the southeastern corner of the state at Eufaula (Barbour County), and far to the north in Huntsville (Madison County), where he also arranged for Negro Republican G. R. Williams, a local landowner and party stalwart, to convass the northern tier of counties in his behalf. In Huntsville his speech "was in good taste and gave general satisfaction to all."[34]

But not all of his public appearances were successful. At Opelika (Lee County), he stepped off a train to address a group of Republicans, but found the depot deserted. "He looked like a strange bird of passage," wrote a reporter who caught a glimpse of the Negro candidate. He stepped down from the car, stood on the platform, waited for a short time, then took the eastbound train without being recognized by anyone. "There were no distinguished white Radicals as in former days to welcome and lead him round. We did not even see a negro speak to him."[35] And at Lafayette, near the Georgia border, he had just begun a speech at a barbeque when an altercation occurred between two Negroes in the audience. Attempting to mediate the dispute, he was soon forced to seek cover as a volley of gunshots rang out. When the smoke cleared, several Negroes, as well as the sheriff, lay wounded on the ground. Even then, after order had been restored, he continued his speech and pressed on with the campaign.

Besides these problems, Rapier faced other difficulties as the first black candidate for state office. Perhaps the most distressing was the indifference, even opposition, of influential white Republicans. Neither the Selma *Press*, nor the Elmore *Republican*, nor the Attala *Union*, financed by Stanton, reported on his canvas; the *Union*, flaunting Smith for governor on the masthead, refused to acknowledge that the gubernatorial candidate had a Negro running mate. And the *Southern Republican* and *Alabama State Journal* failed to reprint any of Rapier's speeches, though they dedicated entire issues to the addresses of the other nominees. In a similar manner, the Huntsville *Advocate* neglected to announce that the Negro

candidate had scheduled a campaign stop in that city. "He spoke
without announcement through Gov. Smith's organ," a Democratic observer sneered. "The white radicals in North Alabama are
like the white radicals in Conecuh, where Ben Turner [the black
nominee for Congress] spoke." They refused to acknowledge "any
nigger."[36]

Such an observation, though coming from such a biased source,
was close to the truth. Southerners and old Union men, as one
newspaper called them, were disgusted with "the tail end of the
ticket."[37] A visitor to several northern Alabama counties during the
campaign commented that some of the most dedicated Republicans
had "given up the ghost; they denounce Rapier," adding that many
had stated publicly that they could not "stomach the rest of the
thing."[38] Admitting his own disaffection, Etowah County committeeman William Caine confirmed the revulsion among upstaters
to the black candidate. "The Negro ticket and the Patona Affair is
all they have on you," he said in a letter to Governor Smith. "I shall
work for the balance except Rapier."[39] Another observer declared
that while Rapier had been canvassing the state, white Republicans
had turned him a cold shoulder wherever he went. "Whatever
becomes of the rest of the ticket, the Rads intend to defeat Rapier so
that his fate may deter other negroes hereafter from seeking more
than crumbs that fall from the master's table."[40]

Two of the most powerful "Rads" working to defeat him were
J. M. Caleb Wiley, judge of the circuit court in the Eighth Judicial
District and a major general in the antebellum state militia, and
William Hugh Smith, the governor, formerly a judge of the tenth
circuit court, and a thirty-year resident of Randolph County. "Our
friends as a general thing will not vote for Rapier," Wiley wrote the
governor after visiting five counties in southern Alabama, "and if
he remains on the ticket, it will lose many votes for the whole
ticket."[41] Wiley declared that even General Jackson, in his best
days, would not have been able to stand up to such popular
revulsion. Though doubting that anything could save the party
from defeat, if the Negro nominee were to withdraw "we yet may
stop the avalanche."[42] As for himself, instead of saying his prayers
before going to bed every night, he devoted about half an hour to
cursing the carpetbaggers, Nicholas Davis, and Rapier—"for they
must think we are as stupid as we are corrupt."[43] At the same time,
William Smith, described by the Mobile *Register* as perhaps the

most conservative of all native Republicans, did all in his power to defeat his black running mate. After descanting for two hours on Democratic corruption and Republican purity at Florence, for example, he closed by saying that, unfortunately, there was only one chance for a man to be a successful candidate for governor in Alabama: "to run on a ticket with a nigger."[44]

Sharing Smith's political views but refusing to prostitute themselves to the "Negro ticket," other Republicans simply renounced their allegiance to the Party of Lincoln and joined the Democrats. Within days after the Selma convention, Albert Elmore, former collector of customs at Mobile; W. J. Bibb, former postmaster of Montgomery; Francis Bugbee, former judge of the second judicial circuit; and Milton J. Saffold, the judge of the first circuit court— all native Republicans and prewar antisecessionists—switched parties. Extremely bitter over the Rapier nomination, Saffold distributed a printed leaflet throughout the state urging other native whites to abandon the party "where a Negro can be bought for any purpose." Even those Republicans who had not renounced their party, prophesied the Montgomery Daily *Mail*, would vote with the Democracy. "They cannot vote for a negro, nor for a party which puts negroes in nomination for office."[45] In all, twenty leading white Republicans publicly, and many more privately, repudiated the party. It was the largest disaffection during Alabama reconstruction.

With their new recruits, the Conservatives hoped to profit by the fissure in Republican ranks. Appealing to white voters in both parties, they nominated J. J. Parker, a lawyer, state legislator (Monroe County), and gallant soldier in the Confederacy, to run for secretary of state. And with Parker they mounted a determined campaign against Rapier solely on the basis of race. Trumpeting his abhorrence to a black candidate, the editor of the Troy (Pike County) *Messenger* asserted that Rapier was "a full-blooded NIGGER," qualified only to hoe a cotton field, or wait on a white gentleman, or serve as a carriage driver.[46] In contrast, another editor described him as a bright mulatto but added that he would make a fine dining room servant. Others said that he was a "nigger" carpetbagger from Canada, that he had been a subject of Great Britain, and indicted him as an ignoramus, "but a very loud talker."[47] There were few whites in the state, his old hometown newspaper predicted, so destitute of respect for the Anglo-Saxon

race as to vote for Rapier, for it could only lead to Negroes ruling
Alabama. Another Democratic journal admitted without apology
that it knew nothing about Parker, but, believing in the divine right
of the white race to rule, supported him rather than his black
competitor.

Though more scientific in its arguments, the Montgomery *Mail*
likewise loathed the thought of a Negro secretary of state. Race was
the deepest dividing line between men, the *Mail* contended, deeper
than politics or religion, deeper than contemporary differences in
laws and manners. Race entered the elements of the blood, formed
the marrow of the bones, and created the size of the brain; it was
the essence of existence and experience, the beginning and end of
history. Was it proper, then, that a Negro should hold the great
seal of Alabama? have the seat of honor next to the governor at
state dinners? receive distinguished visitors at the executive
mansion? Using the same persuasion, the Democratic candidate for
governor, Robert Lindsay, who had begun his career as a lawyer in
1848 only a few miles from Florence, contended that God had
placed the white race in a position of superiority. Though he did
not wish to abridge the constitutional rights of anyone, the white
race must rule Alabama.

Emboldened by such arguments, grimly determined whites
mounted a campaign of violence and intimidation against Black
Belt pro-Rapier partisans. In Greene and Sumter counties, klansmen murdered six politically active Negroes, including Gilford
Coleman, a delegate at the Selma convention, and Henry Miller
and Samuel Clovis, both of whom had been campaigning for
Rapier. When Alexander Boyd, the prosecuting attorney, presented
incriminating evidence against the Klan to a Greene County grand
jury, he, too, was shot and killed (while eating supper). At York
Station (Sumter County) a few days before the election, an
undisguised white man, carrying a double-barreled shotgun,
walked through a car on the Selma and Meridian train and shouted
for Frank Diggs, a Negro state legislator who had been active in the
canvass; when Diggs appeared, the gunman emptied two loads into
his face. Sauntering away from the car, he then turned, raised his
gun, and swept it along the line of the train as if defying pursuit. An
even worse atrocity occurred at Cross Plains, in Calhoun County,
where five Negroes and a white American Missionary Association
teacher, William Luke, accused of political involvement and of

firing on a group of whites, were hanged. "I die to-night," Luke wrote his wife hours before his execution. "It has been so determined by those who think I deserve it. God knows I feel myself innocent. I have only sought to educate the negro."[48] Although Governor Smith, along with former governor Lewis Parsons, conducted a personal investigation of the lynchings, they uncovered no incriminating evidence. But after they had left, Lewis M. Force, who was probably involved in the murders, admitted he was a member of the Klan, stated that the organization numbered ten thousand in the state, and maintained that its objective was to control politically active Negroes.

The atmosphere of violence, the activities of the Klan, the racial arguments of the Democracy, and the repugnance of white Republicans to a Negro nominee, brought Rapier to defeat. In some counties terrified Negroes stayed away from the polls altogether, while in others, white Republicans supported the ticket except for Rapier. In Greene County, for example, though Republicans outnumbered the Conservatives by a three-to-one margin, and though Grant had received an overwhelming majority in the presidential election, Rapier tallied only 1790 to Parker's 1825, with two thousand black voters failing to cast their ballots. In nearby Sumter, where black electors also outnumbered whites about three to one, and previous Republican victories had been in the thousands, Rapier collected a mere 1435 votes to his opponent's 2055 (see table 1), while seventeen hundred freedmen stayed at home on election day. In the few predominately black counties where freedmen cast ballots without fear of the klan, Rapier outpolled Parker by more than two to one, but in ten predominantly white counties, the Negro nominee received fewer than 100 votes. The other Republican candidates each tallied about 4000 more votes than their black running mate in the white counties of the state, and in forty-two of forty-five of those counties, Rapier received fewer votes than any candidate, Republican or Democratic. In the end, Rapier lost by more than 5000 votes, receiving fewer ballots than any candidate on the state ticket.

In contrast, Smith lost by a mere 615 votes (76,290 to 76,905). Charging that violence and intimidation had cost him the election, he ensconced himself at the capitol in November 1870, refusing to accept what he labeled fraudulent election returns. Later, faced with court action, he reluctantly gave up the fight and left

TABLE 1   Rapier-Parker Election Returns for 1870

County	Rapier	Parker	County	Rapier	Parker
Autauga	1508	817	Jackson	400	1573
Baker	121	216	Jefferson	211	1035
Baldwin	532	556	Lauderdale	444	1272
Barbour	3471	2183	Lawrence	965	1336
Bibb	262	847	Lee	1676	1951
Blount	38	657	Limestone	784	1099
Bullock	2941	1547	Lowndes	3558	1195
Butler	686	1532	Macon	1700	1236
Calhoun	327	1843	Madison	2051	2991
Chambers	1239	1610	Marengo	3249	1447
Cherokee	37	993	Marion	16	288
Choctaw	1034	1071	Marshall	84	644
Clarke	535	1207	Mobile	4646	4626
Clay	63	879	Monroe	578	1362
Cleburne	185	539	Montgomery	7320	2613
Coffee	126	626	Morgan	429	1007
Colbert	148	1184	Perry	3902	1357
Conecuh	748	787	Pickens	227	1707
Coosa	561	1094	Pike	495	1824
Covington		587	Randolph	498	677
Crenshaw	130	1170	Russell	1427	1157
Dale	273	1114	Sanford	90	607
Dallas	7372	2099	Shelby	537	1125
DeKalb	327	576	St. Clair	487	789
Elmore	1320	1382	Sumter	1435	2055
Escumbia	158	469	Tallapoosa	402	2286
Etowah	214	788	Tuscaloosa	758	1865
Fayette	151	574	Walker	26	620
Franklin	133	394	Washington	6	551
Geneva	95	163	Wilcox	3678	1407
Greene	1790	1825	Winston	36	137
Hale	3200	1198	Total	72,237	77,306
Henry	429	1632			

SOURCE: Secretary of State of Alabama, Election Returns, 1870. State Department of Archives and History, Montgomery, Alabama.

Montgomery. His departure symbolized the totality of the Republican defeat. The other whites on the state ticket had also lost (by a few hundred votes each), as had two of every three Republican candidates for the state House of Representatives and a majority of the party's congressional candidates. The experiment of placing a Negro on the state ticket had ended in disaster for the Republican party of Alabama and had brought to the surface once again the deep cleavages that had plagued the party from its inception. Unable to accept a black candidate, native white Republicans vigorously struggled to defeat Rapier, and in doing so, made their own downfall certain.

To Redeem a Pledge

At the time of his religious conversion Rapier had pledged himself to improving the education and economic condition of blacks in the South.[1] "If I live and God is willing," he had vowed in 1858, "I will endeavor to do my part in solving the problems of [black poverty and illiteracy] in my native land."[2] The opportunity for Rapier to redeem his promise came during reconstruction.

Despite the 1866 land act designed to provide freedmen with eighty-acre homesteads, property ownership among Southern Negroes had not increased substantially in the years following the Civil War. Though they were able to transfer their families from the slave quarters to tenant cabins, and though able to keep at least a portion of their crops, the great majority of former slaves still worked on land owned by whites. A resident of Dallas County, Alabama, interviewed by journalist John W. Trowbridge, candidly commented on the question of black property ownership: "The nigger is going to be made a serf, sure as you live. It won't take any law for that." Planters already had an understanding among themselves: they would not hire one another's Negroes. "Then what's left for them? Whites are as much the masters of blacks as ever."[3] Indeed, as in antebellum times, Negroes toiled long hours in the fields, lived at a bare subsistence level, and worked on land controlled by white plantation owners.

No better than their economic plight was the educational condition of freedmen in the South. Despite the tremendous enthusiasm of emancipated slaves for learning—W. G. Kephart, chaplain of the Tenth Iowa Veterans, for example, wrote from Decatur, Alabama, in 1864, "I have never seen any people more ready or eager to learn, and so far as I have had an opportunity to observe, their progress is about the same as white children"—few Negroes

experienced the excitement of the classroom.[4] Black youths
fortunate enough to have a "nigger school" in their community
attended school only a few weeks, or months, each year, listened to
ill-prepared, often almost illiterate teachers, and sat in drafty,
dilapidated, and decaying schoolhouses. They went without
books, educational equipment, and in some instances, even paper
and ink. Neither the 1865 Alabama constitution, nor the Democratic legislature under the Johnson plan of restoration, provided
state funds for the support of Negro education, while most whites
vehemently opposed admitting black children to the free public
schools.

Northern missionaries, working with Negroes and Freedmen's
Bureau officials, established a few schools in Alabama, but as late
as July 1866, according to a report submitted to Congress by John
Alvord of the bureau, they had opened only eight schools for
freedmen in the state (compared to one hundred twenty-three in
Virginia), and had sent only thirty-one teachers to the field
(compared to two hundred in Virginia)—the lowest totals in the
South. Even after the adoption of the 1868 constitution, partisan
bickering between the Republican school board and Democratic
legislature plus a lack of sufficient funds made improvement of
Negro education almost impossible. As the nation slumped into a
severe depression in 1873, the state board actually closed the public
schools on the plea of financial incapacity. Because of such
conditions, only a small proportion of Alabama's black children
acquired an adequate education in the first years of freedom.

Throughout his career Rapier strove to correct the economic and
educational inequities facing Negroes. He continually urged blacks
to acquire habits of thrift and frugality, even if it meant saving only
a few pennies each day. To promote this concept—one which he
had grown up with—he accepted an appointment as a director of
the Montgomery Freedmen's Savings Bank, one of thirty-four
branch banks in the South chartered by Congress but under the
aegis of a private board of trustees. During his tenure the Montgomery branch thrived, not only receiving plaudits in the press, but
taking in deposits of nearly $260,000. "We are glad to learn," read
an article in the *Alabama State Journal*, "that this institution is a
success and that the colored people are fast placing themselves on
the credit side of life."[5] But like hundreds of other savings
institutions, the 1873 depression precipitated the bank's failure.

Even then, Rapier continued to work in behalf of its depositors, enlisting local attorneys to press the claims of blacks against companies which had defaulted on loans.

In addition to his work with the bank, Rapier donated personal funds for the construction of Negro churches and schools. "No man in the state has more cheerfully aided our church in erecting places of worship and building places of learning than he," declared Montgomery Negro J. N. Fitzpatrick, who had traveled extensively throughout the state.[6] Indeed, no one in Alabama had done more to give Negroes a business standing.

But Rapier realized that neither the Freedmen's Bank nor personal philanthropy were enough to solve the problems of hunger and illiteracy in the reconstruction South. Consequently, he sought to organize a Negro labor union. Surely, he believed, a nationally organized union, with the support of the federal government, could achieve economic and educational reforms that would improve the Negro's lot. With these thoughts on his mind, he traveled to Washington, D.C., on December 6, 1869, as the lone Alabama representative to the first National Negro Labor Union Convention. Some 156 black delegates from virtually every state came together at Union League Hall on that cold, blustery December day to discuss the condition of black laborers. "We are here to seek the amelioration and advancement of those who labor for a living," Isaac Myers, the black Baltimore shipyard proprietor who had called the meeting, began;[7] and George T. Downing, a Rhode Island Negro chosen permanent chairman, said that to do that the federal government should make homestead land readily available to freedmen. Other delegates asked for a mandatory eight-hour workday, sought to organize state and local labor unions, and suggested a graduated income tax, as one delegate put it, "to make the burden of taxation heaviest upon those who have reaped the lion's share of American toil."[8]

As a newly elected vice-president of the NNLU, Rapier addressed the convention on December 9, expressing his thoughts on these and other subjects as well as offering a program for relief. While dismissing the call for both the eight-hour workday and a graduated income tax as "impractical," he voiced approval for providing Negroes with land. Black farmers, especially in the South, paid enormously high interest rates on borrowed money; they paid equally large amounts for rent; and at the end of the year, they were left with virtually nothing. To ease the burden of the

Negro tenant farmer, he suggested that the federal government make fifty million acres immediately available for homesteading, either in the states of the old Confederacy or in Kansas or Nebraska or the Dakotas, so that former bondsmen could thrive without paying tribute to white landowners. The next day, as a member of the Committee on Homesteads, he put forward a more detailed proposal (unanimously accepted by the convention), which, among other things, suggested that the government establish a land bureau to assist Negroes in obtaining the homesteads.

The Alabama delegate not only suggested that a new federal agency be created, but he also (along with twelve other officers of the convention) sent a memorial to Congress in behalf of Southern blacks. Wages of the average Negro laborer in the South did not exceed sixty dollars a year, Rapier and the others told Congress. Such an amount left him with no surplus, and "when he ceased to labor he began to starve."[9] The remedy, according to the petitioners, was to make landowners of a reasonable proportion of the laborers by subdividing the nearly 47 million acres of the public domain in the Southern states into homesteads so that any freedman who settled on such a subdivision and cultivated it for a year could receive a deed for the land.

To press their demands further, Rapier, Joseph Rainey (South Carolina), John Harris (North Carolina), Sella Martin (Massachusetts), and several other delegates visited President Grant. They asked the president to protect black sharecroppers from the exploitation of grasping landlords, to sanction the cause of Negro land ownership, and to use both his influence and the office of the presidency to establish a federal land bureau. "I heartily empathize with the working men of the country," Grant said in response, "and so far as it is in my power I will endeavor to secure ample protection for them and for all classes."[10]

When Rapier left the White House, he had, in less than a week, met with black leaders from all parts of the nation, served as a committeeman and vice-president at the first National Negro Labor Union Convention, presented a plan for a federal agency to ameliorate the plight of black laborers in the South, and pressed his demands upon the president of the United States. This was, by any test, a remarkable set of experiences for the thirty-two-year-old Alabamian and an auspicious beginning for his career as a black labor leader.

In the following months Rapier waited for federal initiative in creating a land bureau, but gradually came to realize that the promises made in Washington to protect Southern blacks were empty ones. He decided, therefore, to take matters into his own hands. He asked Negro leaders in various sections of the state to gather information about schools, churches, and wages of colored people and issued a call in the *Alabama State Journal* for a state convention to consider the organization of black laboring interests of Alabama.

On January 2, 1871, ninety-eight Negro farmers and farm laborers representing forty-two Alabama counties answered Rapier's call. Assembling at the House of Representatives in Montgomery, they first chose Rapier permanent chairman (in that capacity he appointed the various committees) and then immediately launched into a discussion of possible solutions to the problems facing the state's black citizens. George Washington Cox, chairman of the Homesteads Committee, recommended that freedmen simply leave Alabama. "Here, huddled as we are, so much of the same kind of labor in the market, wages down to starving rates, without land, or a house that we can call our own," Cox said eloquently, "nothing but misery is in store for the masses."[11] He maintained that government homesteads in the state were located in regions where armed bands of disguised men terrorized freedmen, but in Kansas as well as other western states, land was available, and Negroes could exercise their rights. Another committee chairman, William V. Turner of the Committee on the Condition of Colored People, concurred, declaring that black farmers and farm workers were far worse off in Alabama than in any other section of the United States. A black tenant farmer would make a contract for a year, and after twelve months of sweat and toil, he would find himself poorer than at the beginning. After studying information submitted by the delegates, Turner concluded further that the educational facilities provided for Negro children were grossly inadequate. In the cities and some of the larger towns, he sadly admitted, schools were ramshackle and run-down, while in some localities "nigger schools" were not even tolerated. The cure for these evils, according to Turner, was for blacks to emigrate to the "broad and free West."

Although most of the delegates agreed with Cox and Turner concerning the deplorable economic and educational condition of blacks in Alabama, they rejected emigration as a cure for it. The convention adopted a resolution instructing all laboring men under contract for the year to honor the contract, whether it was with a planter or businessman. Outside the convention, interested observers also advised Negroes to stay. William Loftin, the white editor of the *Alabama State Journal*, suggested that black tenant farmers improve their situation by hard work; they should consider settling among a more liberal people only if denied all opportunity for improvement. And the editor of the Selma *Press*, a Republican paper, cautioned blacks not to act hastily. In many localities Negro farmers were doing as well as they could reasonably expect to do anywhere, and those who were prospering unmolested in their rights should deliberate a long time before starting life anew in a strange land.

Conservatives likewise advised freedmen to remain in Alabama, but for quite different reasons. The *Alabama Beacon* (Hale County) contended that Negroes could neither adapt to the cold climate of Kansas, nor compete with white workers there. The Bluff City *Times* (Barbour County) derided the convention members for "consuming so much time discussing the cock and bull stories of political proscription, Ku Klux outrages, destruction of colored churches, denial of school privileges, and the advantages of emigration to Kansas."[12] The *Times* advised blacks to think for themselves, follow their own personal instincts, and disregard the advice of such men as Cox and Turner. The whole notion of leaving the South was a carpetbag idea anyway, the Montgomery *Daily Advertiser* added, trumped up by Northerners, who were desirous of creating a Negro section in Kansas and then securing a congressional nomination. The *Advertiser* cautioned blacks to beware of mischievous schemers and counseled them to remain at home and work honestly and zealously for a living.

As the three-day meeting drew to a close, Rapier called for the report of the Committee on Permanent Organization. The association would be known as the Labor Union of Alabama, an auxiliary of the National Negro Labor Union (NNLU). It was to have a president, an executive committee, and a constitution; and its purpose was to further the welfare and education of the laboring people of the state. Once the plan for the union was unanimously accepted, the delegates selected Jeremiah Haralson, a member of the state legislature from Dallas County, as the first president and elected an executive committee consisting of Montgomery state

legislator Lazarus Williams, Hale County's James K. Greene, a
delegate at the 1867 constitutional convention, and Rapier, all of
whom were to represent the newly established union at the
forthcoming NNLU convention. Shortly before adjourning, the
members thanked "the Chairman of the Convention for his eminent
services in behalf of the laboring people of the South, and his
marked ability as a presiding officer."

Only seven days after he had helped inaugurate the Labor Union
of Alabama, Rapier registered as a delegate to the second annual
NNLU convention in Washington, D.C. Again he was among the
first to address the convention, sharply scolding Congress for
failing to ameliorate the condition of blacks, renewing his plea for a
government agency to assist freedmen in acquiring land, and
deploring the low economic and educational status of blacks. Since
officials in Washington had not heeded his pleas, he said that the
union itself should create a bureau of labor to determine the best
way to colonize blacks on the lands of the public domain. By
distributing available information on homesteads to blacks, the new
bureau would perhaps help alleviate some of the "great suffering
endured by the colored people of the Southern States for want of
land, employment, capital, and pay."[13]

Other delegates quickly endorsed Rapier's idea. George Downing, an officer at the first NNLU gathering, said that Negroes had
gathered together, given speeches, made resolutions, and offered
petitions, "but the essential thing needed, means, is wanting."[14]
Perhaps such a labor bureau, with state and local affiliates, would
give freedmen the necessary means to improve their situation.
Another officer at the first NNLU meeting, Isaac Myers, believed
that such an organization could easily disseminate information to
Negroes about the public domain. The convention soon voted
favorably on the proposal, choosing nine delegates to head up the
new labor bureau—among them Downing, Myers, and Rapier.
Then, at the closing session (January 11, 1871), the membership
empowered delegates from every Southern commonwealth, except
Alabama, to work in cooperation with the bureau in establishing
local chapters of the NNLU. It was not deemed necessary to
empower such a delegate for that state because Rapier, foreseeing
the importance of a grassroots organization, had already established the first local affiliate of the NNLU in the South.

Now somewhat optimistic about the prospects for improving

working conditions among freedmen, Rapier returned to Montgomery and conferred with members of the Alabama Negro Labor
Union. They agreed to call another state convention, but only after
a thorough investigation had been made of the earnings of Negro
tenant farmers, educational opportunities for black children, and
possible sites for Negro colonization.

Nearly a year elapsed before Rapier, in his capacity as executive
chairman of the union, called a meeting. About fifty Negro
delegates from various parts of the state gathered in Montgomery
on January 2, 1872, to hear the results of the surveys. The first
report, submitted by the Committee on Labor and Wages, disclosed that black sharecroppers in Alabama earned on the average
$387 a year, and after paying for food, medical supplies, clothing,
feed, and interest on borrowed money, they were left with virtually
nothing. The report urged Congress to pass a freedmen's homestead bill creating a joint stock company to purchase land for
former slaves. A second report, submitted by the Committee on
Emigration, advocated a far different solution to the wage
problem—emigration to Kansas. Describing the state as mild and
pleasant, with schools in every neighborhood and railroads in all
directions, the report said that Negroes could acquire excellent land
for only $1.25 an acre. An equally sanguine report came from John
Simpson, chairman of the Committee on Education, who announced that the free schools of Alabama were well patronized by
black children and that the state board of education had done all it
could to provide equal educational opportunity. Thousands of
Negro youngsters who had only a few years before never seen the
inside of a school building were happily tramping down schoolhouse paths.

Rapier generally agreed with the reports on wages, labor, and
emigration to Kansas, but he took strong exception to the report on
education. It was impossible, he said, beginning a lengthy address
to the convention, for the poor children of the state to get an
adequate common school education. Schools remained open only
two months a year; state allocations for education amounted to
only $1.20 per student, per year, as compared to $16.45 in
Massachusetts; and hundreds of teachers, unable to work out a
simple sum of interest or to write grammatically, simply put in
their time. In short, Rapier declared, Alabama had no public school
system worthy of the name.

Drawing on his experiences as a student and teacher in Canada, Rapier advanced a farsighted reform plan to improve the educational system of Alabama. He suggested that an examining board, composed of the best scholars (students and faculty) as well as the county superintendent, carefully scrutinize applicants for teacher certification and grade the schools on the proficiency of the teachers. Such a board would eliminate many worthless instructors and make teaching more professional. Realizing that even this would not be enough, he further advocated that the federal government assume a portion of the responsibility for educating Alabama's children. Demanding the appointment of a national superintendent of education with cabinet rank, he offered this challenge: "We want a government schoolhouse, with the letters U.S. marked thereon in every township in the State. We want a national series of textbooks which will teach the child that to respect the government is the first duty of a citizen."[15] To finance the scheme, he suggested using $115 million a year from Internal Revenue; if this sum were divided among the several states, Alabama would receive $2.5 million, an amount sufficient to keep the schools open at least seven months a year; and if the state fund were added to this, schools could remain open nine months a year.

Whites in the state, however, paid little attention to his suggestions. Indeed, few Democratic newspapers so much as mentioned the fact that black labor leaders, representing about half the state's one million people, had held a three-day convention to air grievances and suggest reforms. Speaking for the majority of Alabama whites, the new editor of the Republican *Alabama State Journal*, Arthur Bingham, despairingly commented that the turnout at the Negro Labor Union Convention had been extremely small, not nearly as large as had been expected, and that the proceedings were "necessarily of little interest."[16]

By early 1872, Rapier realized that the strong opposition of white landowners, Republican indifference, and a lack of federal assistance had doomed the Negro labor movement. Though he had advocated the creation of a federal land bureau, served as director of the Montgomery Freedmen's Bank, established the first state affiliate of the NNLU, and demanded reforms in the public school system, the federal government created no land bureau, the bank suffered during the depression of 1873, the Alabama Negro Labor Union made few practical gains for freedmen, and Rapier's educational proposals went unnoticed. Not only had the economic and educational conditions among freedmen not improved during this time, but in some areas they had deteriorated. It was in these circumstances that Rapier again looked for a political solution to the problems of poverty, landlessness, and illiteracy among blacks in the Southern states.

8 Assessor of Internal Revenue

"Mr. Rapier is the leading colored man of our State," Alabama Congressman Charles Hays wrote, sitting at the small desk in his room at Willard's Hotel in Washington, D.C., a gentleman of highest probity, character, and capacity, who justly deserved the unbounded confidence and respect of all citizens.[1] Urging Secretary of the Treasury George Boutwell to appoint Rapier as Assessor of Internal Revenue for the Second District of Alabama, Hays continued: he had organized a Negro labor union in the state; he had performed great service for the Republican party, not only in Alabama but throughout the South; in talent and ability he was the equal of John Langston or Frederick Douglass. Similarly strong recommendations came from three other influential Alabamians: United States Senator George Spencer, Negro Congressman Benjamin Turner, and Montgomery Representative Charles Buckley, who extolled Rapier as a gentleman of the highest character and acquirements. His standing in the community, in every essential, was unimpeachable; his honesty and integrity were proverbial. He was an educated gentleman and a thorough businessman. And, again, in precisely the words of Hays's encomium: "Mr. Rapier is the leading colored man of our state."[2]

With these recommendations at hand, President Grant appointed Rapier as Assessor for the Second Revenue District in April, 1871, making him the first black man to obtain such a high patronage office in Alabama. But even before he could begin his official duties, infuriated whites threatened to kill him if he did not immediately resign. When the new assessor attempted to take charge of the revenue office at Selma (Dallas County) he was unable to do so because of menacing whites, who, according to the Montgomery *Daily Advertiser*, put him "in constant danger of his life."[3] Imputing the appointment to a political conspiracy, the *Advertiser* charged that by designating a Negro to succeed a white man [Dr. George P. Rex], Republicans hoped to goad Southerners into a rebellious act so that Grant could make it a campaign issue. The Democratic Selma *Times* also contended that local Republicans had conspired with the White House, hoping to use opposition to Rapier for political advantage. In the minds of most Conservatives, the appointment of a black assessor could only be a scheme to humiliate the South.

Opposition Republicans also disapproved of Rapier. The leader of the conservative wing, Senator Willard Warner, a former Union general from Ohio, cautioned that such an appointment would be extremely unpopular among whites; and another member of the group, Judge Luther R. Smith, warned that no white assistant with any self-respect would work under a Negro. Former governor Lewis E. Parsons, a Talladega lawyer and a grandson of the famous Jonathan Edwards, predicted that Rapier's taking office would be followed by the resignation of the entire corps of Alabama revenue officers. All three—Warner, Smith, and Parsons—insinuated that Rapier had been selected solely because of his color.

"Make no allowances whatever for my color," Rapier retorted in a letter to Treasury Secretary Boutwell, who had earlier seen the warm letters of recommendation for his appointment which had been sent to the president. "If I prove an inefficient officer, my color should be no shield, but I must go the way of white men who are incompetent."[4] Stung by the racial arguments, he responded by expressing a deeply felt conviction, indeed, his philosophy of reconstruction: if Negroes could not sustain themselves as well as whites, under similar circumstances, then they could make no claims on the party for position. It was thus with a sense of mission in behalf of his race that Rapier undertook his duties as assessor of internal revenue.

He moved from Selma to Montgomery, where he opened a second-floor office at 39 Market Street, downtown, and began accepting applications for positions on his staff. "Finding men has not been the difficulty," he said confidently, in response to the dire predictions of his antagonists, "but finding places for the applicants has been my trouble."[5] Within a short while, he had hired five assistants: two former Union soldiers, William W. Hammel and

Eugene A. Cory; William Loftin, editor of the *Alabama State Journal*; John Hendricks, a Montgomery County Republican leader; and Henry Hunter Craig, the Negro doorkeeper at the 1867 constitutional convention, and had set about administering the affairs of his office. As the great accumulation of papers given over to his keeping were in chaos, he assigned assistants Craig and Cory the task of systematizing the official revenue documents; while the chore of compiling the 1871 tax list, which included assessments on several thousand retail dealers of tobacco and liquor in a twenty-three-county area, he gave to the other three assistants: Hammell, Loftin, and Hendrix. Closely supervising their progress, he also spent time—on one occasion ten consecutive days—listening to appeals and complaints of dissatisfied dealers. Only a short time after he had accepted the assessorship, the *Alabama State Journal* noted with some pleasure that Rapier had entered upon the discharge of the affairs of his office with characteristic energy, enthusiasm, and dedication.

But the responsibilities of his office went beyond the levying and collecting of revenue, and he soon turned his attention to politics. Convinced that conservatives caused perpetual discord within the party, discord that resulted in his defeat in 1870, he undertook to reduce their power. In a long letter to high-ranking Republican George Boutwell, he explained that Alabama Republicans had suffered grievously from the continuing battle between Senators Spencer and Warner. They had each lost an eye in the fight already; the only question was how could it be stopped? When three members of the conservative faction (Parsons, Smith, and Larkin) petitioned the president to appoint Warner as Collector of Customs for the port of Mobile, Rapier answered his own question. Such an appointment would destroy the party. "Nothing but confusion will follow and nothing but defeat can overtake us, if you appoint the 'Chief of the Opposition.' "[6] The only solution was for Warner to leave Alabama. With the head of one, by far the weakest, faction removed, he explained, the wing would probably disband. This, in turn, would mean the disintegration of the Spencer group, and the result would be a unified party "equipped to do battle against the common enemy Democracy."[7] It was in these uncompromising terms—the complete dissolution of what he called the native wing (a faction led in 1871, paradoxically, by a carpetbagger), that Rapier now sought to unify the party.

But his plan to achieve Republican solidarity was ignored by Grant, who decided to appoint Warner anyway and sent his name to the Senate. How fully Rapier's views had come to represent those of blacks in Alabama was vividly illustrated in the subsequent battle to block Warner's confirmation. Negro W. B. Y Bates hastily wrote Massachusetts Senator Benjamin Butler, who controlled a crucial block of votes in the Senate, that the party was badly divided. It would be against the interest of freedmen, Southern Republicans, and indeed, the entire nation, if Warner were accepted, for he, like former governor Smith, held extremely conservative racial views. Congressman Benjamin Turner, a former slave, volunteered that the general had few colored friends in Alabama, and another black spokesman, Albert Gallatin, added that Warner not only suffered the disapprobation of Negroes, but had caused the party's downfall in the previous election. Mobile blacks felt especially threatened, having experienced their only political defeat during reconstruction, when Warner's friends bolted the party and rallied behind the rival ticket. Interrupting a Fourth of July celebration, three thousand Negroes from that city paused to pass a strongly worded resolution against the appointment. Another group of Mobile Negroes circulated a printed address, cordially thanking the president for appointing Rapier as assessor of internal revenue, for Rapier, they said, had the universal support of all former slaves. But they concluded with a dogmatic declaration: "We will never endorse Willard Warner."[8]

Many white Republicans felt the same. Petitions and letters urging the rejection of the nominee piled up in stacks at the Treasury Department. They came from Republicans across the state, including members of the state senate, general assembly, and Republican state and federal officeholders. In one of them, Senator Spencer deplored the appointment as utterly repugnant and distasteful; in another, state senator Q. P. Sibley accused Warner of nothing less than perfidy and deceit in "Bartering the integrity of the Republican Party in 1870 by the nomination of Gov. Smith," misrepresenting the lawlessness in Alabama, and inducing conservative party members to bolt the party.[9] But even more than this, Sibley went on, Warner had vowed to defeat General Spencer no matter what the consequences, even if it meant the disintegration of the party. So white Republicans, far more intemperately than Negroes, denounced the "Conservative Chief."

Though Rapier had exerted every effort to defeat the nomination, he refused to express publicly any opinions on the matter, declaring that it would be improper for one federal official to denounce another. Having seen a petition demanding that the Senate refuse to confirm the nomination of Warner, he questioned the propriety of one federal appointee doing anything openly to prevent the confirmation of a colleague. Yet he hastened to add, in a letter to George Spencer, that Warner, more than any other man, had brought ruin to the party in Alabama. The overwhelming majority of the party's membership in the state, blacks and original Union men, were unequivocally opposed to him. It would never do to turn a deaf ear on their wishes. Who, then, were Warner's supporters? Quasi-Republicans like Samuel F. Rice, Alexander H. White, Lewis Parsons, and John Keffer; men who had done their utmost to defeat Grant in 1868, and even more, men who had exerted every effort to invalidate the reconstruction amendments.

These were strong words; he was accusing members of his own party of depravity. Yet he clearly recognized the anti-Negro sentiments of the conservatives, even though, at times, they were subtle and disguised. Realizing that any accommodation between the two groups would be impossible without blacks conceding their political integrity, Rapier demanded nothing less than full acceptance of the Fourteenth and Fifteenth Amendments; he pledged, "I shall ever be found at my 'Post' battling for our cause."[10] Conservatives, on the other hand, were working in various ways to nullify the amendments. "My honest opinion is that under the garb of Republicanism," one perceptive observer noted in the midst of the struggle, "we have men in Alabama, some in high places, who are seeking to make themselves acceptable to the Democracy."[11] Indeed, like the Democrats, conservative Republicans sought to abrogate the constitutional guarantees of full citizenship for blacks, while "radicals" fought to conserve those guarantees. It was a strange definition of conservativism and radicalism. In the end, Grant withdrew the nomination, but only after the fight had seriously shaken the party.

The battle over Warner's confirmation, as well as the similar interparty disputes occurring across the South, posed a dilemma for Rapier and other Negro leaders who understood that party unity was essential for victory, but who also realized that they could never forsake the principle of black citizenship. To solve this dilemma, Negro spokesmen from seventeen states gathered in Columbia, South Carolina (October 1871), at the Southern States Negro Convention. Answering the initial roll call were several of the nation's most eminent black reconstructionists, including, in addition to Rapier, Josiah Walls (Florida), John Quarles (Georgia), P. B. S. Pinchback (Louisiana), Isaac Myers (Maryland), James Lynch (Mississippi), Alonzo Ransier, Joseph Rainey, Robert Elliott, Richard Cain (South Carolina), and Frederick Douglass. Gravely aware of their power and responsibility, they contended that, as the freedmen's vote would elect the next president, they should carefully scrutinize the views of the candidates concerning equal rights for Negroes. They had not gathered together as a race to organize against another race, as was alleged in quasi-Republican newspapers, but only "to preserve our own rights and privileges and subserve the best interest of the community."[12]

Rapier offered three resolutions at the outset designed to do exactly that—subserve the best interest of the community. He first proposed that the convention raise five hundred dollars for the victims of the Chicago fire (October 9–10) to benefit "a suffering humanity." Reminding the gathering that Lincoln, who had led Negroes to physical emancipation, and Grant, who had led them to political emancipation, had both received the Republican nomination in Chicago, he said that the Windy City was one of the most progressive cities in the nation. Then, to chart a political course for Southern freedmen, he asked the gathering to endorse unanimously the principles of the current administration and to issue a strongly worded statement saying that Grant was blacks' choice for president. The *New National Era* regarded the resolutions as among the most important and farreaching to emerge from the week-long convention, but the storm of protest that followed suggested only that they were among the most controversial.

"We are not here in a political capacity at all," proclaimed B. A. Bosemon, Jr., of South Carolina, beseeching the delegates to discard the Rapier proposals. Southern Negroes should not ally themselves with either party, nor adopt any resolution binding themselves to a particular candidate, nor endorse any administration. Another South Carolinian, Congressman Robert Elliott, also refused to support any aspirant, insisting that it was not the duty of the membership to sanction the renomination of Grant. Others deemed it impolitic to anticipate the nomination of the Republican party, and even the influential Louisiana editor, P. B. S. Pinchback, who had earlier extolled the president as a great military chief and praised federal patronage as "a crowning act of elevation for colored people," withheld his approval.[13] In the end, the convention voted 30 to 18 against the Rapier resolutions, thus rejecting any plan to endorse the Republican party. By their action, or inaction, the convention had shown its unwillingness to mark out a political course for Southern blacks.

Rapier had meanwhile turned his attention to other matters. As a member of the Committee on Education and Labor, he presented a comprehensive report to the assemblage, wherein he demanded equal educational facilities for Negroes, recommended the organization of Negro labor unions, and restated his proposal for a national bureau of labor. It was the responsibility of each state legislature, he said, to provide funds not only for free common schools but also for Negro high schools and normal schools; it was the duty of Negro leaders to create unions of black mechanics and tenant farmers; and it was the obligation of the federal government to protect the rights of workingmen. On the question of emigration, he suggested that such an alternative be given serious consideration, and when a member of the committee dealing with that subject described the old Confederate states as a land of civil liberty and equality, Rapier implored the members to reject such a gross distortion. Though he made a motion to recommit the entire report of the emigration committee, he was overruled.

But all was not lost. He strongly approved of the speeches delivered by Josiah Walls and John Quarles on October 25, the closing day of the convention. As chairman of the Committee on Outrages, Walls condemned the murderous acts of the Klan, while praising the president's suspension of the writ of habeas corpus in South Carolina as "wise and beneficial" for the black race. Speaking on the social changes in the South since emancipation, Quarles cited the magnitude and complexity of the challenge facing blacks: it was one thing to attack a gigantic system of wrong and to wipe it out, but it was quite another to discover what should be substituted in its place. It required wisdom and foresight to devise a new and better system. "Revolutions may sweep away old social systems in a day, but it requires great wisdom and profound statesmanship to inaugurate new ones."[14] Yet when the Columbia convention adjourned, it was clear that a majority of the delegates had demonstrated neither the "great wisdom" nor the "profound statesman-ship" necessary to institute a better society.

Discouraged, though not disheartened, Rapier returned to Mont-gomery, but no sooner had he resumed his routine in the revenue office than he was summoned by Treasury Department Supervisor M. D. Stanwood to an inquiry into the management of his office. To make matters worse, he soon learned that he and his staff were charged with malfeasance in office, gross neglect of duty, and fraud upon the government. If the charges could be proven, he might be impeached; if he were impeached, his political future would be ruined.

For three days Rapier responded to a barrage of questions from Stanwood, a long-time Alabama resident and strong anti-Spencer Republican:

"Do you know of any Assistant Assessor under you who has drawn pay when he has not rendered service?"

"I did not know of it until this day at one o'clock."

"Who informed you of such being the case?"

"John C. Hendricks, Assistant Assessor for the Second Division."

"Who did he say had done so?"

"He told me that Assistant Assessor William W. Hammell . . . had done so."[15]

Stanwood then read the first charge: entries in Hammell's pay accounts for July, August, and September, 1871, listed full pay on every working day, but he had been absent from the district for nearly a month during a political canvass. The supervisor produced the accounts of other revenue officers. How long had Craig been working in the office?

He had been employed about four months.

What was the nature of his employment?

He had worked as a clerk, except during a three-week absence when he, too, was engaged in a political canvass.

What were his duties?

To deliver letters to the post office, to file, package, and label official papers, to organize the bulk of the office's material received from the previous assessor.

Had he written the labels?

He had not.

Had he done any writing for the office?

He had not.

Producing a booklet, *Instructions for Revenue Officials*, Stanwood read aloud that clerks were responsible for all the writing. His next questions concerned the affairs of John Hendricks, a recent bridegroom.

Had he come to work late on the Monday following his wedding? Had he taken time off to attend a political meeting in Montgomery, August 8, 1871? Had he performed any labor for the government on those occasions? Was Rapier aware of the regulation which required assistants to report fractions of a day? To these questions Rapier answered that he was not aware of Hendricks's activities, but he was familiar with the fraction-of-a-day regulation.

Two witnesses whom the supervisor called to testify on Thursday, Friday, and Saturday, November 2 through 4, 1871, were especially critical of assistants Cory and Craig. One said that Cory had been so involved in Republican politics that he had not properly canvassed his division. Another, Montgomery Marshall Charles Scott, a personal friend of Stanwood, testified that Craig had spent most of his time during the summer months talking politics with Negroes. Neglecting revenue business, Scott said, he had sought to indoctrinate his brethren on streetcorners or at political meetings or at the drinking saloons for colored men in the city.

A transcript of sworn testimony, which filled twenty-two pages, along with a seven-page personal report, which led off with the claim that the accused had mistaken their relationship, was mailed by Stanwood to Commissioner of Internal Revenue John Douglass. From the beginning, Stanwood charged in his reports, Rapier had been under the impression that he would be opposed by the supervisor, either because the latter was a friend of Spencer's, or because Rapier was black. Untrue, wrote Stanwood. All he required was a faithful discharge of duty. Yet the Negro assessor had approved illicit pay vouchers, allowed his staff undue liberties, and even encouraged them to become involved in politics, despite the fact that he had explicitly instructed Rapier on the official duties of the office.

Responding to the allegations in a long letter to Commissioner Douglass, Rapier defended each member of his staff. He affirmed that although Hammell had been absent from the district for a number of days, he was an efficient officer and had frankly acknowledged his absence; the service would suffer without him. In the same manner, Craig, who was responsible for most of the office routine, had been engaged upon necessary work and should be absolved of any neglect of duty. He also excused the absences of Hendricks, who had attended the Montgomery meeting with Rapier's full knowledge and consent. Rapier requested exoneration of Cory, who had canvassed his division thoroughly. Believing that the charges were political and racial, he accused Stanwood of abusing Negroes in the foulest language, intimidating revenue officers in a tyrannical and ungentlemanly manner, and publicly denouncing Spencer's appointees. He called attention to the fact that Stanwood had long wanted to dismiss him, even if he had to appoint another Negro in his place, and described the supervisor as "a man of extraordinary vigilance" and firmness that many thought amounted to oppression. As for the whole proceedings, Rapier proudly stated that he would, at any time, invite an investigation of himself and his staff, certain that it would do credit to the revenue service. Apparently Rapier's rebuttal convinced the commissioner, as no action was taken. But the inconclusive inquiry had served once again to intensify factional antagonisms.

While Republicans fought among themselves, Conservative whites, as they had in 1868 and 1870, launched a campaign of terror—intimidating, terrorizing, and murdering Negroes. In some areas violence became a way of life. In Sumter County, Klansmen whipped Negroes, burned black schools and churches, and lynched Zeke High, a Negro accused of a crime. In one attack, though they were unsuccessful in their attempt to kill their victims, whites drove a wealthy black landowner, Robert Fullerlove, and his family from their home, forcing them to sleep in the woods for several months. Klan members bludgeoned Marengo County Republican Pierce Burton (Rapier's 1870 running mate) and threatened to kill Hale County judge William T. Blackford, both of whom soon fled from Alabama. "There is a very deplorable state of things," United States Marshall John Minnis reported. "Bands of disguised men have committed all sorts of depredations."[16] One such depredation occurred when a band of ten disguised men raided a house near Montgomery where two Negroes, a white woman, and two young children lived; they shot the black men to death, whipped the children, and then locked the woman in the house, poured turpentine on the porch, and set it ablaze, cheering as the woman "slowly roasted to death." The atrocity was recounted in March, 1872, by

Judge Richard Busteed, whose court had convicted a number of Klansmen. The   pretext for the diabolism, he wrote, was the intermarriage of a white woman and a black man.

During the fall of 1871 Rapier made a number of speeches condemning the activities of the Klan. At a meeting in Montgomery, he repudiated the murderous rampages, calling for federal intervention to protect innocent freedmen. At another, flanked by Minnis and Benjamin Norris, the latter a delegate to the 1867 constitutional convention, he demanded drastic action to curb the reign of terror. Negroes in many areas ran at the sight of a white man, fearful that some atrocity would be perpetrated against them. At yet another gathering, Rapier again called for federal intervention. "The slaves had a big pow-wow up at the Capitol this week and kicked monstrously, expressing indignation over the fearful doings of the Ku Klux," the Marion *Commonwealth* (Perry County) noted derisively, describing the last of these meetings. The "nigger" Rapier detailed some "blood-curdling narratives of their ravages."[17] Unhappily for Negroes, the narratives were true.

Despite three federal laws, called Force Acts (1870–1871), prohibiting abridgement of a person's right to vote because of race, empowering federal judges to appoint election supervisors, and subjecting Klan members convicted of criminal activity to imprisonment, the government seemed unable to halt the lawlessness. To such specific misdeeds as whipping, conspiracy to commit assault, or murder, dispositions simply read "escaped," "broke out of confinement," "eluded arrest," or "witnesses refused to testify." For crimes ranging from breaking and entering to murder, federal law enforcement officers in the state brought more than three hundred indictments in the fall of 1871, but only ten Klan members were found guilty as charged.

Though congressional legislation and federal prosecutions failed to halt the white terror, Conservatives regarded the government intervention itself as an odious tyranny. The overwhelming majority of Democrats either actively supported or tacitly condoned the activities of the Ku Klux Klan, vehemently condemning any prosecution of Klan members. Newspapers like the Montgomery *Advertiser* said that the federal courts intended to compel social equality, protect miscegenation, and encourage the mongrelization of the South. Its arch-Conservative editor, John Tyler, Jr., the son of the former president, asked rhetorically, How long would the

Southern people suffer such unendurable wrongs and usurpations? Another rhetorical question came from editor John M. Withers, of the Mobile *Tribune*, who described the federal courts as a travesty— judges and military guards holding bayonets to the throats of local juries. "Is this the 'best government the sun ever shone upon'?"[18] Such irony expressed genuine resentment, as Democrats believed, all evidence of flagrant crimes aside, that the prosecution of Klansmen was an attempt to abrogate the rights of the people.

The indictments, however, continued. In early 1872 United States Officer Minnis, Federal Marshal Robert Healy, Montgomery sheriff Paul Strobach, and Middle District judge Richard Busteed, captured, prosecuted, and sentenced a number of Klan members. Even a Montgomery jury of twelve white men found seven Klansmen guilty of murder, so overwhelming was the evidence. "This offensive warfare against them has brought terror to their ranks," Marshall Healy proudly disclosed, adding that he did not anticipate nearly as much trouble from marauding whites in the future.[19] Healy praised Lincoln-appointed Judge Busteed, who, long determined to punish Klansmen, had imposed stiff sentences. Though Conservatives called him a toad, ermine, base radical, and betrayer of his race, Busteed was a hero to Rapier. "He is the only hope for the Republican party in this state," Rapier said, again recalling the 1870 election, when violence had cost him a victory. "Without the U.S. Courts we are powerless, but with them giving protection, as they now do through Judge Busteed, we are confident in carrying the state from five to six thousand."[20] Thus as the Klan was gradually brought under control, Rapier anticipated a fair and peaceful election that he believed would surely bring victory for his party. His optimism proved to be well founded.

It was almost impossible to persuade a native to vote for a Negro, an exasperated Robert Healy, chairman of the Alabama Republican Executive Committee, explained to his national counterpart William Chandler. Citing the disastrous election of 1870, when Rapier had run for secretary of state, Healy went even further: it was impossible to induce a native Republican to vote for anyone who had not "come with the Indians."[1] Proposing that the 1872 slate consist entirely of native Alabamians, as opposed to Northerners or blacks, he contended that this was the only way the Republicans could be victorious in the coming election. In effect, he was willing to surrender the leadership of the party to the conservative faction.

Rejecting any such capitulation to the opposition, Rapier announced he would make a bid for a seat in Congress from Montgomery's Second District. Though confident he could secure the nomination, even win the election in November, he faced many obstacles in his first bid for national office. Arthur Bingham, editor of the *Alabama State Journal*, had already mounted a campaign for the renomination of two-term incumbent Charles Buckley, who, despite being a Northerner, had the support of most conservatives in the party. The *Journal* was the only Republican newspaper in the district. Moreover, Democrats and conservative whites would be repelled by the nomination of a Negro, yet they comprised nearly half of the forty-two thousand eligible voters. To win, Rapier would probably have to poll at least a thousand white votes. And if these difficulties were not enough, he also had to contend with the Liberal Republican disaffection in the North: long-time party members like Lyman Trumbull were denouncing Grant as a simpleminded fool. Despite this, Rapier remained optimistic about his chances for victory.

Even the weather seemed to presage a change. As he boarded a
Montgomery train for the nation's capital in January 1872, Rapier
looked out over four inches of snow—the first in the Alabama
Black Belt in more than twenty years; and, arriving in Washington,
in the dead of winter, he was greeted by a warm, sunny, springlike
day. Having made the journey to obtain endorsements in his bid
for Congress, he immediately conferred with a group of prominent
Republicans, including John Chandler, George Spencer, and Frederick Douglass, receiving their unqualified support, as well as a
promise of some financial assistance. Rapier was a diligent worker
in behalf of his race and party, said Douglass, as reported in the
New National Era; he thoroughly understood the needs of the
South and what was necessary for the progress of her people—both
black and white. An even greater tribute came at a dinner party in
his honor at Gray's Hotel, where Rapier received endorsements
from Negro leaders John Sampson and Charles Purvis and heard
the main speaker acclaim: "The State of Alabama would do itself a
great credit by sending Rapier to Congress."[2]

Returning to Montgomery, Rapier made a down payment on a
used printing press, rented a small office, and on Thursday,
April 1, 1872, he issued the first number of the *Republican Sentinel,*
a newspaper dedicated to the Republican party, the welfare of
freedmen, and the reelection of Ulysses Grant. Serving as editor-in-
chief, he printed political announcements of the National Committee, launched an attack on Democrats and conservative Republicans, and voiced support for the Regulars (as opposed to the
Liberals) in Washington. The first black-owned, black-edited, and
black-organized journal in Alabama, and among the first in the
deep South, the *Sentinel* came out weekly until three months after
the election, displaying in its columns a deep, unabiding loyalty to
both the Republican party and the reconstruction amendments.

Only three days after the first issue of the *Sentinel* had appeared
on the streets, Rapier registered as a delegate at the Southern States
Negro Convention in New Orleans, the second such convention in
six months. Almost immediately he expressed his views concerning
the disaffection of the Liberals, offering a resolution repudiating the
anti-Grant labor convention (which had met in Columbus, Ohio)
and the forthcoming national convention of Liberal Republicans.
Making the proposal in behalf of Southern Negroes, he again, as he
had in Columbia, sought to chart a course for his brethren in the

presidential election, but this time he had the backing of the
influential Frederick Douglass. The Republican party was the
national party, explained Douglass, who only a few weeks before
had endorsed Rapier as a candidate for Congress. It had given
blacks their freedom, their citizenship, and their voting rights.
"Grant is the man for whom I expect to vote."[3] Before the black
leaders left the Crescent City, they voted in favor of Rapier's
resolution; he had at last succeeded in mapping out a political
direction for Southern blacks.

A short time later the Liberal Republicans gathered in Cincinnati
to nominate a candidate for president. With the support of Lyman
Trumbull, the nomination went to the once-vigorous abolitionist
and editor of the New York *Tribune*, sixty-one-year-old Horace
Greeley, who, in accepting the honor, announced a stand for states'
rights. Local governments guarded the liberties of citizens more
securely than any centralized power, he said, and added, with
reference to reconstruction, that the public welfare required the
supremacy of civil over military authority. Greeley would permit
each of the several states and municipalities to protect the rights
and promote the well-being of their inhabitants by such means as
the judgment of their own people should prescribe. Though such
conservatism belied the name of the party, Liberals were using
strict construction arguments to attract Northern Conservatives
and Southern Democrats, and, at the same time, by nominating an
old friend of freedom, they hoped to lure the ballots of the recently
enfranchised. They were thus relying upon the attractive power of
a popular candidate, a politically clean slate, the backing of the
Conservative press, and the possible shift in the vote of Southern
blacks away from the Regular Republicans.

But Greeley's candidacy would attract fewer Negro votes in
Alabama than would the nomination of Jefferson Davis, Rapier
predicted with an air of authority, leaning back in a swivel chair in
his Internal Revenue office in Montgomery. Negroes could not be
bought, bribed, or even influenced by the nomination of a former
abolitionist. "I only speak for Alabama, for I was born and raised
here, and know what I say to be true. No colored man in the state
has more extensive acquaintance with colored men than myself."[4]
He explained that he had traveled in every Black Belt county and
that his office served as headquarters for Republicans from across
the state. Speaking to a correspondent of the *New National Era*,

who was making a tour through the South to determine the extent
of Negro support for the Liberal party, he continued: in Montgomery, Negroes could not be enticed away from the Regular
Republican organization, no matter who had been nominated in
Cincinnati. "They go in a body and with the organization."[5]

How many blacks in the northern section of the state would
support the new party?

In a few counties where the Klan was still active, the defectors
might receive a handful of Negro ballots, but not as many as
Horatio Seymour had received in 1868, Rapier said confidently.
Anyway, the Ku Klux had been driven to cover by the federal
enforcement laws in most areas, allowing freedmen to cast their
votes without fear of intimidation.

Greeley's name, then, carried no weight?

Not in the least; not in the least. In the entire state of Alabama he
would not get fifty more colored votes than would any Democrat
who might be nominated. The idea that his name would carry any
weight among former slaves was simply absurd.

How about the white Republican vote?

That, too, was for Grant. Rapier knew of perhaps a dozen white
Republicans who supported Greeley. Scattered in various counties,
with only limited influence, they would make a very small showing
on election day.

As he spoke, several Negro Republicans who had been testifying
against the Klan in the district court entered the office. "Though
they did not express themselves as fluently and intelligently as Mr.
Rapier," the correspondent wrote, "they too succeeded in saying,
'We are all for Grant.' "[6]

The following day, the correspondent telegraphed a detailed
report to Washington. "Mr. Rapier is the best intellect under a
colored skin in Alabama," he exclaimed, offering as proof the fact
that he had visited thirty-odd counties and had interviewed hundreds of Negroes.[7] At the "head and front" of the Republican party,
the leading colored man in the state, Rapier was another Frederick
Douglass, and his views were essentially correct. It could be said,
subject to a few trifling exceptions, that the Negroes of the South
would not vote for Horace Greeley.

And when Republicans of the Second District gathered at
Johnson's Hall in Union Springs, May 15, 1872, to choose delegates
to the national nominating convention in Philadelphia, they were

united behind Grant. The editor of the prewar journal *Cotton Planter*, Dr. N. B. Cloud, who had run on the state ticket with Rapier in 1870, resoundingly eulogized the president, as did United States District Attorney Minnis, who praised Grant for signing the enforcement laws. Dissension arose, however, when the Committee on Credentials selected Rapier as permanent chairman, subject to the vote of the members. The Negro state legislator from Montgomery, Holland Thompson, descanted for more than an hour in opposition to the selection. Accusing Rapier of seeking a congressional seat, "the irrepressible Thompson," said one observer, "fought against the ratification with zeal and earnestness," charging that selecting his opponent chairman would give him an unfair advantage in pushing his ambitions.[8] Despite the lengthy oratory, in part prompted by Thompson's own congressional aspirations, the report of the committee was ratified with only four dissenting votes. With Rapier presiding, the convention chose three judges— Richard Busteed, whose court had driven the Klan to cover, Elias M. Keils, and John V. McDuffie—to represent southeast Alabama at Philadelphia. After again endorsing Grant, this time by resolution, the delegates adjourned. Rapier now concentrated on his own nomination.

"I have long wished to try for membership in Congress," he wrote his old teacher, William King, expressing his fond remembrances of the log schoolhouse in Buxton. He had profited greatly from those experiences, as had many of his old classmates: Abraham Shadd, who was a lawyer in New Orleans; John Riley, who was a minister in Louisville; and Jerome Riley, who was a doctor in Washington, D.C. How much had he benefited? "Let whatever positions I have occupied and now occupy speak for me."[9] Rapier then proudly traced his rise in Alabama politics, concluding that, "No man in the State wields more influence than I."[10]

With this bold assertion, he began his campaign for Congress. In the sweltering heat of late July and August, he crossed and recrossed the district for political rallies, mass gatherings, and meetings with party leaders. Before several hundred Negroes in Montgomery, he spoke in favor of Grant; and in front of five hundred freedmen in Eufaula, accompanied by city judge Elias Keils, he delivered another speech in behalf of the Regulars. At a mass meeting in Union Springs he made what some listeners considered a powerful defense of Republicanism. "He gave Mr. Greeley full credit for everything he had done," the Conservative Union Springs *Times* reported, "but said he had wandered from the faith."[11] Even the devil himself had once been an angel in heaven. And at a Republican convention in the same town a few weeks later he sought the support of the Bullock County nominating committee, only to return quickly to the capital for yet another engagement. "Hon. James T. Rapier then addressed the convention on the great issues of the day in a most excellent speech," one observer wrote, noting that Rapier was the featured speaker at Montgomery's nominating convention.[12] His terse arguments against the Liberals were received with prolonged applause by the predominantly Negro audience.

Yet even white Conservatives expressed admiration for the black aspirant, as he was variously described in the Democratic press as intelligent, effective, energetic, forceful, and "a fine looking man."[13] Following his address at the Union Springs nominating convention, a Conservative newspaper was almost effusive in its praise: knowledgeable, quick-witted, and clever, Rapier had made tremendously effective thrusts at the "Philosopher in the White Hat," as Greeley was called, as well as at the Democratic party.

The opposition, however, was formidable. States-rights Democrats, Conservative blacks, and native Republicans all strongly opposed what they called the Radical ticket. Though there seemed to be less bitterness in 1872 than at any previous time during congressional reconstruction, most Democrats mustered behind the opinion of the Montgomery *Advertiser*: Grant partisans were revolutionaries seeking to deprive white people of their right to govern and to instigate another era of Negro rule (Republicans had been defeated in 1870). Rapier was attempting to play blacks against whites to the deep injury of both. A few Negroes, perhaps 5 percent of the voting freedmen, argued against the radical candidates from a more practical standpoint. Conservatives controlled their economic livelihood. Black bricklayers, carpenters, railroad hands, and barbers owed their means of living to the magnanimity and noble generosity of Democrats, intoned former Radical George Washington Cox, who had earlier spoken so eloquently in behalf of emigration at the Alabama Labor Union Convention. Negroes would have a holiday six days a week if it were not for whites. "We should not fight the breast that gives us milk. Vote for Greeley."[14]

Conservative Republicans likewise embraced Greeley. Willard Warner, a former Senator, compared him to Abraham Lincoln: both were honest, sincere, and true candidates of the people. The former slave would accept Greeley, too, when he intelligently understood the situation, he said in a letter to journalist Whitelaw Reid, for the Liberal movement offered the black man equal rights. Both the *Elmore Republican* and the *Alabama State Journal* displayed "Greeley for President" on their mastheads, and the *Journal*'s editor, Arthur Bingham, pressed for the renomination of Charles Buckley, who, he said, had arrived in Alabama at a most embarrassing time, but nevertheless had gained the confidence and respect of the entire community. "It would be egregious folly to exchange a certainty for the sake of an experiment."[15]

Rapier answered the opposition in the columns of the *Republican Sentinel*. The Democracy, he said, was led by young, reckless politicians; Conservative blacks had little influence; and conservative white Republicans did not represent the wishes of the people. "We have heard from the representative men of the sixty-seven thousand colored voters in Alabama," a front-page editorial in the *Sentinel* read. "Indeed, it has been our privilege to mingle freely with the colored people in the black belt since this nomination."[16] Yet there was not one prominent Negro who supported Greeley for the presidency. Other articles censured Congressman Buckley for discriminating against Negroes in the distribution of patronage jobs and attacked him for introducing legislation in Congress which benefited firms outside the district. How effective were the editorials? "I issue 1000 copies weekly and flatter myself that much good has been accomplished," Rapier boasted, "as we reach a class of reader who get no other paper [the *Sentinel* was free], and knowing mine to be edited by one of their own race, have confidence in it."[17] The paper cost him only fifty dollars a week to produce, with thirty dollars of that coming from his own pocket. It was well worth the cost. Read and reread, the *Sentinel* became the anti-Conservative voice of many thousands.

Buckley was angered by the critical editorials. He charged that, though the Negro aspirant congratulated himself on the gentlemanly manner of his campaign, his newspaper was ablaze with falsehood, slander, and venomous hatred. Buckley proclaimed himself proud of his record in behalf of freedmen. Having graduated from Beloit College in Wisconsin and from the Union Theological

Seminary in New York, having served as chaplain in the Forty-Seventh Regiment, United States Colored Infantry, and the Eighth Regiment, Louisiana Colored Infantry, he had taught Negroes to read and write, urged them to attend school, and demonstrated a sincere interest in the freedmen's well-being. Later, as super-intendent of education for the Freedmen's Bureau in Alabama, he had established Negro schools and distributed federal funds for Negro education. "He labored with earnest christian [sic] devotion to extend the benefits of education among freedmen," the *Daily State Sentinel* had observed in 1867, "and the colored people whom he protected in their rights will always hold him in grateful remembrance."[18] But as a congressman, Buckley had introduced a bill to establish a collection district in Florida, had appointed only two Negroes (Joshua McNeal and James T. Harris) to patronage positions, and had aligned himself with the conservative Repub-licans. It was this betrayal that Rapier attacked.

In the midst of the campaign, Rapier wrote a letter to his cousin Sarah Thomas, who, through the recommendation of John Rapier, Jr., had secured a teaching position at a freedmen's school in Mississippi. Describing the loneliness of public life, he said that during the past five years he had made very few close friends. "I am at my office nearly all the time. Sleep there. My associations are wholly of a business character."[19] He then admitted that he did not intend to marry—"The days of poetry are over"—but that he looked forward to a summons from the people to run for Congress. He would reap whatever pleasure there was in a political life, since he had been "impaired of doing my thing in a social way."[20] It seemed strange that Rapier, who had struggled so long to secure equal rights for Negroes, now on the verge of success, should feel more deeply than ever his own ostracism from Southern society.

The campaign was well under way when Republicans of the Second District gathered at Eufaula on August 16 for a one-day congressional nominating convention. Forty-two delegates, repre-senting eleven counties, convened at the city hall; they selected Lazarus Williams, a Negro, as permanent chairman and then put forward four candidates for the Republican congressional nomina-tion. On the first ballot Rapier received twenty-five votes, Buckley, nine; Philip King, eight; and Holland Thompson, one. In a brief speech, Rapier thanked the convention and reaffirmed his adherence to the great principles of the Republican party.

At first Conservatives reacted favorably to the nomination. In a letter to the editor of the Eufaula *Daily Times*, one Democrat said, as a Southerner and true friend of the Negro, that he preferred "an intelligent colored man who pretends to be honest," rather than a carpetbagger or scalawag. And the editor rejoiced at the choice. Happily, he said, Buckley was at last "up the spout."[21] But once the official canvass began, Democrats united behind William C. Oates, the candidate of the party. Famous for losing an arm while leading the Fifteenth Alabama Regiment to the heights of Gettysburg, and for his relentless defense of the Lost Cause, Oates had the backing of every Conservative newspaper in the region. In his campaign he subordinated the race issue to Republican inefficiency, carpetbag corruption, and the need for liberal reform in Washington. At Benton (Lowndes County), in a spirit of paternalism, he even professed: "I will protect the interests of the Second District in Congress and stand forth as the friend and champion of Southern men, WHITE AND BLACK, knowing no distinction of race or color among my constituents."[22] By using such language, he hoped to lure ex-slaves into the ranks of the Democratic party.

Ironically, it was a Republican who injected the race issue into the campaign. Arthur Bingham asserted that the nomination of a Negro for Congress would only kindle racial animosity. He would not oppose the candidacy of anyone solely because of skin color, other things being equal, Bingham rationalized, but it was obvious in this case that other things were not equal. It was suicidal folly on the part of Negroes to nominate one of their own race for Congress simply because he was black, because the nominee probably would have "not even the ability to read the English language."[23] Employing phraseology reminiscent of 1870, he called black Republicans "poor deluded creatures," threatening: "They can't control us, this is one thing certain. We will see if ignorant negro dupes can control this state."[24] Following this manifesto, he pressed John M. Wiley to run as an Independent, but this connivance failed when Wiley was unable to garner support.

Despite the determined opposition of conservative Republicans, Rapier carried on a strenuous campaign. He even journeyed outside the district, to Uniontown, Perry County, to speak to a huge mass meeting. He took the speaker's stand twenty-six times in as many far-flung towns and stations in a span of only thirty-six days during September and October. A stirring address at the Montgomery

Courthouse climaxed what was described as one of the most orderly and enthusiastic meetings ever held in that city. At Richards Beat in Barbour County, he "buried Horace Greeley" and formed a Grant-Wilson (Massachusetts Senator Henry Wilson, the vice-presidential nominee) club of one hundred thirty charter members. He considered it significant that longstanding Democrats were joining Grant clubs and that a large number of Conservatives were organizing against Greeley. At stations, beats, and villages, he shared the stand with William V. Turner, William Loftin, Peyton Finley, Lazerus Williams, N. B. Cloud, Joshua McNeal, even Charles Buckley and Arthur Bingham. On a hectic tour through the six white counties of the district, he spoke beside Lewis Parsons, Adam Felder, and Montgomery sheriff Paul Strobach. Everywhere he called for party unity and peace at the polls. At Fitzpatrick's Station, Union Springs, Chunnenugga Ridge, and in localities never before visited by political speakers, crowds listened as he discussed the issues with humor and irony as well as gravity. Toward the end of the campaign, as both sides pushed the canvass with unprecedented vigor, he reviewed the chances for a Republican victory. "We have a good ticket in the field, and the party is more than usual united in full accord with Senator Spencer and Representatives Hays and Turner."[25] On the eve of the election he boldly predicted that the Republicans would carry the state by a majority of seven thousand.

Election day, November 5, 1872, was peaceful and calm everywhere in the district. According to the Montgomery *Daily Advertiser*, blacks assembled early at the polls, and by noon every Negro had cast his vote. No quieter election had been held anywhere; a spirit of universal good feeling prevailed as whites and blacks mingled together in friendly rivalry. The Union Springs *Times* also remarked about the tranquillity of the election. Crowds had gathered from all parts of the county; the streets were lined with a living, moving mass of humanity; the friends of the different candidates worked diligently. "But everything was done in good humor. There was no undue excitement. We heard no quarreling— no difficulty of any kind."[26] In Eufaula, too, a paper observed that the election passed in a quiet manner. Not only this, but nearly 70 percent of the district's voters went to the polls, and Alabama, with a 65 percent turnout, led the entire South.

When the ballots had been tabulated, Rapier had won by 3175

votes—19,397 to 16,222. He swept the Black Belt (Lowndes, Montgomery, Bullock, Barbour) two to one, and even polled 2513 votes in the white counties (Butler, Coffee, Crenshaw, Dale, Geneva, Henry, Pike). He received the support of nearly all of the 18,000 eligible Negro voters and about 1500 whites. In addition, Republicans regained every state office, and Grant won by a margin of nearly a million in the popular count and a total of 286 electoral votes, compared with 66 for Greeley. One Montgomery Conservative observed that the great mistake of his party during the campaign had been to underestimate the strength of the opposition. "We could not be successful unelss we carred with us many of the negroes," he said, but blacks remained completely loyal to the Party of Lincoln.

Rapier had achieved the organization of the party in the Second District and had rallied the voters to Grant Republicanism; he had defeated a formidable and highly respected adversary and had reaffirmed a government by the people—both black and white. But the wider implications of his victory were even more significant. By omitting any discussion of race, by concentrating solely on the issues, and by emphasizing harmony on election day, a Negro had been elected to Congress from the capital of the old Confederacy.

10

**Rapier in Congress,
1873-1874**

Although elected to Congress in November 1872, Rapier would not take his seat until the Forty-third Congress convened in December 1873. He would thus have a full year to prepare himself and put his affairs in order. He was by no means idle during this period. Tendering his resignation as assessor in the winter of 1873, he thanked Commissioner Douglass for his kindness and consideration, especially during the Stanwood inquiry, and promised to remain active in revenue affairs if his services could be of any benefit to the department. It was not long afterward that he received a request to appraise the nomination of Louis H. Mayer as Collector of Internal Revenue for the First (Mobile) District. Recalling that Mayer had campaigned in behalf of Negroes, had backed the congressional acts from the beginning, and had always been a loyal Republican, he enthusiastically recommended the appointment, but, he explained in a letter to the commissioner, conservative Republicans were even now attempting to prevent Mayer from raising the necessary bond. Rapier requested an extension of the deadline, pointing out that it was not an easy matter to post such a large sum (sixty thousand dollars) in a short time: for one thing, he explained, wealthy white Southerners, who usually financed the bonds, traveled to the North in the spring, returning only after the summer heat had broken. A resulting extension and the eventual appointment of Mayer reflected Rapier's growing influence in the party.

It was also in early 1873 that Rapier was appointed as commissioner to the Fifth International Exposition in Vienna, Austria. A few days before his scheduled departure, however, he was stricken with a virus of some kind and forced to remain in bed for several weeks, but early in May, though still weak and debilitated, he decided to leave anyway. He journeyed by train to Washington, then New York City, and secured passage on a British steamer for the Continent. It was late in the month when he made his way slowly up the gangplank, leaning heavily on his father's gold-headed walking-cane, but as he stepped on board, Rapier felt a sense of rejuvenation, even exhilaration. "The moment I put my foot upon the deck of a ship that unfurled a foreign flag," he recalled in a House speech some months later, "distinctions on account of my color ceased."[1] When he registered at the luxurious Archduke Carl Hotel in Vienna, more than a month later (July 2, 1873), the same thought was on his mind, and he later expressed delight at being able to sign the register without the slightest fear of a humiliating incident.

During his stay in the Austrian capital, he toured several exhibition buildings, including the enormous Circular Hall, with a dome four hundred feet in diameter, and the huge main exhibit building, which was more than a half-mile long; he assisted in preparing the Alabama display, which included specimens of marble, lithograph stones, and cotton plants; and he observed displays from the various European counties, as well as a host of other nations, including Russia, Japan, Australia, China, Brazil and Morocco. While in Vienna, Rapier also entertained his uncle, James Thomas, who had stopped in Austria during a grand tour of Europe. Together they dined at the delightful sidewalk cafes, listened to band concerts in the Prater—a beautiful park over-looking the Danube—strolled through the flower gardens, and attended the opera. Such an enjoyable and relaxing social milieu made memories of those early years in Nashville seem like a long-forgotten dream.

Before returning to the United States, Rapier visited Germany, France, and England, with a special view, he said, toward obtaining an understanding of the conditions for the workingman in those countries. Then, in early September 1873, he boarded a ship for home. "James T. Rapier has just returned from Europe, where he has been spending [five] months profitably studying the customs of the most advanced nations on the Continent," announced the *New National Era* upon his arrival.[2] He had returned completely re-stored in health and anxious to begin his duties in the next Congress. But even before Congress convened, he took up the responsibilities of his office. Learning that a yellow fever epidemic was sweeping through Alabama and that it had claimed forty-three lives in Montgomery, he quickly telegraphed the Democratic city council with an offer of federal relief assistance in the form of rations and medicines. But he received a curt rebuff. Private individuals were making donations, the City Fathers declared, and government aid, especially from a Negro official, would simply be returned. Even then, he attempted to persuade them to accept federal assistance, but received a second, more threatening, rejection.

These overt anti-Negro declarations reflected the widespread alienation of Conservatives and blacks in Alabama. It was certain that Negroes aspired to rule, the Montgomery *Daily Advertiser* asserted, and it was absolutely necessary for the safety of whites, and the good of Negroes themselves, that they should not do so. In more frightening terms, the Birmingham *News* declared: "We intend to beat the negro in the unending battle for life, and defeat means but one thing—extermination."[3] Though it did not expect the repeal of the laws, the *News* refused to recognize the rights guaranteed in the Fourteenth and Fifteenth Amendments and intended, by using whites' superior intelligence, stronger muscle, and greater energy, to make them dead letters on the statute book. The Eufaula *Times* promised a violent dissolution of the relations between the two races if "the indolent thick skulled and unaspiring wooly-heads" dared to advance against the rights of the generous and conceding white man, rights that belonged to the superior race.[4] The Troy *Messenger* claimed that the black man possessed no qualifications for leadership: he was a laborer, not a legislator. So even before Rapier assumed his duties in Congress, the campaign to redeem Alabama (for a second time) and to drive him from politics was well under way.

Rapier took his seat in the United States House of Representatives on December 1, 1873. A correspondent for the St. Louis *Dispatch* noted that Rapier had received a liberal education, was an insatiable reader, and possessed a marvelous sense of humor. Another reporter said he was an original thinker, a forceful and eloquent orator and a bachelor of means who had "recently enjoyed an extended tour of Europe without hinderance of wife or pocket."[5] Even white Conservatives spoke of him with respect and admiration. It seems that Rapier possessed those personal and intellectual qualities that demanded recognition—even from his adversaries.

Besides Rapier, six other Negro congressmen, all experienced
legislators, answered the first roll call in the Forty-third Congress.
From South Carolina came Joseph Rainey and Robert Elliott, both
of whom had served in previous congresses; Richard Cain, who
had been a state senator; and Alonzo Ransier, who had been
lieutenant governor. Josiah Walls of Florida had served in the
Forty-second Congress, and John Roy Lynch of Mississippi had
been a state legislator. Of the seven blacks in Congress, the *New
National Era* said that Rapier was a man of mind, nerve, and
fidelity, who would be seconded in his labors by the parliamentary
experience of Elliott, Walls, and Rainey; and in the presence of such
men as Cain, Lynch, and Ransier, "our cause ought not to suffer."[6]
Though white Southerners scoffed, and Northerners whispered
"White Man's Tool," the *National Republican* said that the Negro
members were intelligent, diligent, and persevering. The eyes of the
entire nation would be upon them, but they promised to fulfill even
the greatest expectations. The Negro representatives joined 189
other House Republicans, 88 Democrats, and 4 Liberals, and in
doing so became part of the largest single-party majority (percent-
age-wise) in fifty years and the largest numerical majority in the
nation's history.

With a coterie of able black colleagues, and with an unprecedented Republican majority, Rapier began his duties with great
optimism. Only a few days after the opening session, he, along
with several other members of the Committee on Education and
Labor, offered legislation to improve the common school system of
the South. They submitted a bill (H. R. 477) which proposed the
establishment of a five-million-dollar federal school fund designed
to insure a proper education for Negroes. The money, to be derived
from the sale of public lands, was to be distributed on the basis of
illiteracy; the proposed allotment for Alabama was $135,000. Only
three other states (Georgia, North Carolina, Virginia) would
receive more, while a northern state like Iowa, with a population
equal to Alabama's—though with a greater literacy rate—would
receive only $16,000. Of his home-state colleagues, three (Frederick
Bromberg, Charles Hays, and Charles Pelham) quickly sided with
Rapier, but four others (Democrats John Caldwell and Joseph
Sloss, Republicans Christopher Sheats and Alexander White)
opposed any form of federal aid to education. And their sentiments
reflected the general mood of the House. Such a proposal was

unjust, unequal, and in violation of the Constitution of the United States, Southerners exclaimed. It was class legislation in the interest of the blacks, to the detriment of the white race. After only a few minutes of debate, the House voted to table the bill, and Rapier was defeated in his first attempt to sponsor legislation.

As a prominent national black leader Rapier's duties went beyond offering legislation and on December 9 he attended the Negro Civil Rights Convention in Washington, where he listened to representatives from twenty-five states speak on the question of equal rights for blacks. One delegate who, like Rapier, had attended the Columbia and New Orleans conventions, complained that black citizens were denied accommodations on railroads, steamboats, and common carriers; they were refused equal treatment in hotels and excluded from the best schools. In short, he said, "we are denied the hospitalities and civilities of communities."[7] The convention urged Congress to prohibit any attempt by a chartered society, private company, or public school to discriminate against any person because of color or race. Rapier and the other Negro congressmen present (Rainey, Ransier, Elliott, Walls) listened with eager attention as the convention declared: "We want Congress to give us a civil rights bill."[8]

But discussion on the several pending equal rights proposals in the House and Senate was indefinitely postponed shortly after the Christmas recess when Henry K. Dawes, who held the influential position of chairman of the Ways and Means Committee, demanded legislation to improve economic conditions. Pointing to the failure of the great investment banking house of Jay Cooke (September 1873), the high unemployment rate, the decrease in demand for goods, declining farm prices, and a growing number of bank and business failures, he reluctantly acknowledged the onset of a national depression.

Although Congress soon turned its full attention to economic matters, it moved slowly, and not without major disagreements. In the protracted debates that followed, two basic plans emerged, both of which sought to institute reforms in the United States monetary system. On the one side there were Southerners and Westerners, who, like Kentuckian Edward Crossland, spoke out in favor of increasing the circulating currency. "We must have money to avert the impending calamities," Crossland explained. "I shall vote for an increase in the present bank circulation to meet the wants and relieve the needs of the destitute sections."[9] On the other side there were congressmen from the Northeast, who, like New York Representative Samuel Cox, backed a plan called specie payments to stabilize the economy. They advocated a decrease in the money supply by a gradual withdrawal of greenbacks—the nonspecie-backed paper currency issued during the Civil War. Gold was the only true standard by which the value of commodities could be properly measured, Cox maintained, speaking for his section, and the circulating medium should be gold, or a currency convertible to gold at the pleasure of the holder. Greenbacks or legal-tenders, he insisted, were inflationary, unhealthy—broken and worthless promises. Though there were variations on this theme, generally the inflationists (soft-money men) of the agrarian sections confronted the deflationists (hard-money men) of the industrial Northeast.

Rapier did not participate in the debate, though he, like most Southerners, advocated some increase in the circulating medium. Having witnessed the rapid decline of Alabama cotton prices (from thirty-five cents to fifteen cents), the enormous rise in interest rates, and the financial difficulties caused in his section by tight money, he believed that more currency might improve the situation. Joining Southerners, the other Negro representatives, and Westerners, he voted for a measure to increase the money supply and cast his ballot against a proposal (H. R. 1398) that called for withdrawal of bank notes from circulation. Only nine of the eighty-five Southern congressmen (four Republicans and five Democrats), and five of the thirty-two Western members, voted in favor of withdrawal. Rapier also supported a House bill, which passed in a sectional vote, to keep the legal limit of greenbacks in circulation at a relatively high forty-four million dollars, but it was vetoed by the president. The currency and banking bill that finally became law (S. 1044) instructed the United States Treasury to redeem United States notes until only three hundred thousand dollars remained in circulation and after January 1, 1879, to reclaim in coin all legal tender outstanding. Rapier and ninety-eight other congressmen, mostly from the South and West, strongly opposed the law.

Sectional voting in the House was not confined to the money question. Congressmen from the southern, north central, and western parts of the country also stood against the power of railroad companies to fix rates. Even before Congress had convened, the *National Republican* had reminded representatives of

their responsibility to make railroad rates equitable, and early in
the first session, members openly criticized the railroad companies
for undertaking construction without proper capital and for
setting exceedingly high rates on passenger and freight service.
William Louthridge of Iowa spoke for the farmers of his section
when he said that the rates charged by railroads for carrying
western produce to market were unreasonable. Instead of going
into the pockets of the producers, Louthridge charged, anticipating
the arguments of the Populists a generation later, profits had gone
to swell the fortunes of railroad kings. The cure: the strong arm of
the government should be brought to the aid of the people. The
same coalition also asked for federal aid to transportation. Tennessean Barbour Lewis, for example, pointed out that a mud bar at
the mouth of the Mississippi River kept the internal commerce of
half the nation from reaching the ocean; it was the responsibility of
the government to remove it.

Again, like most Southerners, Rapier and his Negro colleagues
supported railroad regulation, voting for a bill (H. R. 1385) which
demanded that railway lines collect only fair and reasonable rates
for the transportation of freight and passengers. Though Republicans from the Northeast strongly opposed the bill, it passed the
House by six votes and was eventually signed into law. Rapier also
favored a bill (H. R. 2694) requiring the United States government
to construct a two-hundred-foot-canal connecting the Mississippi
River and the Gulf of Mexico. Southern Conservatives championed
the measure despite its stipulation that Louisiana cede the jurisdic-
tional land to the federal government. The votes of thirty north-
eastern Republicans, however, canceled those of thirty Southern
Republicans, and the bill failed.

The vote symbolized the deep sectional divisions within the
Republican party. For the first time in nearly a generation, the
agrarian South and West stood against the commercial Northeast.
The currency and transportation questions were disastrously dividing the party, James Blaine wrote, and even more seriously, the
sections. "You have no conception of the intensity of the struggle,"
New Englander Edward Atkinson added. "It is civil war in the
Republican ranks and there can be no harmony."[10] Another party
member lamented that Republicans had seen their last victory. The
depression, then, was not only an economic disaster, but a catalyst
that intensified the already deep divisions within the party.

Besides voting with the South on economic questions, Rapier

submitted two bills to improve the transportation system of
Alabama. The first (H. R. 1818) requested fifty thousand dollars to
dredge the Pea and Chochawatche rivers. Submitted at the behest
of the mayor of Geneva, Alabama, (a town in the wire-grass
country on the Florida border), and designed to stimulate commerce in the predominantly white counties of Dale, Coffee, and
Geneva, the bill never came up for a vote. The second (H. R. 899)
asked that Montgomery, Alabama, be constituted a port of delivery within the collection district of Mobile, providing for a deputy
collector of customs with an annual salary of fifteen hundred
dollars. Coming up for consideration only a few weeks before
adjournment, the Montgomery Port Bill, as it was called, met stiff
opposition, especially among retrenchment-minded conservatives
from the Northeast. Vermont Republican Charles Willard, for
example, reminded his colleagues of the great need to cut spending—
not to increase it by paying a salary to a Montgomery customs
official. But other members vigorously defended the proposal. An
influential member of the Commerce Committee, Omar Conger of
Michigan, said that a large amount of business was transacted in
the Alabama capital. Explaining that foreign imports had increased
substantially since the war, he proposed that Montgomery could
become another Memphis, St. Louis, or Pittsburgh. Equally enthusiastic was Alabama Republican Frederick Bromberg, who boosted
the city as the new commercial center of the deep South. Such
supportive argumentation had its desired effect: the bill soon
passed the House, but in the Senate, it was amended by Commerce
Committee chairman Zachariah Chandler, who added a proviso
that would have repealed an 1858 law constituting Selma as an
Alabama port of delivery. The revised bill, then, came up for
reconsideration in the House June 20, 1874, just three days before
the end of the first session.

Fearful that the bill might die in the House, Rapier immediately
asked for a suspension of the rules in an attempt to put the proposal
up for immediate passage, but only eighty-nine members voted for
the suspension, while fifty-six voted nay, six votes short of the
necessary two-thirds. The bill was then sent to a conference
committee which included Rapier, Bromberg, Conger, and Senator Spencer; after eight long hours of discussion, the committee
finally struck the Senate's amendment. Then, in the waning hours
of a Senate session which lasted until three thirty Sunday morning

June 21, George Spencer wearily rose and asked his colleagues to
concur. Exhausted from sixteen continuous hours of debate, the
Senate voted to delete the provision, passed the bill, and the next
day, only a few hours before the end of the session, it was signed
into law by the president. Montgomery would now have a port of
delivery.

Hundreds of similar bills had been bogged down in committee,
been tabled, or met with failure in the Senate. Rapier had worked
tirelessly to bring foreign trade to the heart of the Black Belt, and he
had succeeded. Yet no Alabama newspaper even mentioned the
victory. Instead, conservative Republicans launched a vigorous
attack on the Negro congressman, charging him with favoritism
and failure to discharge his official duties. Both charges stemmed
from the cancellation of an eight-hundred-dollar-a-year federal
contract that had previously gone to the *Alabama State Journal* for
printing the laws of the United States. Editor Arthur Bingham
demanded an explanation for such arbitrary and unjust treatment,
and Rapier felt obliged to reply. In an open letter, he explained that
Congressman Alexander White had insisted that the *Journal* did not
want the contract. "In the face of his statement and in the absence
of any advice from you," he told Bingham, "you can easily see how
awkward it would have been for me to press the claims of the
Journal."[11] The Democratic Montgomery *Advertiser*, which de-
tested everything Rapier stood for but admired him as an individual,
substantiated Rapier's claim: it had been White who had persuaded
his House colleagues to cancel the contract, not "the faithful and
intelligent Rapier."[12] It was not without a certain amount of irony
that Bingham, whose connivances against Rapier had amounted to
treachery, wrote a short time later that newspapers with government contracts, doled out by those in power, could not be true to
the great principle of equality.

During the first session of the Forty-third Congress Rapier not
only voted on economic matters, wrote important legislation, and
answered critics at home, he also listened to the first skirmishes of
the House debate on civil rights. If there was one truth that stood
out above all others in the history of the United States, the former
vice-president of the Confederacy, Alexander Stephens, began,
reading from a manuscript placed on a pile of law books stacked on
his desk, it was the seminal principle that Negroes and whites were
inherently *unequal*. "Yet, I do maintain the great truth," he added,

"however paradoxical it may appear, that all men are created equal."[13] Black congressman Robert Elliott, who had studied law and served as a member of the South Carolina reconstruction convention, wasted little time answering Stephens. Occupying the seat vacated by antebellum proslavery fanatic Preston Brooks, Elliott argued persuasively that the Constitution should always be interpreted in favor of human rights, that the Civil War had settled forever the question of those rights, and that the bill proposing equal accommodations for Negroes in public places was just and equitable. "We are at last politically free," he told a silent House, "the last vesture only is needed—civil rights."[14] In response to Elliott's words, great applause resounded from the gallery, and congressmen rushed forward to congratulate the Negro speaker. No more dignified and skillful tearing down of the false theories of caste was ever witnessed in a legislative hall, one exuberant observer exclaimed, and the New York *Times* declared that the speech had electrified the entire nation.

House Democrats scoffed at the speech. Insisting that blacks were innately inferior and incapable of citizenship, they claimed that a civil rights law for the South would be tantamount to inciting a war between the races. Though the Negro could outdance, outlaugh, and outfrolic the white man, North Carolina congressman William Robbins said, blacks lacked will, vigor, and force of character. The Negro was an inveterate servant. Robbins claimed further that an equal rights law would ruin the public school system of his section and explained that whites had already provided Negroes with equal, though separate, educational facilities. Southerners would rather perish, insisted Hiram Bell of Georgia, articulating the views of his Conservative cohorts, than submit "to the humiliating degradation of social equality with emancipated free negroes."[15]

Rapier answered the Democrats on June 9. In this, his first speech to the House, he denied that Negroes were innately inferior, accused Conservatives of wanting to establish a system of caste, and stated unequivocally that the school clause called only for equal school facilities, not mixed schools. Recalling the arguments of Stephens, he asserted that the old ideas of states' rights, along with the institution of slavery, had been swept away by the Civil War. He refused to equivocate on the question of equal rights for Negroes. If he were to be content with fewer liberties than the white man, he would furnish the best possible evidence that blacks did not understand the responsibilities of citizenship and freedom. Anyway, the entire Conservative argument boiled down to one word—*caste*. Other countries had rigid class distinctions based on wealth or religious differences, but in America the distinction was color, and the system was far more brutal than in any other part of the world. The lowest, most ignorant, most dishonorable white man stood above the highest, most intelligent, noblest Negro. "I cannot willingly accept anything less than my full measure of rights as a man, because I am unwilling to present myself as a candidate for any brand of inferiority."[16] Though there was little immediate response to his speech, nine days after he had given it the *New National Era* paid Rapier a supreme compliment: he had delivered an address on civil rights second to none; it would be read by Negroes everywhere with a deep sense of pride.

At one time or another all the Negro representatives spoke on civil rights. The first Negro congressman, Joseph Rainey, defined social equality, the phrase so often used by Conservatives, as a congeniality of feeling, a reciprocity of sentiment, and a mutual social recognition among men according to taste and desire—not as the right of Negroes to be admitted to public places. The twenty-six-year-old son of a white plantation owner and a slave, John Roy Lynch, demanded a national civil rights law because it would place blacks in an independent position. Spurning the Conservative prophesies of racial conflict, he said such a law would bring about a more friendly feeling between the two races. The highly educated Richard Cain also asked for equal opportunities for blacks, challenging Democrats to open the schoolhouse door for all children, rather than taunt Negroes about their ignorance. Cain's speech was brilliant and magnetic, acclaimed the *Daily Critic*; he spoke eloquently for his race. Josiah Walls demanded the enforcement of the spirit as well as the letter of the reconstruction amendments. Without this needed legislation, he said, the channels for advancement would be forever closed by law, prejudice, or indisposition. One of the few black men to hold state office during reconstruction, Alonzo Ransier, proposed that state governments prohibit the use of the word *white* in any statute, ordinance, or law.

To dramatize the pressing need for an equal rights law, Negro congressmen narrated their own experiences in the South. Rapier had been refused sleeping berths, ejected from hotels, and denied

service in restaurants. There was not an inn between Montgomery
and Washington, a distance of more than a thousand miles, that
would accommodate him to a meal and bed. On a visit to
Richmond, Virginia, Rainey had been brutally thrown from a
fast-moving streetcar marked "FOR WHITES ONLY"; and after board-
ing a train in Jackson, Mississippi, Lynch had been forced to
occupy a filthy smoking car with drunkards, gamblers, and
criminals. "I was treated not as an American citizen, but as a
brute."[17] Such testimonials prompted one observer to say that the
black congressmen had done their full duty. "Filled with a sense of
their new responsibilities, [they] are certainly a credit to their
race."[18]

The Negro congressmen realized, however, that recounting a
thousand similar indignities would not influence the attitudes of
white Conservatives, many of whom took delight in such incidents.
And they also understood the extreme difficulty in enforcing
legislation concerning individual rights. Even as they spoke, and
despite a strongly worded Washington, D.C., statute providing for
a forfeiture of a business license to anyone refusing to serve or
accommodate a well-behaved person, Negroes were excluded from
most of the capital's restaurants, boardinghouses, hotels, barber
shops, and even portions of the capitol itself. When the dignified
university professor John Langston, later a congressman himself,
asked for a table at the district's fashionable Harvey's Restaurant,
he was not only denied service, but assaulted and thrown into the
gutter. When two well-dressed blacks entered the barbershop at
Willard's Hotel, they also were refused service. And when several
Negroes sought accommodation at a nearby hotel, they were told
quietly to leave. Even in the gallery of the House of Representatives, the exceedingly handsome, stylish, light-skinned Mrs. Robert
Brown Elliott was refused admission to the pen, a section set aside
for members and their families. Acutely aware of these and other
incidents, the black reconstructionists nonetheless pushed ahead
with their effort to codify the rights promised in the Declaration of
Independence. Perhaps some day the laws protecting blacks would
be enforced.

But their cause suffered a serious setback in March 1874, with the
death of Charles Sumner, the articulate national spokesman for
Negro rights. Rapier immediately expressed his "solemn gloom and
great bereavement" at the loss of such a great champion of racial

equality. Along with a number of other black leaders, he paid his last respects to Sumner at a memorial ceremony in Union League Hall; at the conclusion of the ceremony he was selected to chair a committee to raise funds for a statue in honor of the late senator. After several weeks, he disclosed that the committee was hopelessly deadlocked over the question of how much money should be solicited for such a purpose. Rapier suggested an expenditure of no more than thirty five thousand dollars; the other members, including A. M. Greene, Charles Purvis, and George Downing, recommended larger amounts, that ranged up to one hundred fifty thousand dollars. The disagreement elicited sharp criticism. Committee members were full of resolutions and points of order, a Negro who attended one of the open committee meetings charged, but they were unwilling to donate a dollar themselves. "A more corrupt gang cannot be found in any community of colored men." Though such accusations were groundless, the committee finally settled on a figure of twenty thousand dollars, which was eventually used for a statue honoring Sumner in Boston.

Many whites also paid homage to the civil rights leader. Ironically, one of the most memorable and politically significant eulogies to Sumner was delivered by an antebellum secessionist and ex-Confederate, Lucius Q. C. Lamar of Mississippi. Lamar was invited to address the House by Massachusetts congressman George Hoar, who was in charge of making out the list of speakers. When Lamar learned that he was scheduled to speak after black reconstructionist Robert Elliott, he went immediately to Henry Dawes, who had also been invited to speak. "I can't follow a nigger," he told Dawes privately. "It would be political death to follow a nigger."[19] Persuading Dawes to rearrange the schedule secretly so that he would follow Hoar, Lamar used the occasion to deliver a major address, calling for peace, prosperity, and a reconciliation of the differences between the North and South, a speech hailed across the nation, by Republicans and Democrats alike, as an eloquent expression of the new Southern sentiment. Yet the Lamar-Elliott episode tragically symbolized the exclusion of Negroes from any political settlement between North and South; it was even more tragic that Sumner's death offered the occasion for such a betrayal of the Negro.

The civil rights bill that Sumner had introduced early in the first session finally passed the Senate in May 1874 and went to the

House of Representatives. The strongly worded bill (S.1) prohibited discrimination in public places, including schools, and stated
that all persons or corporations convicted of such discrimination
were subject to a fine of up to five thousand dollars for each
offense. The civil rights leader in the House, Benjamin Butler,
moved to suspend the rules, put the bill up for debate, and vote on
its passage; it received the yea votes of 154 Republicans, including
Rapier, but 78 Democrats and 7 Republicans voted nay, and the
motion failed, 6 votes short of the required two-thirds. Five times
during the next month the same motion was defeated, though on
each occasion Rapier and all but a few Republicans voted in favor
of it. The final defeat came only three days before adjournment,
when the House voted 140 to 91 in favor of suspending the rules, 14
votes short; exactly that many Republicans voted against the
resolution (see tables 2 and 3). Thus, the first session of the
Forty-third Congress adjourned without having passed any civil
rights legislation. Ironically, the party responsible for six equal
rights laws in seven years had also been responsible for the defeat
of the strongly worded Sumner proposal.

The defeat reflected the mood of the nation. Americans were
becoming tired of abstract questions in which the overwhelming
majority had no direct interest, the *National Republican* editorialized. The Negro question, with all its complications, and the
reconstruction of the South, with all its interminable embroilments,
had become dead issues; and the civil rights question was best
subordinated to the interest of the overwhelming majority of the
people. The *Daily Critic* likewise asserted that the North should
cease agitating about the black man if a watered-down version of
the equal rights bill were passed. Negro rights had been debated
and debated, one disgusted observer wrote, but legislation against
social or racial prejudice was never successful. "Such a bill might
have been justifiable 8 or 10 years ago, but the time has passed for
it. The necessity for it has gone ..., and the power to enforce it
also."[20] James Rapier was soon to learn the painful truth of these
words.

TABLE 2 Voting in the Forty-third Congress

	Jeremiah Wilson Resolution January 19, 1874			Contraction of Currency Amendment (H.R. 1398) March 23, 1874			Railroad Bill (H.R. 1385) March 26, 1874			River Improvement (H.R. 2694) June 5, 1874			To Take Civil Rights Bill (S.1) off Speaker's Table in House June 20, 1874		
	Yea	Nay	Abstain	Yea	Nay	Abstain	Yea	Nay	Abstain	Yea	Nay	Abstain	Yea	Nay	Abstain
Southern Democrats	26	6	7	5	29	7	1	32	4	14	20	7	0	40	1
Western Democrats	9	3	—	3	7	2	0	7	5	6	3	3	0	10	2
North central Democrats	11	4	—	2	10	3	0	12	3	6	5	4	0	12	3
Northeastern Democrats	—	17	5	15	4	3	0	16	6	4	10	8	0	15	7
Southern Republicans[a]	22	12	10	4	24	16	32	5	4	33	5	6	26	8	9
Western Republicans	15	1	4	2	17	1	17	1	3	18	0	2	13	3	4
North Central Republicans	43	9	8	7	53	2	52	6	8	42	8	12	44	2	16
Northeastern Republicans	9	46	19	32	27	15	19	36	21	22	30	21	57	1	18
Total	135	98	53	70	171	49	121	115	54	145	81	63	140	91	60

[a] Negro vote is included in Southern Republicans.

TABLE 3   The Negro Vote on Important Issues in the Forty-third Congress

	Jeremiah Wilson Resolution January 19, 1874			Contraction of Currency Amendment (H.R. 1394) March 23, 1874			Railroad Bill (H.R. 1385) March 26, 1874			River Improvement Bill (H.R. 2694) June 5, 1874			To Take Civil Rights Bill (S.1) Off Speaker's Table in House June 20, 1874		
	Yea	Nay	Abstain	Yea	Nay	Abstain	Yea	Nay	Abstain	Yea	Nay	Abstain	Yea	Nay	Abstain
Negroes[a]															
Cain		x				x	x			x			x		
Elliott		x				x	x			x			x		
Lynch	x				x		x			x			x		
Rainey		x			x		x					x	x		
Ransier	x				x		x			x			x		
Rapier	x				x		x			x			x		
Walls			x		x		x			x			x		

a Negro vote is included in Southern Republicans.

11

A Reign of Terror: The Election of 1874

Encouraged by the inaction of Congress, Alabama Conservatives became more determined than ever to wrest the control of the state from so-called Negro Rule. Expressing the attitude of the overwhelming majority of Democrats, the Montgomery *Daily Advertiser* asserted that neither specious pleas nor vague sophistry could avert the inevitable confrontation between whites and blacks for political supremacy in the South. Those who believed in the white race were arrayed under the banner of the Conservative party; those who believed in the domination of Negroes were marshaled under the label of the Republican party. If blacks were to rule, the *Advertiser* concluded, the white man must ultimately leave the state. Thus, according to Conservatives, political defeat in 1874 meant the end of white civilization.

Observing this deterioration of race relations, Alabama blacks called a meeting of the state's Equal Rights Association at the capital in June, hoping somehow to ameliorate the situation. Though still in Washington, Rapier wholeheartedly endorsed the conciliatory spirit of the call. For a Republican victory in the upcoming election, he said in a letter to the delegates, it would be necessary to maintain peaceful relations between the races; and, as honorary president of the association, he urged the members to pass a resolution favoring the most amicable relations with whites.

Thanking the Alabama congressman for his earnest, devoted, and zealous labor in behalf of equal rights, the convention quickly launched into a discussion of one of the most controversial issues facing Alabamians: the public school section of the Sumner civil rights bill. Although several delegates—among them north Alabama educator William Councill, who later, in bitter despair, turned to the Conservatives, and the youthful Negro state legisla-

tor, Thomas Walker, barely twenty-four years old—demanded
mixed schools to insure Negroes an equal educational opportunity,
most association members said they only desired adequate school
facilities for black children. In an obvious effort to placate white
Alabamians, the convention resolved that in declaring themselves
in favor of the civil rights bill, they were not favoring mixed
schools; they were only asking that their children enjoy the benefits
of a sound education.

Rapier understood the necessity of getting into the fray early and
immediately launched his campaign for renomination to Congress
when he returned to Alabama in July. In his first speech, at a
Bullock County Republican convention in Union Springs, July 20,
he set forth his position with regard to the pending civil rights bill.
It did not require mixed schools, nor social equality, he said,
explaining the immense difference between social and civil rights,
much as he had done at various times since the beginning of
reconstruction. He assured his listeners that he did not wish to
make such a drastic change in the public school system, but, like
the Alabama Equal Rights Association, he wanted blacks and
whites to have an equal opportunity for schooling. In many states
where there was a mixed school law, there was not a single mixed
school, he pointed out, but state and federal funds in those states
(the latter in the form of assistance to land grant schools) were
distributed to benefit Negroes as well as whites. Though he argued
against mixed schools per se, he favored the Sumner bill to insure a
proper education for blacks.

Most Republicans in the district accepted this argument and
supported Rapier for a second term. Recognizing his past services
in behalf of liberty, justice, and equality, Republicans meeting in
Bullock County pledged him their support for a second term. A
convention of Barbour County Republicans expressed unqualified
approbation of his ability, patriotism, and statesmanly conduct in
Congress. Other conventions thanked him for his vindication of
Republican principles, his conscientious efforts on behalf of the
state, and his faithful discharge of duty; they pledged anew, as one
resolution read, a hearty and earnest support to the able and loyal
James T. Rapier.

Conservatives, on the other hand, misrepresented the Negro
congressman on every controversial question. The Montgomery
Daily Advertiser accused him of advocating not only mixed schools

and miscegenation, but nothing less than perfect equality in all things. Republicans, one *Advertiser* editorial said, were taking the social equality pill in sugarcoated form, that is, they were coating it with Rapier and then swallowing it. Another Conservative writer, though he recognized Rapier's preeminent influence in party affairs, asserted that every radical, from Rapier to Spencer, favored compelling white men to concede social equality, with or without the law. The Union Springs *Herald and Times* warned that unscrupulous politicians like Rapier, in their blind zeal to force racial interbreeding, which was falsely labeled civil rights, were threatening to bring about a second Civil War, one that would be even more disastrous than the first.

Ten days after Rapier opened his campaign, the Democrats held a state convention in Montgomery. In an opening speech, Robert Tyler, chairman of the State Executive Committee, described the pending civil rights legislation in the House of Representatives as a flagrant and dangerous invasion of the ancient conservative principles of personal liberty and free government. It was a palpable violation of the federal Constitution; it sought license for the sexual deviations of blacks; and it presented an issue of vital importance to the American people. Congressman James Pugh, a former Confederate, who had long been hostile toward freedmen, told his Conservative colleagues that the iniquitous civil rights bill was sure to produce a racial conflict. A black demon had appeared upon the stage to disturb the peace and harmony, but the Caucasian race would fight it and save their race. The first plank of the Democratic platform established the direction of the Conservative campaign. The radical and dominant faction of the Republican party, by false and fraudulent representations, had influenced the passions and prejudices of Negroes against whites, and it was therefore necessary for white men, in self-defense, to unite to preserve white civilization.

Democrats from the Tennessee Valley to the Gulf of Mexico expressed sentiments similar to those affirmed in Montgomery. Calling for a rude demarcation line between the races, the Conservative Montgomery *Ledger* said that in the coming election, the physical, intellectual, and political supremacy of the white race would be decided forever. "We will ACCEPT NO RESULT BUT THAT OF BLOOD."[1] The Mobile *Register* put it simply when it said that the only issue in the campaign was whether the elevated white

man or the debased Negro would govern the state. No political
issue since the secession crisis, contended the Birmingham *Iron Age*,
had created such an emotion-charged atmosphere; whites were determined, at any cost, to redeem the state. Democrats in Troy (Pike
County) passed a resolution to protect their homes and the purity
and integrity of their race; Conservatives in Bullock County claimed
that the vindictive, unreasoning, intolerant, and partisan spirit of
Rapier and the Republican party had made it impossible for the two
races to live together harmoniously. And in nearby Eufaula
(Barbour County), antebellum slave owner Eli Shorter, concluding
his remarks at a Democratic gathering, turned to a few Negroes in
the audience and said threateningly that he had been attempting to
persuade them for years to follow their former masters. "We are
not going to ask you any more to go with us. If you don't come
with us, we will exterminate you as we did the poor Indians."[2]

Rather than promising to exterminate Negroes, other plantation
owners simply refused employment to black Republicans. Hundreds of witnesses afterward told of such economic coercion. A
great many freedmen were turned out of their jobs because they
supported the Republican ticket, complained a black tenant farmer,
Asa Barber. Negroes either signed a pledge supporting the Democracy or had to leave the plantation. A black shoemaker in Barbour,
Edwin Odon, testified that colored men in his area joined the
Democrats because whites told them that if they did not, they
would never be able to feed their families. The successful Negro
entrepreneur Robert Wittaker, who owned sixteen mules, eight
drays, and ran a prosperous hauling business in Montgomery, was
forced to sell out when white store owners refused to give a Negro
Republican their business. Democrats freely admitted the truth of
such ruthless tactics. When the material interest of an employer
was placed in jeopardy, the platform of a White Man's Club
declared, it behooved him to protect himself by hiring only those
who would aid in ridding the nation of the incubus of bad
government.

Besides discharging Negro employees, Conservatives also dis-
rupted Republican political meetings, socially ostracized white
members of that party, and in some cases resorted to violence.
"Democratic War Begun—A Republican Speaker Driven from the
Stand," read the headline on a late July edition of the *Alabama
State Journal*.[3] The paper stated that at a Republican gathering in

Clayton (Barbour County) Democrats brandishing knives, pistols, and clubs had fired on a number of whites, knocked down and slashed several Negroes, and completely disrupted the meeting. The same newspaper reported that Conservatives had shot at Adam Felder, a white, during a campaign speech at Greenville (Butler County) and had kicked, cut, cursed, and abused blacks attending a Republican conclave near Montgomery.

Democrats also avoided social connections with white Republicans. Bullock County legislator Charles Smith said that it was understood among white ladies that they would not speak to the wives or the families of any man who supported the Republican party. They abused, ostracized, and attempted to crush completely all Republicans; "there never was a more bitter warfare, politically, anywhere then [sic] in Alabama during 1874."[4] Troy Democrats resolved at a public meeting that nothing was left for the White Man's Party to do but to ignore socially all who acted, sympathized, or sided with the Negro party or who supported the odious, unjust, and unreasonable measure known as the Civil Rights Bill.

Some Democrats, however, concluding that economic coercion, political disruption, and social banishment were too mild, employed more radical tactics. In Sumter County a revitalized Ku Klux Klan shot and killed Walter Billings, chairman of the County Republican Executive Committee, and murdered Thomas Ivey, an active Negro Republican. Prior to his assassination Ivey wrote Governor Lewis, saying that leading Democrats were determined to prevent the colored population from voting. "They Say if any man, or set of men, come here in this county to Speak, or to make an address, to the colored men, they never will Leave here because they will be killed."[5] Because he had a premonition that he was marked for execution, Ivey kept twenty-five men guarding his home day and night and begged the governor for protection. "Please Let me hear from you Soon," he wrote, "as you get this, I am expecting these men to attack me."[6] A few days later, he was fatally shot. Also seeking protection from the governor was Choctaw County Negro Jack Turner, who beseeched the chief of state to use his influence to stop the intimidation of blacks. Some years later he was lynched for his political activities.

But these frightful occurrences took place outside the Second District. What were the conditions in southeast Alabama? "There was a Killing 7 miles from here last Saturday," Barbour County probate judge Elias M. Keils, a resident of Eufaula since 1837, wrote excitedly. "The man Killed was a colored man, rather earnest in politics."[7] He had been murdered in his home by fifteen Democrats, who killed him, though he was unarmed. For the sake of life, liberty, and justice, Keils demanded that a state of martial law be declared in the area. The mob had inaugurated "a perfect *reign of terror,*" openly declaring they would never submit or surrender.[8] The reign of terror Keils described included several other brutal, racially motivated murders in the district. Near the Florida border whites killed two blacks and laid their bodies across each other on a public road; at Clayton a group of whites lynched Abel Cotton and Jack Horne, two Negroes accused of theft; and in the same vicinity a white peace officer, John D. Glass, shot and killed George Hollis, a Negro, for refusing to obey an order. Questioned about the incident, Glass retorted, "But he was nothing but a nigger."[9] Even before the campaign had officially begun, Conservatives were using every means to insure a victory in November.

Ironically, when the Republicans of the Second District gathered in Union Springs to nominate a candidate for Congress, the threat of violence came not from the Democrats, but from a group of Republicans. Bitter antagonisms had developed during the summer between two factions of Republicans in Montgomery County, one headed by the erratic young lawyer Robert Knox, a native Republican who had earlier (1871) been convicted of jury tampering; and the other led by Vienna-educated party stalwart Paul Strobach, who had served as state commissioner of immigration, a member of the general assembly, and sheriff. Both groups included Negroes, native Southerners, and Northerners, but the first found its major strength among a coterie of Republican conservatives, including Arthur Bingham, William Buckley, Pat Robinson, and Samuel Rice, while the other faction found its most ardent supporters among Negroes Charles Steele, James Foster, and Peyton Finley. Besides the desire for local office, the main issue at stake between the two groups concerned the pending impeachment of Richard Busteed. Though there were differences within each organization, Knox, seeking to placate some of his black followers, opposed impeachment, while Strobach, despite his admiration for Busteed's 1871 war against the Klan, reluctantly admitted that the judge was probably guilty of several impeachable offenses.

Throughout the controversy Rapier had refused to support either group. Determined not to become involved in a local fight, he said that the decision about which faction should be recognized by the party should be left to the Republican state convention. Foreseeing the ruinous effect such factionalism might have on his forthcoming bid for Congress, he hoped some sort of agreement could be reached, but as he prepared to leave for the district convention, the feud became so intense that violence erupted and one man (a Strobach follower) was shot and killed.

It was a pleasantly cool August afternoon when Rapier boarded the Montgomery-Eufaula railway coach for Union Springs, accompanied by an entourage of leading Republicans, including Third District congressman Charles Pelham, Internal Revenue Collector John Hendricks, Spencer envoy H. W. Betts, and Negro politician Charles Harris. Upon arriving, Rapier quickly found accommodations at a Negro boardinghouse (operated by Lewis Johnson) and then arranged for a meeting of his followers. At eight o'clock that evening, in the probate office of the recently completed county courthouse, he chaired a preconvention caucus. "What may be styled the Rapier delegation," a reporter for the Union Springs *Times* observed, "conducted themselves in a quiet and orderly manner, and their presence would scarcely have been noticed had it not been known that they had arrived in town."[10] Despite the quietude, the most important question discussed at the preconvention gathering—how to bring the two warring factions of Montgomery Republicans to some sort of agreement— was still not answered when Rapier retired shortly after ten.

Then, at half past the hour, Robert Knox, Pat Robinson, and a host of "Busteed's Bummers," as the Knoxites were scurrilously called in the press, arrived in Union Springs on a special train. Forming a procession, preceded by a brass band, they paraded to the courthouse, took possession of the probate office, and held a boisterous meeting, where Knox ranted about the thieves, scoundrels, and liars in Republican ranks and vehemently condemned his archrival Strobach. Then they staged another torchlit parade down the main street, yelling, drumming, trumpeting, swearing, and cheering, as one Union Springs resident observed. Entering Baumont and Rostenthi's Saloon, Knox attempted to provoke a fist fight with the self-restrained Rapier partisan Charles Harris. "It seemed as if hell itself had let loose it's [*sic*] legions upon our town," the same reporter who had earlier described the Rapier delegation, wrote. "It was fully two-o'clock in the morning when the mob showed signs of fatigue and went to sleep."[11]

Tensions were high at the courthouse the next day. No sooner had the delegates entered the hall than shouts of "Liar," "Traitor," "Scoundrel," and "Bolter" rang out. Even before the delegates took their seats, a heated debate erupted concerning membership on the Credentials Committee. Knox demanded the appointment of a five-member committee, with at least three of his sympathizers as members, including John Wiley, who had labored so diligently to defeat Rapier in 1870; while A. E. Williams, a friend of Rapier's since he had first arrived in Montgomery, asked for a more balanced seven-member committee. According to witnesses, what followed was confusion which amounted to chaos: the delegates and would-be delegates crowded around the speaker's stand, shouting, interrupting each other, and raising innumerable points of order; the chairman's gavel hammered away continually. It seemed as if an outright brawl was inevitable when Rapier appeared before the convention. He was greeted by the waving of hats, and antagonisms subsided for a time, but then the Knoxites reiterated their demands, and once again it looked as if the convention would break up in a bloody fight. A second time Rapier took the stand, calling for calmness and moderation, and once again the delegates quieted.

"I had stood all day between angry disputants, sometimes even forcing them to put up their deadly weapons," Rapier later recalled, "and now the danger seemed more imminent than ever, if peace was not at once restored."[12] He therefore decided, despite his desire not to become involved in a local dispute, to seek some kind of a compromise, and along with Betts, Hendricks, Knox, and Robinson, he adjourned to a back room of the probate office to discuss the situation. As the meeting began he received two urgent notes, one from Charles Pelham, who pleaded with him to make some agreement to avoid riot and bloodshed, and the other from Bullock County probate judge W. H. Black, who felt that without some sort of accommodation with Knox, there would surely be a serious disturbance. Any terms would be preferable to a continuation of the fighting. Other town officials also pressed Rapier to make some compromise; any terms with the Knoxites would be for the good of Union Springs. After two hours of negotiations, Rapier decided to sign a pledge saying that he would do nothing detrimental to the Knox-Robinson faction in the coming election, that he believed their ticket to be the legitimate one, and that he would even promote their success and use his influence to defeat the impeachment of Judge Busteed.

The delegates then adopted the Credentials Committee report, placed Rapier's name in nomination, and when the chairman called the roll of the county representatives, thirty-one members voted in the affirmative; only the inscrutable Knox cast his vote against the Negro nominee. As the chair declared Rapier duly nominated, ten exultant delegates hoisted him to their shoulders and carried him out of the courtroom and down the street to the depot. "The air was filled with shouts," an onlooker wrote, "and even the rain that set in could not dampen the enthusiasm of the sable politicians."[13]

Rapier began his official campaign by retracting the pledge he had signed at Union Springs. It was well known that upon his return from Washington he had vowed not to take part in local politics, especially the fight which was then going on in Montgomery County, he explained in an open letter to the editor of the Montgomery *Advertiser*. At the district convention a serious confrontation was imminent; it could have meant bloodshed in Union Springs and could have cast a stigma on the Republican party that nothing afterwards could have effaced. Hence, he had signed the pledge, though he had refused to accept the same terms during the day. But he did not feel that the public would hold him to a pledge obtained under such circumstances, especially when he could prove beyond any doubt that his nomination was assured even before the convention had assembled.

But Democrats quickly accused Rapier of making a corrupt bargain in order to secure the nomination. Before the war, an article in the Union Springs *Times* said, white men sold Negroes, but here was a case where a Negro had purchased several white men. The only difference between such a sale and those of antebellum times was that when a white man obtained a slave before the war, he had to pay fifteen hundred dollars; now Negroes could pay a few pennies for their white chattel. Conversely, an article in the Montgomery *Daily Advertiser* concluded that Rapier had sold himself and that his humiliating confession was too thin to deceive anyone. Severely chastising the black incumbent, the *Advertiser* added that the facility with which he had broken his sacred pledge and forfeited his honor should be a warning to Republicans everywhere not to trust the word of a Negro. Siding with the Democrats and expressing pain and humiliation at Rapier's recantation, Robert Knox felt chagrined that such a pledge should have been made under any circumstances, but especially as the purchase price for the nomination to a political office.

Most of the criticism leveled at Rapier was unfair. He had neither sold himself nor paid for the nomination. Indeed, ten days before the convention, the Union Springs *Times* had said that it was understood that the Negro incumbent would receive the nod of the party, as there were no other aspirants in the field. And he rightly feared that violence would have resulted if he had refused to sign the compromise; he entered the arena of local politics only to avert an impending riot. Yet by retracting his promise, no matter what the circumstances, he had not only committed a political blunder, but had left himself open to valid criticism from the Democrats.

Still, the atmosphere of violence was the real issue. Realizing that his only hope for victory was a fair and peaceful election, Rapier journeyed to the nation's capital in the hope of securing federal protection for voters. Only three days after writing his letter of recantation, he explained the troublesome situation in Alabama to Attorney General George H. Williams—the outrages against Alabama freedmen, the unsettled political state of affairs, the threats of Conservatives to carry the election at any cost. He urged the attorney general to dispatch federal soldiers to protect voters during the election. Upon returning to Montgomery, he felt confident that some help would be forthcoming.

Such was not the case. At the very time Rapier was seeking governmental assistance to end the reign of terror in Alabama, federal authorities were formulating a more passive policy toward the South, arguing that the force acts had been miserable failures; federal intervention, instead of curtailing lawlessness, had actually encouraged illegal acts; and the Klan no longer constituted a threat. Williams had even issued an order requiring federal prosecutors to dismiss all pending indictments if the charge was "merely that of belonging to the Klan." Moreover, while instructing United States marshals to punish the perpetrators of serious crimes, the attorney general, under instructions from the president, promised white Southerners that federal troops would not be used, except when called upon by local officials, most of whom, in Alabama, were Democrats.

And the violence continued. Two weeks after the attorney
general issued his instructions, a black resident of Sumter reported
that a group of white men had declared war on the Negroes in his
section. A special agent for the Justice Department, investigating
the climate of murder in Alabama, had much the same to report.
Though he had traveled in almost every country on the globe, he
had never witnessed such deplorable conditions. Seeking to interview freedmen and freedwomen about the white leagues in various
areas, he was unable to obtain any firsthand information because
the Negroes, upon seeing a white man, would frantically run off
into the woods. The old Klan had been revived across Alabama,
United States Attorney Charles Mayer disclosed, and in no
Southern commonwealth was it more active, more cruel, or more
hellish. From Montgomery another federal attorney, Nicholas S.
McAfee, wrote that outrages were becoming frequent in at least
eight Black Belt counties, including Montgomery and Barbour.
Inspired by the race issue, the Klan was daily becoming more
murderous. Carrying new, breach-loading double-barreled shot-
guns, they threatened violence against the enemies of the white
man's race, the white man's government, and any friend of
"Nigger Equality."

Conservatives who did not actually participate in these misdeeds
condoned the actions of the wrongdoers. The Mobile *Register*
theorized that the only weapon of defense left was the most fearful
known in the history of nations desperately oppressed—the
weapon of assassination. "And so terribly urgent and pressing has
been the provocation to resort to it, that we look upon it as one of
the marvels of this monstrous and phenomenal era of reconstruction."[14] On another occasion the same newspaper observed that
mob law was unquestionably essential in any free and well-
governed society.

Despite Conservative hostility toward blacks, Rapier vigorously
canvassed the Second District in the months before the election. He
spoke in Montgomery, at Pike Road and Barnes Beat in Montgomery County, at Hayneville in Lowndes County, and at Midway
and Fitzpatrick's in Bullock County, attempting, as he had in 1872,
to carry his message personally to every corner of the district. At
each place he advocated the passage of the Sumner civil rights bill
and impressed on the minds of his listeners the importance of a
Republican victory in November. Rapier was forced to cancel a
scheduled campaign stop at Geneva when Democrats threatened

his life. "The Democracy told us that Rapier should not speak," Dr.
N. B. Cloud testified before a congressional investigating committee, "if he did they would kill him."[15] Paradoxically, it was this
very county that would have benefited most from the river
improvement legislation proposed by Rapier at the first session of
the Forty-third Congress.

Threats were only part of the Democratic campaign against the
Negro congressman. A Union Springs Democrat demanded a
replacement for "that yellow-nigger Rapier," who had misrepresented him for two years.[16] Another Conservative pointed an
accusing finger: if, as Rapier claimed, he had signed the infamous
Union Springs pledge only to prevent bloodshed, why had United
States officials, under the Enforcement Acts, not prosecuted any of
the wrongdoers? The shameful moral obliquity of the Negro
representative, continued the editor of the Troy *Messenger*,
shocked the manly and religious sentiments of white people everywhere. And the polished Southern gentleman, lawyer, former Confederate officer, and Conservative candidate for Congress, Jere N.
Williams, of Barbour County, told an audience that no respect-
able white man could vote for Rapier, who had sold himself to a
faction in his own party and then repudiated the sale. "Better by far
to have died at his post a fearless martyr to principle."

If the White Man's Party represented Rapier as a devious,
immoral, self-aggrandizing "yellow nigger," Republican newspapers did little to correct the slander. In fact, editor Arthur
Bingham blamed him for wantonly and wickedly dividing the
Republican party. Though there was a large Republican majority in
the district, he pointed out in an editorial in the *Alabama State
Journal*, the intraparty conflict which he had created and so
mischievously sustained was ruining any chance for victory.
"Unless the Congressman himself shall exert himself to cure the
division, which he did so much to sustain, we shall not be surprised
if he is hoisted by his own petard."[17] Though he refused to support
Rapier during the canvass, on election day Bingham begrudgingly
asked Republicans to vote for the entire ticket, even Rapier. By
then, however, it was too late.

Fearing that the intensity of the campaign might lead to violence
on election day, Rapier telegraphed Attorney General Williams
with an urgent request for protection for the voters of the district.
"Please order a detachment of soldiers to Union Springs," he said,
basing his request on the fact that a near riot had occurred during

the August Republican convention, "to aid the United States Commissioner in preserving the peace at the election."[18] His premonition proved unfounded so far as the county seat of Bullock was concerned, but in Barbour County a riot did occur. On the morning of November 3, hundreds of blacks streamed into Eufaula from the surrounding countryside to cast their ballots. Shortly after noon, a scuffle broke out in the street. Soon a shot rang out, then a volley of shots, and when the smoke had cleared a few minutes later, the main street was strewn with bodies. According to several witnesses, the firing came mostly from the roofs of buildings and from a group of whites hidden behind a pile of lumber, though other observers suggested that the first shots came from armed blacks. Whoever fired first, only eight whites received gunshot wounds, all superficial, while a hundred Negroes were killed or wounded in the melee. Yet, to Rapier's dismay, a detachment of 35 United States soldiers stationed in the vicinity (there were 679 in Alabama) did absolutely nothing to prevent the riot. Under the command of one Colonel Daggett, the troops went about their daily routine as the dreadful moans of wounded and dying freedmen echoed through their encampment.

United States soldiers also ignored the violence at Spring Hill, twelve miles from Eufaula, on election day. Shortly after the polls closed, a group of Democrats burst into the old store used as a polling place, shot sixteen-year-old Willis Keils three times in the leg and once in the abdomen, and absconded with a box containing 600 Republican and 132 Democratic ballots. Following the Eufaula and Spring Hill incidents, the Montgomery *Advertiser* expressed the sentiments of Conservatives concerning the election day violence: "We hope the negroes will learn a lesson from this, and understand that they cannot run 'ruffshod' over white men, and go unpunished."[19]

Ballot box stealing as well as other irregularities occurred in other parts of the Second District. It was common knowledge that prominent white Democrats had been seen bribing citizens in Columbus, Georgia, with new, half-dollar coins to cross the border and vote in Alabama. Gangs of these Georgia repeaters went to Montgomery and then voted at every depot from there to the Georgia line. Even an ex-Confederate, A. A. Mabson, admitted (or boasted) that Democratic supervisors in Bullock threw out ballot boxes containing 700 Republican ballots.

Election returns showed an overwhelming Conservative victory.

As in 1870, Democrats had gained all the state offices, two of every three seats in the state legislature, and a majority of the congressional seats. And as in 1870, Rapier had lost, but this time by only 1056 votes out of a total of 39,000. In Geneva County, he had not received a single popular vote, in Coffee only 72, in Dale 260, and even in Barbour, a Black Belt county, he lost by over 100 votes. Serving notice that he would contest the election, he charged that 500 black voters in Eufaula had been driven from the polls by armed men and that due to intimidation, voting irregularities, and fraudulent returns, he had been cheated out of an additional 788 votes, which would have been enough to insure his victory in a fair election.

Conservatives answered with charges of their own. Congressman-elect Jeremiah Williams accused Rapier of spreading vicious rumors among the superstitious Negroes that if they failed to vote the Republican ticket, they would be remanded to slavery. Moreover, he continued, the Negro incumbent had terrorized Conservative blacks, making them afraid to vote; had coerced thousands of others into becoming Republicans, "like so many unreasoning animals"; and had fraudulently garnered more that four thousand votes.[20] The Montgomery *Advertiser* offered its own calumny, charging that Rapier had used federal rations earmarked for the victims of the flooded Alabama, Tombigbee, and Black Warrior rivers to bribe Negro voters. Although only two counties in the district were affected by the flood, the paper charged that Rapier had shipped bacon to Troy, about fifty miles away, as well as Eufaula and Union Springs, both some distance from the flooded area. "He is a very proper person to charge fraud on the Democrats," the *Advertiser* sarcastically remarked. "The truth is the present Congress ought to expell [him]."[21]

Rapier refused to dignify the charges with an answer. Such outlandish slander, he said, would collapse of its own weight. By comparing the Second District's 1872 and 1874 returns, he could easily prove the validity of his own contest (see table 4). In riot-torn Barbour, as well as in Bullock and Montgomery counties, the Republican vote had fallen off substantially in 1874, by a total of 1525 votes, or about 10 percent; in the peaceful Black Belt county of Lowndes, though, Rapier had increased his 1872 margin by 432 votes, or 11 percent. As to the *Advertiser*'s charge, it was not even his responsibility to supervise the distribution of overflow bacon, but the job of Governor David Lewis.

TABLE 4   Comparison of Congressional Elections: Alabama
                   Second District, 1872 and 1874

County	1872		1874		Democratic Republican increase (+) or decrease (–)	
	Oates	Rapier	Williams	Rapier		
Barbour	2349	2742	2791	2683	+442	–59
Bullock	1263	3100	1588	2497	+325	–603
Butler	1518	1097	2189	1470	+671	+373
Coffee	949	7	1382	72	+433	+65
Conecuh [Crenshaw]	1025	309	1615	382	+590	+73
Dale*	1194	266	1734	260	+540	–6
Henry	2022	281	2020	736	–2	+455
Lowndes	929	3726	1189	4158	+260	+432
Montgomery	3051	7047	3295	6184	+244	–863
Pike	1900	552	2377	727	+477	+175

*Geneva was included in Dale County returns.

After a three-month investigation, a congressional committee
concluded that the Democratic majority had been obtained by
fraud, threats, violence, and murder. Had the canvass been fair and
undisturbed, the Republican candidates would have all been elected.
"The whole election was an imposition upon popular rights, and
the result attained was but the accomplishment of the threat of the
democratic leaders when the campaign opened, 'to carry the
election at all hazards.' "[22]

The most important question confronting Rapier upon his return
to the lame-duck session of the Forty-third Congress, then, was
violence in the South. He invited a group of prominent Negroes,
among them Downing, Langston, Pinchback, Arkansas judge
Mifflin Gibbs, Alabama editor Philip Joseph, North Carolinian
George W. Price, and Frederick Douglass, to his rooming house
(1619 K. Street NW) to discuss civil disorder. The lawlessness in several Southern states threatened the stability of the national government and jeopardized the lives and property of loyal citizens, he said
in an opening resolution; it demanded an expression of sentiment
from all friends of justice and humanity, but especially from
representative blacks. After several hours of discussion, Rapier and
the others drafted a declaration in behalf of the Negro population
of America, expressing outrage at the revolutionary atmosphere as
well as at the spirit of assassination that prevailed in Arkansas,

Louisiana, Mississippi, and Alabama. Considering the bitter persecution of those whose Republican affiliation was evidenced by their
complexions, they declared that Congress should institute appro-
priate laws to protect persons, property, and political rights.

Only days later, a bill to protect blacks' civil rights finally came
before the House. The proposal differed from the original Sumner
bill by imposing a maximum fine of only one thousand dollars and
completely excluding the mixed-school provision. In the debate
that followed, native Alabamian Alexander White declared that
Negroes in his state desired separate public facilities anyway and
offered a substitute bill which set forth the principle of separate
but equal accommodations. Rapier was quick to his feet. "My
colleague from Alabama has not properly represented the sentiments of the people of my State."[23] Alabama Negroes demanded all
the civil and political rights, privileges, and immunities extended to
white citizens under the Constitution of the United States. They
would be satisfied with nothing less. Though the civil rights bill
that finally passed Congress in February 1875 contained neither a
separate but equal clause, nor an equal school section, it did
promise blacks full enjoyment of accommodations in inns, conveyances, theaters, and other public places.

To celebrate, Rapier and a number of other Negroes slushed
through the sleety streets of Washington to a party at Wormley's
Hotel. "The nation's leading colored gentlemen were present," a
reporter for the *Sunday Herald and Weekly National Intelligencer*
observed; that group included Rapier, Downing, and Douglass,
"the white-maned lion of the tribe."[24] As he walked slowly through
a flower-bedecked suite of parlors to the main banquet room,
Rapier observed statues of Jefferson signing the Declaration of
Independence, Lincoln signing the Emancipation Proclamation, as
well as oil paintings depicting other significant events in black
history. During the festivities that followed, he offered several
toasts, listened to speeches by Douglass and others, and sipped
French brandy, though he usually did not drink. It was early in the
morning before the celebrants finally returned to the then frozen
and icy streets of the capital. The next day a newspaper reporter
described the celebration: the most "touching incident" of the
evening, he said, had occurred when Republican editor Elijah P.
Brooks, standing next to a statue of Lincoln, had fondly embraced
Rapier, who was at the time "in the bronze clutches of the author of
the Declaration of Independence."[25]

The reporter had unwittingly suggested the major goal of Rapier while in Washington: to give meaning to the words of Jefferson. Alabama's Negro congressman had spoken forcefully in favor of equal rights for blacks, voted to bring the Sumner bill up for consideration, held meetings in his home to discuss strategy, and in the end, played no small role in the passage of the Civil Rights Act of 1875. In addition, he had favored expansion and improvement of America's commercial waterways, government regulation of the railroads, an increase in currency, and had introduced legislation to subsidize internal improvements. At no time had he endeavored to keep alive racial friction, neglected his white constituents, or demonstrated a "race supersensitivity"; rather, in a dignified, confident, and conscientious manner, he had struggled for the economic uplift of the South and the fair treatment of his race.[26]

Before returning home he took up the cause of blacks for the last time as a congressman when he suggested that his good friend Elias Keils be appointed district judge to fill the vacancy created when Richard Busteed resigned. He should be confirmed with as little delay as possible, Rapier wrote, as his services were greatly needed in the state. Learning that Alexander White had nominated conservative Republican and former governor David Lewis for the judgeship, Rapier led a delegation of Alabama Negroes to the White House. Lewis would declare the Enforcement Acts unconstitutional, he and the others, including Selma editor R. A. Moseley, congressman-elect Haralson, and Montgomerian A. E. Williams, told the president. With him as judge, Negroes in the state would be in a worse predicament than they had been as slaves. But in the end both Keils and Lewis were passed over, and a third candidate, former provisional governor Lewis E. Parsons, received the post. Rapier was forced to acquiesce, as Parsons was the lesser of evils, but the appointment not only suggested the indifference of Grant to the wishes of Negroes, but had once again brought to the surface the breach between the two groups of Alabama Republicans. As if to dramatize the irreconcilable differences between the factions, Lewis soon joined the Democrats.

At the end of the last session, Rapier, along with ten other members of the House Committee on Education and Labor, submitted a final report. Highly critical of the management of land grant colleges in the South, the committee charged that there had been serious mismanagement of funds at Auburn Agricultural and Mechanical College. The report stated that the school had invested some $216,000 of public funds, derived from land sales, in bonds, called Alabama Eights, but the highest price recently offered for such bonds was only 50 percent of their original market value. The committee recommended that Congress take stern measures to secure a promise from Auburn that the remaining principal in the fund would be preserved undiminished, but the suggestion was not acted upon before Congress adjourned.

Despite Rapier's efforts, as the Forty-third Congress drew to a close many observers sharply censured the Republican members. One Conservative editorialist insisted that the Civil Rights Act could not give Negroes rights and privileges; there was an equal rights law for the district, but blacks were refused accommodations in the best restaurants and hotels, even in the very shadow of the Capitol. Even the *National Republican,* a paper strongly wedded to the policies of the party of reconstruction, called the Republican representatives despicable failures, termed civil rights a piece of sentimentalism, and accused congressmen of only tinkering with the great problems of despair and depresssion. The result had been disgraceful struggling and faltering whenever questions of vital interest to the country had been presented. Though these castigations were unfair, when Rapier left Washington in March 1875, the depression had worsened, discrimination and segregation still existed almost everywhere, and violence in the South had increased rather than diminished.

12

Following Reconstruction: Politics and Emigration

The redemption of the state by the Conservative party ended the four-year experiment with reconstruction and so-called Negro rule in Alabama. Now the Democrats moved swiftly to consolidate their power. Gerrymandering the boundaries of the congressional districts, the state legislature scattered nine Black Belt counties into six different districts, which, at least according to previous election returns, would all become Conservative, and grouped five others (Dallas, Hale, Lowndes, Perry, Wilcox) into a new, overwhelmingly Republican Fourth District. To control the Negro vote in that district, the legislature passed a law requiring all electors to register and vote in the precinct or ward of their residence, thus allowing white plantation owners the opportunity to supervise closely the political activities of their tenant farmers. In addition, the Democrats overturned the reconstruction constitution by reducing salaries in the General Assembly, prohibiting state railroad construction or internal improvements, lowering property taxes, and abolishing the public school board. By late 1875, Conservatives were well on their way to recovering complete political domination and reinstituting a one-party system.[1]

Although defeated and out of power, the Republicans continued to nominate candidates, campaign for office, cast ballots, and send delegates to national political conventions. But the disparate factions that had fought so bitterly since the beginning of reconstruction soon divided into two separate parties. At a convention in Montgomery on May 16, 1876, long-time Rapier foe William Smith announced the formal reorganization of the party and urged the selection of Samuel Rice, Willard Warner, and Jeremiah Haralson as delegates to the national nominating convention to be held in Cincinnati. To head the all-white state ticket, Smith recommended state supreme court judge Thomas Peters of Lawrence County. Only a week later, at a second Republican convention in Montgomery, Rapier denounced the earlier gathering, declared their delegate selection process fraudulent, and backed the nomination of Senator Spencer, Congressman Hays, and Negro A. H. Curtis, a former state senator, to represent Alabama at Cincinnati. Elected as a Presidential Elector, and serving on several committees, including Credentials and Business, he successfully urged the convention to adopt a resolution favoring a return to specie payments (a deviation from his congressional stance on the issue); but he was less successful in seeking an uncommitted delegation to the national convention, as the delegates chose to support Indiana Senator Oliver P. Morton for the presidential nomination. Thus, as one Republican despaired, the party in Alabama, torn by internal feuds, was disorganized, disrupted, and demoralized.

Democrats, of course, rejoiced at such discord in the ranks of the opposition, and, as they had in the past, played on these differences. Concerned neither with the consistency of their arguments, nor the accuracy of their statements, Conservatives battered the Republicans with a barrage of hostile editorials. Typical of these was a column in the Mobile *Register* which chastised the Smith faction for truckling to a Negro, Haralson; rebuked them for nominating Peters, who believed in indiscriminate sexual intercourse between whites and Negroes; and at the same time complimented them for their intelligence, moderation, and ability. Another Democratic editorial contended that philosophically the two Republican factions were exactly alike but went on to stereotype one as "Nigger and Carpetbagger" and the other as "Scalawag."[2] Other articles played on this theme: Though each faction hated the other intensely, though they were represented by the *Alabama State Journal* and the *Alabama Republican*, and though they had different leadership, their principles were identical.

Such observations, however, were naive. The Smith group, though they professed being in favor of equal rights for blacks (as indeed, had the Democrats), entertained grave doubts about the capacity of freedmen for citizenship, especially in leadership roles. Conservative Willard Warner went so far as to admit frankly that for Republicanism to prosper in the South, it would have to represent all the political elements "except Douglas Democrats and colored men."[3] The opposing faction, led by Rapier, demanded full

and complete recognition of the Fourteenth and Fifteenth Amendments, while recognizing fully the covert activities of some Republicans to use blacks as voters when necessary, but never to allow
them more than, as he put it, "crumbs from the Master's Table."
Nor was the leadership a matter of Negro and carpetbagger vs. native Southerner. The four most powerful figures in one group in 1876
included Smith and Rice, scalawags; Warner, a carpetbagger; and
Haralson. Their counterparts in the other camp included Pelham
and Hays, scalawags; Spencer, a carpetbagger; and Rapier. From
the first months of reconstruction, and through 1876, principles,
not personnel, had divided the Republican party.

Recognizing the basic conservativism of Smith, Warner, Rice,
and others, Rapier had battled continuously to uphold the principle
of full equality for blacks. And in 1876 he was determined to
continue the struggle. He had rented a small house and several
hundred acres of plantation land in Lowndes County, a few miles
from Montgomery, and now he announced his intention to run for
Congress in the recently gerrymandered Fourth District. He immediately launched into a third campaign for national office. But
for the first time in his political career he was competing against
another Negro, incumbent Jeremiah Haralson, who had the backing
of the Smith faction. Consequently, Rapier began a canvass nearly
a month before the nominating convention, speaking in each
of the five county seats comprising the district in an attempt to
woo convention delegates. After one speech in Greensboro (Hale
County) a Conservative newspaper observed that in less than three
weeks Rapier had already garnered enough delegate strength to
oust Haralson. It seemed certain that the incumbent would be
defeated at the district convention. "The man who will walk Jere's
log is James T. Rapier."[4]

The confrontation between the two Negro aspirants became even
more intense in Marion (Perry County) September 13 and 14, when
Republican representatives gathered to nominate a candidate for
Congress. In a bitter fight over credentials, Haralson demanded the
seating of his delegation from Dallas County and moved to reject a
group led by A. P. Wilson, who sympathized with Rapier.
Acrimonious debate continued for two full days until finally the
Credentials Committee decided to seat both delegations from the
county in question. Haralson then "rolled up his sleeves and
pitched into the committee like a thousand bricks," a journalist

wrote, "speaking of a stocked concern gotten up to defeat him."⁵
After a two-hour harangue, he walked out of the convention,
declaring that he would run as an Independent. The remaining
delegates then settled down to the work at hand, and Negro
Alexander H. Curtis, his voice husky with emotion, nominated
Rapier for Congress. The motion, wildly seconded, carried by
acclamation. "He is a man of fine abilities and education, ranking
with Fred Douglas [sic]," an article in the *Alabama State Journal*
noted several days later.⁶ His nomination afforded great satisfaction to Alabama Republicans, for as a congressman he had won the
respect of all—Democrats and Republicans—by his upright conduct. But the *Journal* confessed ambivalent feelings toward Rapier.
He was not the paper's first choice, but since he had been properly
nominated by the convention, "we feel it our duty as a party paper
to give him our support."⁷

With characteristic energy, Rapier canvassed the district during
September, October, and early November. Opening his official
campaign at Hayneville, in Lowndes County, he spoke with force
and eloquence to an enthusiastic crowd of over a thousand
freedmen. Standing on the steps of the courthouse, he asked for the
support of all loyal Republicans. Back in Marion again, he
announced to a large audience that he had just received a telegram
from the national executive committee declaring him the regular
nominee. But when a group of avid Haralson supporters shouted
"Withdraw, Withdraw," and started a row, he was forced to call in
the sheriff to restore order.⁸ In his concluding remarks, he made a
plea for party unity. In Selma, speaking from a platform at the
corner of Broad and Alabama streets, he warned an attentive
assembly of Negro listeners that only a split ticket could give
General Charles Shelley, the Democratic party's candidate from
Dallas County, a chance for victory.

In a further attempt to heal the wounds of party dissension,
Rapier dispatched three of his followers to canvass the smaller
towns and stations in the district and asked them to reiterate his
message concerning the necessity of Republican solidarity. To
Lowndes County he sent Charles Harris, the Negro who had
attended the tumultuous Union Springs convention two years
before; to Wilcox, T. D. McCasky, a white resident of Camden and
well-known property owner; and to Dallas, twenty-three-year-old
Jesse Chislom Duke, a schoolteacher who ran a country store at

Minter's Station. Following explicit instructions, they each spoke of the dire consequences of a split ticket, explaining to voters that Rapier was even willing to withdraw, if Haralson would do the same, in favor of a third candidate who could unify the party.

But Haralson was not willing to compromise. Even after the national committee had refused to recognize his candidacy, he steadfastly maintained that he was the regular nominee. Such defiance had been characteristic of his career: in 1868, against the preferences of the regular Republican organization, he had stumped the Black Belt for Seymour and Blair; in 1870 he had run as an Independent for a seat in the state Senate, defeating a Republican aspirant by several thousand votes; and in 1874 he had won a seat in the Forty-fourth Congress, again running against a Republican. Described by one newspaper as genuinely black, burly, shrewd, insolent, uncompromising, and bold, he struck consternation into the souls of white Alabamians.

It seems ironic, then, that during the 1876 campaign, he received a good deal of support from native Southerners. Suppressing for the moment their antipathy toward blacks, men like William Smith, Samuel Rice, and Dallas County editor John Saffold went through the district soliciting votes for Haralson, while denouncing his Negro opponent. At a Republican meeting in Marion, for example, Saffold cautioned that Rapier's 1870 nomination had nearly ruined the party. His arrogant conduct during the canvass, his incitant handling of the race issue, and his foolish belief that a Negro would make an acceptable secretary of state had brought defeat to the entire ticket. Besides, because Rapier lived in Montgomery, he had no right to present himself to the voters of the Fourth District. What were his motives in seeking the only sure Republican office in the state?—only an insatiable personal ambition.

Haralson received sympathy as well as support from many Democrats. Some of the most vindictive and alienated Conservatives in Wilcox County supported the incumbent, plantation owner M. J. Candee of Camden observed during the canvass, but they denounced Rapier because he had voted for the civil rights bill. It was a sad commentary that Haralson might again represent the richest district in Alabama, a Conservative newspaper explained, but he had the sympathy of most Democrats, as one could not be a disinterested spectator, even in a dog fight. Another Conservative paper, the *Wilcox Vindicator*, apologized for taking part in Republican politics, but said that if its vote could decide between the two blacks, that vote would certainly be for Haralson. Why? Because he was not the regular nominee, because he was breaking up the party, and because he could be controlled by the superior intelligence of whites. He was certainly preferable "to that darkie Rapier, who believes a negro is as good as a white man."[9]

Despite the complexities of political loyalties in the district, there was no animosity between the two black candidates. "Neither of us abused any body during the campaign," Haralson testified before a Senate committee after the election. "Rapier and I are perfectly friendly and always have been."[10] Such was the case at a political rally in Hayneville, when the two sat down on a park bench and, for nearly an hour, discussed matters completely unrelated to politics. Later the same day, though they did not share the speaker's rostrum, both spoke to a large audience—Haralson in the morning, Rapier in the afternoon.

Emnity did develop, however, between the two candidates from Dallas County. The ex-Confederate general and Democratic nominee Charles Shelley, sheriff of Selma, harbored a special hatred for Haralson, who had a reputation as having been a recalcitrant slave during the antebellum period. Late in the canvass Shelley arrested him on a charge of vagrancy. "You called me a 'good Republican,' " he said during an interrogation. "You God damned black son of a bitch, you have to take that back or I'll murder you right here." Then, in spite of his threat, the infuriated Shelley pointed a derringer in Haralson's face and shouted, "Don't open your mouth."[11] After two hours of such harassment, he finally succeeded in getting Haralson to withdraw from the campaign. Because he knew that he would lose the fight, Haralson announced in the Selma *Times*, surely aware of the double meaning of his words, he had decided to withdraw from the race for Congress, but he earnestly urged his followers to vote for Shelley, believing that his chances would be better in 1878 if Rapier were not elected.

But on November 7, both Negro aspirants went down to defeat, even though, together, they received a total of 61 percent of the vote (see table 5). The split ticket had been the major cause for the Republican debacle, but there were other factors: the growing apathy among Negroes who, in previous elections, had turned out 22,000 strong; the spirited campaign by Conservatives to redeem the only

TABLE 5   Congressional Election Returns, Fourth District, Alabama, 1876

	Shelley	Haralson	Rapier
Dallas	2490	2979	67
Hale	2170	48	2340
Lowndes	1312	163	3904
Perry	2168	2563	261
Wilcox	1484	2922	664
Total	9624	8675	7236

Republican citadel in Alabama, as indicated by a 35 percent increase in the Democratic vote; the discounting of ballots in several traditionally Republican precincts; and the new election law requiring voters to remain in their precincts. In the Alabama election of 1876, a Senate investigating committee concluded, fraud had been substituted for violence; Negroes were denied voting privileges solely because of skin color. So in a district where blacks outnumbered whites nearly four to one (110,000 to 30,000), and where Republicans had previously outvoted Conservatives three to one (23,000 to 7000), a Democrat had won a seat in Congress. It was Rapier's last campaign for public office.

Turning away from politics, he devoted himself to managing his plantations. Borrowing seven hundred dollars from Lehman, Durr, and Company, the largest cotton merchant in Montgomery, he expanded his plantation acreage in Lowndes; hired seven Negro tenants; provided them with mules, horses, oxen, wagons, and farming implements; and, as he had done a decade before in the Tennessee Valley, supervised the planting of a cotton crop. The following year, he again borrowed from Lehman and Durr, provided his tenants with necessities, and planted a crop, but now he also began to serve as a private moneylender for a number of Negro farmers in the region. He advanced sharecroppers like O. O. Thomas, Samuel Ransome, and S. B. Reid, low interest loans ranging from twenty-five dollars to one hundred twenty-five dollars so that they could purchase teams, farm tools, and supplies. At the end of the second year, he harvested nearly eighty bales of cotton, clearing over two thousand dollars.

Yet, as in the past, economic success meant little to him while the condition of blacks remained substantially unimproved. And when election time rolled around in 1878, he returned to the political arena, using profits from his cotton sales, as he had in 1872, to rent a printing press, lease an office, and establish a Negro newspaper in Montgomery. This time, however, he hired as editor-in-chief a well-to-do Negro banker, Nathan Alexander, who, though still in his twenties, had a number of business interests, including a chain of drugstores, in the capital. In the first issue, published September 21, the new *Republican Sentinel and Hayneville Times* scolded Conservatives for drawing the color line in Alabama politics, but at the same time censured Republicans for going to the other extreme: nominating a Negro candidate to sway black voters. The candidate referred to was the irrepressible Jeremiah Haralson, who, with the withdrawal of Rapier, had secured the congressional nomination in the Fourth District. Rapier explained that when any candidate sought the nomination for a political office, he should do so because of his stance on the issues, not because he was a white man or a black man. Yet, as the publisher of the only Republican newspaper in the state, he felt obliged to support the party's nominee, and during the fall campaign, the *Sentinel* carried under the masthead: "For Congress, Fourth District, Jeremiah Haralson."[12]

Perhaps because of his long-time party loyalty, Rapier was nominated that same year as Collector of Internal Revenue for the Second District, one of the most prestigious and powerful patronage positions in Alabama. The nomination was vigorously supported by several high-ranking Republicans. He was the best, most reliable, and most competent Negro in the state, wrote former congressman Pelham, who had been Rapier's companion at the Union Springs convention four years before. He had the confidence and esteem of all good men; he could easily post the required sixty-thousand-dollar bond; and he was extremely capable of discharging the duties of the office. His appointment was perfectly satisfactory with Spencer, who also praised Rapier as able, competent, and honest, and with Secretary of the Treasury John Sherman, who told President Hayes: "From my own knowledge of Mr. Rapier, formerly a colored member of Congress, he would make a most faithful officer."[13]

But almost immediately conservative Republicans mounted a skillful campaign to defeat the nomination, claiming that Rapier had weighed down the ticket in 1870, had "carpet-bagged" himself into the Fourth Congressional District, and had caused discord within the party by his uncompromising stance. According to

Samuel Rice, William Smith, and Charles Buckley, his appointment would be offensive to the great mass of honest white people in both parties; anyone, even a Spencer man, as long as he was white, would be preferable. In an even blunter statement, Huntsville's William Bradley, who, even before reconstruction, had doubted the wisdom of allowing Negroes citizenship rights, told Hayes that such an appointment would do more to aid the opposition than any other act. It was not a question of skin color, but of efficiency. "Do not understand me to say that I have any objection to Rapier because of his African descent," Bradley wrote, and then, as if to reassure himself, repeated this contention several times, finally adding, "for on principle we could not."[14] These last six words had long been the creed of conservative white Republicans, who, since the beginning of congressional reconstruction, had professed an allegiance to black equality but had done everything in their power to stifle the aspirations of Negroes. And perhaps Rapier, who had relentlessly fought to maintain the inviolability of the postwar amendments but had confronted resistance within his own party at every turn, understood this better than anyone.

The campaign against him quickly gained momentum. Conservative Republicans across the state, but especially in the northern regions, claimed that the nomination would greatly aid the opposition and suggested that the antebellum state senator William Bowen, of Macon County replace Rapier. Playing on Hayes's conservative Southern policy, they deluged the White House with letters saying that if Republicanism were to survive in Alabama, men like Bowen must be pushed to the front ranks in the party. A person of property, integrity, and a thirty-year resident of the state, his qualifications were of the highest order, plus he had "the unswerving endorsement of the conservative masses of the people."[15] Influenced by these arguments, Hayes sent a sharp note to Sherman. The dispatches indicated that the nomination of Rapier was a mistake; take "no action about it until we look into it."[16] Despite this pressure, Sherman refused to withdraw the nomination, and in July 1878, after four months of bitter controversy, Rapier became Collector of Internal Revenue for the Second District—the first black man to attain such a position in Alabama.

About the time he began work for the Treasury Department, Southern Negroes again became the focus of national attention. Protesting conditions in the post-reconstruction South and following such men as the self-professed patriarch Moses "Pap" Singleton, blacks in Louisiana, Mississippi, North Carolina, Tennessee, and Alabama left their home states, and, in a great migration, moved to the North and West. Tenant farmers along the lower Mississippi, many of whom had emigrated from Alabama after the 1874 election, gathered together their worldly goods and boarded steamers for Kansas, while sharecroppers in North Carolina boarded trains for Indiana. Correspondent Henry King of *Scribner's Monthly*, dispatched to Wyandotte, Kansas, in April 1879, estimated that at least twenty thousand blacks had already sought refuge in the Sunflower State. Within a fortnight after his arrival, he reported that no less than a thousand Negro migrants— men, women, and children, carrying diverse barrels, boxes, and bundles—had disembarked from up-river steamers. When questioned as to why they had come, they were evasive; but when asked if they planned to return, they were positive and resolute: "We will never go back to the South."[17] By May the total was estimated at fifty thousand, a figure that represented the greatest single migration of blacks in the nineteenth century.

The exodus posed a dilemma for Rapier, who, during reconstruction, had consistently opposed radical movements—land confiscation, land redistribution, the complete disfranchisement of ex-Confederates—but who now faced the most radical movement of the postwar era, the mass migration of blacks out of the South. Moreover, even while in Canada, he had always looked upon himself as a Southerner. Yet he also realized that the migrants had legitimate grievances: the crop lien system, the lack of educational opportunities, the low wages of Negro workers, violence against freedmen, and a legal system based on caste. It seemed that despite reconstruction, despite the promises of white politicians, and despite the strenuous efforts of Negroes themselves, the plight of the ex-slave had not changed. Discouraged by this state of affairs, he came to the realization that emigration, a concept he had previously considered and rejected, was now the only viable solution to the problems facing blacks. And it was fitting that the first public declaration of such a radical stance would come in a city where he had so hopefully and optimistically begun his political career, Nashville, Tennessee.

One of one hundred forty black representatives who gathered for the Southern States Emigration Convention at the state capitol May

6, 1879, Rapier was among the first to speak. Describing the injustices that Negroes had endured since the war, he said that the insults received by the famous Fisk Jubilee Singers by Southern Railroad officials a month before symbolized the treatment of Negroes everywhere in the South. In the minds of whites, black political and civil equality was the consummation of all that was repugnant and dishonorable. Now deeply convinced that true equality was impossible in the states of the ex-Confederacy, he charged the convention to take a stand in favor of emigration.

The delegates responded with near unanimity. Flee from the oppressors to the land of freedom, cried the usually moderate former congressman Joseph Rainey. Blacks were a proscribed people not because they had crucified a Saviour, but because they had a different skin color. James Napier of Tennessee, who had attended school with Rapier, and who had also opposed extremism after the war, affirmed that Negro rights in the South were abridged and curtailed in every conceivable manner: politically, educationally, and economically. Napier, too, urged emigration. Another of Rapier's old Nashville school friends, now an Alabama lawyer, Samuel Lowery, complained that human rights, even the right to make a decent living, had been stealthily snatched from blacks. "Shall we toil day and night only to make more cotton for the landlord?"[18] For three days such was the tenor of speeches; the delegates indicted the South as a land of inhumanity.

Rapier had participated only briefly in the discussions. As chairman of the Committee on Migration, he had spent the three days evaluating hundreds of resolutions, petitions, and letters and writing an extensive report on the black migration. Late in the afternoon of May 9, he informed the delegates that a statement had been drafted; he moved that the convention adjourn briefly and then reconvene to discuss the document. At eight o'clock that evening he presented the report to the assemblage. The four-thousand-word, handwritten document answered two questions: What had caused the migration? and Should it be continued? In response to the first question, the committee concluded that a host of injustices had caused blacks to leave the South, injustices that included oppression, intimidation, violence, denial of rights granted in the Constitution, reactionary state constitutions, and a white man's government. The movement was based on the determined and irrepressible desire of Negroes to escape the cruel treatment and continued threats of the dominant race. Observing that thousands of former slaves and their children had bettered their condition by emigrating, the committee recommended that the convention "encourage and keep in motion" the migration of Negroes to the North and West, at least until those who remained behind were accorded every right and privilege guaranteed by the Constitution.[19] After twenty-three speeches of endorsement, the delegates unanimously adopted the report shortly before midnight and adjourned *sine die*.

Although the sentiment at Nashville was overwhelmingly pro-emigration, several prominent blacks counseled their followers to stay in the South. Interviewed in Washington, D.C., by a special correspondent of the Baltimore *Gazette*, former Alabama congressman Jeremiah Haralson said that he opposed emigration. The South was the proper place for the black man; it was his native land; it had a mild climate especially suited to his impoverished and ignorant condition. It took a hardy and thrifty foreigner, Haralson explained, to thrive in such a cold and forbidding country. Frederick Douglass believed that conditions in the Southern states were improving so steadily that ultimately blacks would realize "the fullest measure of liberty."[20] Anticipating the later arguments of Booker T. Washington, he wrote that, in his judgment, there was no section of the United States where an industrious and intelligent Negro could better serve his race than on the soil where he was born. And former congressman Robert Smalls of South Carolina described Beaufort County as a haven for Negroes. It was impossible for a black man to be lynched in Beaufort, Smalls claimed, no matter what his offense.

Rejecting these arguments, Rapier remained a steadfast emigrationist. And in August 1879, at the urging of Senator William Windom, he visited Kansas to inspect possible sites for a Negro colony. He spent three weeks touring the eastern part of the state, conferring at length with J. W. Henderson, the editor of the *Colored Citizen* in Topeka, and also seeking the views of Judge Mifflin Gibbs of Arkansas, who accompanied him to Wyandotte. Returning to Montgomery in September, he began a round of speaking engagements, attempting to persuade black tenant farmers in Alabama to emigrate to Kansas.

"He may induce a few to go," a Democratic newspaper noted, "but those who have tasted the bitter disappointments realized in

Liberia and Mississippi will never again leave the sunny plain of Alabama."[21] Conservatives accused Rapier of planning to build a political empire in Kansas. As he was fairly well off and had some cotton acreage, editor John Tyler said, he could purchase land for some of his deluded followers, and in time he might represent Kansas in Congress. But there was nothing to worry about. Negroes were impervious to the arguments of base Radicals like Rapier, whose only aim was to fill his own coffer. Why? Because the Southern people were by no means dependent on the Negro. His place would be filled as fast as he chose to leave. Whites only hoped that Negroes would not be misled by "unscrupulous mischief-makers like Rapier," who paraded before the imagination a thriving paradise in the West.[22]

But he continued the fight. In a grueling two-day examination before the Senate Committee on Emigration in Washington, he explained why he so strongly favored the mass migration. He pointed to discriminatory laws, inadequate schools, and intolerable economic conditions. One law that affected Alabama Negroes, he said, made it a felony to buy or sell cotton, corn, or wheat between sunset and sunrise, thereby forcing Negro tenant farmers to trade only with white property owners. The black witness read another state law. It prevented any person from buying or selling seed cotton in nine counties of the Black Belt except to, or from, a landlord, with a penalty of two to five years in prison upon conviction. This law, too, circumscribed the trading power of Negroes, placing all seed in the hands of white plantation owners. But a third law was the most severe. It made it a felony, grand larceny, to steal any part of an outstanding crop or personal property exceeding twenty-five dollars in value. Under it, freedmen had been sent to the state penitentiary for stealing one ear of corn. "Do you think stealing is a purely technical word?" North Carolina's Civil War governor Zebulon B. Vance asked sharply.[23] Anyway, had the witness not said that a felony was stealing something valued at more than twenty-five dollars? "No, you have not got it right yet," Rapier retorted.[24] An ear of corn was part of an outstanding crop, and any man caught stealing a portion of a crop could be convicted of grand larceny. The last law brought to the attention of the committee provided that five commissioners, appointed by the governor, should choose grand and petit jurors, but again only in certain predominately Negro counties. "The proper heading of the law might have been 'An Act to Keep Negroes off Juries,' " Rapier sarcastically remarked, adding: "It is the application of these laws and the opportunity they afford for oppression that we complain of, and from which the colored people are trying to get away."[25]

Though the Negro witness offered oppressive laws as perhaps the primary reason for black emigration, he also contended that extreme poverty had caused many blacks to migrate. In most instances the whites furnished the land, implements, stock, and feed, he explained, while the laborer boarded himself, cultivated and prepared the crop for market, and received one-half of the proceeds from the marketing of the crop. He offered a list of figures showing the average cost of supplies for Negro farmers to reinforce his argument (see table 6). Forced each year to pay 100 percent

TABLE 6   Cost of Supplies to Negro Farmers

Supplies	Market cost	Planter's price
Meat (180 lbs.)	$12.15	$22.75
Corn (13 bushels)	5.20	13.00
Hats (2)	2.00	4.00
Shoes (2 pairs)	2.50	4.50
Jeans (6 yds. of material)	1.50	3.00
Coat (4 yds. of material)	1.00	2.00
Shirts (9 yds. of material)	.90	1.50
Pants (6 yds. of material)	.60	1.00
Salt (12 bushels)	.25	.50
Tobacco (4 pounds)	1.80	4.00
Total	$27.90 [sic]	$56.25

SOURCE: United States, Congress, Senate Reports, 46th Cong., 1st sess., 8, no. 693 (1880): 465.

interest on the planter's price for supplies, making the total cost $112.50, as well as rents for land, mules, and feed which in monetary terms equaled $170, the Negro farmer who took his 6-bale cotton crop (worth $300) to market was left with $17.50 after a year's hard labor. In the West, he continued, Negroes could demand as much as three dollars a day for their labor. "The colored people are leaving to better their condition, and I think they can do it anywhere except in the Southern States."[26]

After listening to the testimony, an anonymous Alabama Democrat wrote that Rapier, who had heretofore been regarded as a representative Negro, had maligned and slandered the people of

Alabama. His statements that black people had left the state because of poverty, poor schools, and prejudicial laws were "quite too thin for the times."[27] Other Conservatives termed the testimony a "fancy sketch worthy of the best Louisiana liars" and mourned that Rapier had now been thoroughly radicalized by his Radical associates.[28] For the first time in his career, Democrats thus denounced Rapier as a radical. Indeed, he had come a long way from reconstruction days, when he had advised freedmen to proceed with moderation; after reconstruction, he gradually became convinced that the only opportunity for blacks to improve their condition was to go "anywhere except in the Southern States."

13
Following Reconstruction: Politics, Principles, and Patronage

Despite his feelings about emigration, Rapier still clung to the hope that perhaps some political solution could be achieved to assist blacks in their quest for individual dignity. A courageous president, determined to turn the tide against racism, could accomplish a great deal in the South. But who? He rejected President Hayes, who, due to internal party dissension, was not a viable candidate anyway; he refused to consider Grant, who by this time had virtually abandoned the Negro; nor was he willing to back Blaine, who seemed more concerned with urban problems than with the plight of Negroes. But he could, in good conscience, support Treasury Secretary John Sherman, one of the authors of the Reconstruction Acts, a long-time espouser of black political equality, and a man who had consistently spoken out against white terrorism in the South. It had also been Sherman who had so faithfully stood by him during the bitter controversy over the collectorship. Consequently, as early as the fall of 1879, he promised to use his considerable influence among Southern blacks in behalf of the secretary. "Whatever influence and energy I have," he told Sherman during a private meeting at the Treasury Department in Washington, "are at your service and you can command them at any time."[1]

The command came quickly. How important was the vote of the Alabama delegation at a national convention? Were there any prominent Republicans in the state who opposed his candidacy? If so, could anything be done to neutralize their influence? In response, Rapier stressed the historical significance of the Alabama delegation: as the leadoff state, its vote had traditionally affected the vote of other states; and at two recent national Republican conventions, the Alabama vote had decided the entire contest.

Henry Wilson, for instance, had defeated Schuyler Colfax for the
vice-presidential nomination in 1868, and Hayes had won over
James Blaine in 1876, both times by less than the voting strength of
Alabama. As to the internal opposition, he said that it was
formidable and that it included two of the most influential white
Republicans in the state, namely, United States Attorney Charles
Mayer, and United States Marshal George Turner, who were both
strongly pro-Grant. Like other federal officials, Rapier explained,
they had a tremendous opportunity to mold public opinion. "You
can see at a glance what an opportunity they have to spread their
views."[2] But, as both were men of obvious talent, he did not
suggest their removal. "We want will, but we must have ability."[3]
But to offset their influence, he promised to canvass the state in
Sherman's behalf, seeking delegate pledges for the forthcoming
state convention in Selma. He would leave immediately, in fact, for
the United States District Court session in Huntsville, where he
would meet with Republicans from across Alabama.

Conservative Republicans also backed Sherman, but not because
he had supported the aspirations of freedmen. Willard Warner
advised the secretary not to engage in partisan bickering over
Negro equality; rather, he should emphasize the issues of political
and economic reconciliation, as set forth in Lamar's speech to
Congress. If this were done, small businessmen, manufacturers,
bankers, and merchants across Alabama would enter the Sherman
camp. Probate Judge John V. McDuffie of Lowndes County,
chairman of the state executive committee, went even further,
openly declaring his desire to cooperate with the Democrats; while
Joseph Speed, another native Republican, pledged to advance
Sherman's cause in the business community because it could be
correctly claimed that the great business revival in the state was the
result of his efforts.

Such support placed Rapier in a predicament. If he continued his
fight against the conservative wing of the Republican party, he
would be working against the man he hoped would become president, but if he ceased agitation against the Warner-Smith group, he
would be compromising the principles he had been advocating
since the inception of reconstruction. Having fought too long and
too hard to yield principle for the sake of politics, he decided to
continue his battle against those who would advance economic
prosperity at the expense of Negro rights. In the spring of 1880 he

began yet another campaign against the anti-Negro Republicans, attacking with particular vehemence Judge McDuffie, who had harshly meted out long jail sentences to Negroes convicted of such minor violations as selling produce after sunset. In a round of speeches in Lowndes County, he urged blacks not to reelect the judge, who, he said, was a man of neither compassion nor humanity. McDuffie had it in his power to release Negroes accused of petty offenses, but he had failed to do so; instead, he had used his authority as an instrument of brutal oppression. So effective was Rapier's campaign that the judge asked Sherman to intervene, but even after the secretary suggested to him the impropriety of speaking out against McDuffie, or any fellow Republican, Rapier stood his ground, asserting that McDuffie's atrocious mismanagement of the criminal justice system had amounted to tyranny.

Conservative Republicans consequently accused Rapier of deceit, duplicity, and faithlessness. "I can fight Enemies but I am afraid of treachery," Warner scribbled in an almost illegible hand at the bottom of a letter to Sherman.[4] He knew the members of the Spencer faction personally; not one of them could be trusted, least of all Rapier, who had stood where he could have corrected the ignorant direction of Negroes, but who had not done so. Furthermore, Rapier's deputy collectors, Christopher Sheats, Robert Bryan, and Robert Reynolds, were actively campaigning for Grant. Reports had come to him from many quarters that such was the case. "I cannot discredit them, for I know from experience Rapier's treacherous character."[5] Other Republicans made equally harsh accusations. Former governor Smith, Judges Samuel Rice and Charles Buckley, and former Republican committeeman Robert Barber also impugned Rapier's integrity, describing him as disloyal, traitorous, and unfaithful. They, too, said that his deputies, with the assent and devious assistance of their chief, were speaking out against Sherman. Yet they reluctantly acknowledged the truth of Rapier's boast eight years before that he was the most powerful Republican in Alabama. Native whites could not control the delegates at the state convention unless pressure were brought on the Negro leader to do his duty; otherwise, as Barber admitted painfully, disastrous consequences would result. Even Warner agreed that pro-Sherman Republicans would be successful only if Rapier were brought into line.

After evaluating these imputative communications, Sherman

promptly dispatched a personal envoy, George Tichenor, to Montgomery to size up the situation. After consulting with Warner,
Smith, Rice, and Buckley at the Exchange Hotel, Tichenor observed that everyone seemed completely demoralized because
Rapier's deputies, as well as other federal officers, had been
actively campaigning for Grant. As the deputies were utterly
profligate—having been affected by money, falsehoods, and offers
of political appointments—he recommended that they should be
immediately discharged from government service. The outlook was
discouraging, even disheartening, he despaired, but if Rapier could
be influenced, there still might be a chance for a Sherman victory.

When Rapier entered the spacious and comfortably furnished
lobby of the Exchange Hotel the following day in response to a
summons from Tichenor, he was perplexed by the situation in
which he found himself. Though he could not bow to the Warner
faction, he decided that he would emphasize his genuine admiration for the treasury secretary rather than his antipathy for
opposition Republicans. In a long interview with Tichenor, he
explained that he would continue, as he had in the past, to work
earnestly in behalf of Sherman, promising to relay his preferences
to all federal employees in his service.

Everyone seemed satisfied. After their interview, Tichenor expressed a newfound optimism concerning Sherman's candidacy in
the deep South, remarking as he left Alabama that he was now
more hopeful than ever. Though not quite as optimistic, Smith,
Rice, and Buckley also said that there was a good chance that a
majority of the Republicans at the upcoming convention could now
be brought around. Even Warner, who had earlier said: "I don't
speak to Rapier of course. Can't talk to him," wrote that following
a brief conversation with Rapier, "I am satisfied he will now stand
by us."[6]

But Rapier had no intention of submitting to the opposition. At
Selma, he declined the nomination for temporary chairman offered
him by Judge McDuffie, and even when Warner and Smith
entreated him to accept the position, he refused. As a result, it went
to George Turner, a white lawyer who supported Grant for a third
term. According to Warner, the Grant chairman was arbitrary and
unfair to the last degree, adding bitterly that even when it became
obvious that the delegates were not going to back Sherman, Rapier
had done nothing. "We were beaten by foul."[7] Echoing the

sentiments of native Republicans and Bourbons alike, Warner charged that there were few, if any, blacks who could be trusted. Negroes had deserted their best friends and sold themselves to the enemy. "I don't hesitate to say that Rapier's refusal to take the advice of Genl. Warner," another Republican added in support, "was the starting point against us."[8] Thus, the bitter dilemma which had dogged him since his interview with Sherman a year before was now out in the open. Yet, he had refused the chairmanship not out of any ill will toward Sherman, who he still hoped would secure the nomination, but because he still refused, no matter what the political pressures, to capitulate to the conservative wing of the party.

The effect of his refusal, however, was the defeat of the pro-Sherman forces, as the delegates voted overwhelmingly (117 to 38) to support the former president for a third term. On the last day of the convention the members held district caucuses to elect representatives to attend the national convention; Republicans from the Fourth District (Dallas, Hale, Lowndes, Perry, Wilcox) selected William J. Stevens, an articulate young Negro from Dallas County, and Rapier. But shortly before the meeting adjourned, Grant partisans gathered in their own caucus, resolving that the entire state delegation should pledge themselves to the dictates of the majority.

This resolution, requiring every delegate to come forward and make a public pledge to support Grant, Rapier noted a few days later, was certainly an afterthought. Never before had such a resolution been passed at a Republican convention. But this did not deter the third-termers, who quickly sent him a telegram demanding that he make a declaration in writing promising to abide by the wishes of the majority. His election was subject to his acceptance of this pledge; if he refused to make such a declaration within twenty-four hours, his credentials as an Alabama delegate would be withheld. Quipping that an answer might require twenty-five hours, Rapier ignored the command.

But on May 31 when he arrived at the Palmer House, headquarters for the Alabama delegation in Chicago, he discovered that another delegate had been given his seat. Rapier quickly presented a claim to the Credentials Committee, asking whether a state convention had the authority to control the votes of district representatives? One newspaper, the Chicago *Times*, saw

this question as among the most important in American political history. If Rapier and two other delegates, Warner and
Smith, were admitted to the convention, the *Times* said, they
would be joined by five others in opposing Grant, but as things
stood, these duly elected delegates would be deprived of the right to
represent the wishes of their constituency. Could any state convention take away this right? Another observer went so far as to
declare that the survival of the Republican party depended upon
the equitable settlement of this very question. After a day-long
hearing, the Credentials Committee declared Rapier the properly
elected delegate from his district.

On the first ballot to nominate a presidential candidate, 93
delegates, including Rapier, voted for Sherman; 284 supported
James Blaine; and 304, only 70 short of the necessary majority, cast
their ballots for Grant. But after a solid week of balloting, despite
the maneuverings of Senator Roscoe Conkling, Commissioner
Raum, and others to secure the nomination for Grant, the former
president's total remained exactly the same at 304 votes, though
neither Blaine nor Sherman had mustered enough support to secure
the nomination. Then, on the thirty-fifth ballot, the deadlock was
broken when a number of Sherman partisans switched to a
dark-horse candidate, James A. Garfield, and on the following
ballot the convention chairman announced Garfield as the Republican nominee for president. When it was decided by his friends that
Sherman could not pull through, Tichenor wrote his chief from
Chicago the next day, the Sherman partisans all turned to General
Garfield. "In that sense you dictated the nomination." Included
among those friends were three Alabamians: Warner, Smith, and
Rapier, who voted for the secretary until the final ballot. Thus,
three bitter political adversaries had remained faithful to
Sherman—Warner and Smith because they wanted peace and
prosperity, and Rapier because he dreamed of a time when blacks
in Alabama and the South, free from intimidation, could vote, hold
office, and participate in the decisions that molded their destiny.

But such a dream was as fleeting as a summer thundershower,
and Rapier, who had always been more of a pragmatist than a
visionary, quickly returned to his efforts to resettle blacks in the
West. Accompanied by William Ash, a prominent Alabama Negro,
he traveled once again to Kansas, inspected a number of possible
sites for the colonization of Southern blacks, especially in Saline,

Shawnee, and Wabaunsee counties, and finally decided to purchase
an eighty-acre stretch of land (in Wabaunsee) along the route of the
Kansas-Pacific Railway. Returning to Montgomery, he and Ash
mounted a determined campaign to convince sharecroppers in
Alabama that Kansas offered them an unequaled opportunity for
economic advancement. Negroes there were prosperous, had built
neat and comfortable homes, and were gradually acquiring their
own farms. It was a glorious country. Following a quick succession
of emigration meetings in Hayneville, Montgomery, and Union
Springs, the Montgomery *Daily Advertiser* nervously noted that
two of the most radical Negro politicians in the state were on the
stump urging tenant farmers to leave the South. But a short time
later, with a sigh of relief, the same paper observed that though
Rapier and Ash had exerted every conceivable effort to induce the
Negro masses to join the movement, they had met with little
success. Nine out of every ten blacks had not taken a jot of interest.

But Rapier remained convinced that blacks should leave the
South. He journeyed to Kansas a half dozen times during the early
1880s, and each time, upon his return to Alabama, made a new
round of speeches urging his brethren to emigrate. Interviewed by a
Washington correspondent after one such speech, he lambasted
Alabama, where, he said, there was more poverty and more
ignorance among freedmen than there had been during reconstruction. Prospects for any improvement seemed extremely remote.
Short crops, small returns, enormous prices, worn-out soil, a lack
of available land, and white oppression had caused virtual desti-
tution among the masses. He prayed that he could persuade his
brethren to strike out on their own for a land that promised larger
returns and better soil.

Rapier even considered moving West himself, and during a
fifteen-day leave of absence as collector he investigated the possibility of purchasing more land in the Sunflower State. Returning
home via Madison County, he explained to the Negro editor of the
Huntsville *Gazette*, Charles Hendley, that the West was a region
where every man could depend on his own resources. He saw this,
in itself, as being a powerful inducement for Negroes to emigrate
from the South. But because he was beginning to suffer from
prolonged coughing spells and a steady deterioration of his health,
he decided against leaving Alabama, though he continued to be
deeply wedded to the concept of black migration.

Neither his declining health nor his extensive travels, however, seemed to curtail his business activities. Between 1880 and 1883, in part to finance his emigration schemes, he greatly expanded his cotton acreage. In the first year, he borrowed over a thousand dollars from Meyer Lehman, of Lehman and Durr and Company, purchased the necessary teams, provisions, and farming implements, employed fifteen tenant farmers, and rented acreage on three plantations (Lee, Shelby, and Bell plantations, in Lowndes County), planting, cultivating, and harvesting some one hundred fifty bales of cotton. The following year, he secured a two-thousand-dollar loan, further enlarged his operations (to Jones, James, Watts, and Caldwell plantations in the same county) and marketed nearly two hundred bales. In 1882, he borrowed nearly three thousand dollars, again enlarged his acreage, now employing thirty-one Negro tenant workers, and in the fall of that year, he took three hundred bales to the cotton exchange in Montgomery. Selling it for forty dollars per bale, he made a net profit of five thousand dollars. Such an income elevated him to a position of wealth and economic standing, even in the white-dominated society of postwar Alabama. Although his success was due in part to a reviving economy, it also stemmed from a long family tradition of business enterprise.

Several of Rapier's tenants, as well as other Negros in the area, also achieved a measure of economic self-sufficiency. Sharecropper O. O. Thomas, who started out in 1878 harvesting only three bales of cotton, by 1882 was employing ten farmhands, operating on a budget of three thousand dollars (including a seven-hundred-sixty-dollar loan from Rapier), and transporting forty bales to the exchange. After expenses, Thomas cleared over a thousand dollars, an income that made him the equal, in purely monetary terms, of many middle-class whites. In the same year, another cropper, Charles Alexander, harvested two hundred fifty bushels of corn, two hundred stalks of sugarcane, one hundred fifty bushels of potatoes, and twelve bales of cotton; and David Norman, a tenant near Calhoun Village, made two hundred bushels of oats, six hundred bushels of corn, and nine bales of cotton. Despite these success stories, Rapier realized that the vast majority of blacks lived in grim poverty, barely subsisting from day to day, and consequently, he never swayed from his belief that the West, or the North, offered the best hope for economic advancement. It was only through emigration that blacks could hope to achieve America's promise of economic prosperity.

During this period he also administered the office of Internal

Revenue. Shortly after beginning his official duties (July 1878), he published the revenue regulations in the columns of the *Republican Sentinel and Hayneville Times*, explaining that the law required (1) all liquor distillers to register with the Treasury Department, (2) wholesale dealers to pay an annual tax of one hundred dollars, (3) retail dealers, who sold less than five gallons at a time, to pay a twenty-five-dollar yearly tax, and (4) tobacco dealers to pay four dollars, though the latter provision did not include planters who sold tobacco to their hands as a convenience. He also issued a stern warning: any violators of that law would be quickly prosecuted. To demonstrate the sincerity of this admonition, he mounted a statewide campaign, seizing illegal stills, caps, and worms, confiscating tobacco, beer, and whiskey, and requiring law-breakers to appear for trial in Montgomery. He personally journeyed to the Isaac Cantrell plantation in Marion County to destroy a huge private distillery, which was producing two thousand gallons of beer and one hundred gallons of whiskey a month; and he dispatched an armed force of revenue agents to the northern part of the state. His rigorous enforcement of the revenue statutes brought illegal distilling in Alabama to a virtual standstill.

Local residents, as well as Treasury Department officials, carefully scrutinized the work of the only high-ranking black official in the state. It was the opinion of one Mr. Greil, owner of a wholesale grocery store in Montgomery, that since Rapier had become collector the revenue laws had been better enforced and legitimate dealers better protected, than at any other time in Alabama history. Even greater praise came from Treasury Agent P. H. Downing, who, during a thirty-state inspection tour, asserted that Rapier was one of the most efficient officers in the entire nation. He was first class in every respect; his district was in superior condition; his deputies were all active, vigilant, honest, capable, and acted in perfect accord with the collector. Completely satisfied with the administration of the Montgomery office, Commissioner Green B. Raum wrote Rapier that he was extremely pleased with the suppression of illegal distilling in Alabama. "This excellent condition of your office, maintained under the pressure of extra work, indicate [sic] a gratifying degree of energy and zeal on the part of yourself and four assistants. Your grade is first class."[9]

Yet, opposition Republicans, though foiled in their attempt to block his confirmation as collector, continued a strenuous campaign to have Rapier removed from office. As might have been expected, a coalition of Warner, Smith, Rice, and McDuffie argued that Rapier was devious, immoral, and unreliable, had caused the factional fights between Republicans, had brought the party down to defeat in 1870 and again in 1874, and had betrayed his constituency at the Chicago convention. "With a good native Republican in Rapier's place," Warner wrote, "we will be pretty well rid of the Spencer gang in Alabama."[10] Unexpected, though, was a printed leaflet, signed by several hundred blacks, denouncing the Negro collector as utterly profligate and lacking in the essential qualities of honesty and integrity. Repudiating him as their leader, they, too, demanded his removal, claiming that his hypocrisy, bad faith, and acts of selfish aggrandizement were intolerable. Swayed by these arguments, President Arthur suspended Rapier in September 1882, pending an investigation.

By this time Rapier's declining health had become increasingly apparent. He was afflicted with deep chest pains and prolonged coughing spells and was under the intermittent care of a physician. Nevertheless, he rose to his own defense. In a ten-page letter to the president, he emphasized his past loyalty: he had helped organize the Republican party in Alabama; had remained faithful to Grant, even when such loyalty had nearly cost him his life; and had run for Congress on an equal rights platform, later speaking out in behalf of a national civil rights law. He also said that he had given full satisfaction to the Treasury Department by almost completely suppressing illegal whiskey-making in his district. In sum, he concluded, "My Republicanism has never been questioned. I am sure I have done something to popularize Negro suffrage. My stance in business circles is good. My office is first class."[11]

To further his cause, he traveled to Washington, discussed the attacks on his character with Commissioner Raum, and soon received Raum's unqualified endorsement: he was one of the most earnest, most conscientious, and most practical of the representative blacks that freedom and citizenship had brought to the fore. But a Negro newspaper in the city noted shortly after his visit that Rapier had been in poor health for several months and that during his stay in Washington the evidences of his physical debilitation had become even more noticeable.

The response of hundreds of Alabamians—white and black, Democrat and Republican, Northerner and native—to the assault on his character was a moving tribute to Rapier as a man and a leader. No man stood any higher in the esteem of fair-minded Alabamians than he, a white Republican exclaimed: he was educated, accomplished, and had discharged the duties of his office with ability, fidelity, and honesty. Expressing the same thought, another white observer said that his wisdom, honesty, and ability commanded the respect of all Southerners, regardless of complexional differences. Analyzing the political milieu of reconstruction Alabama, B. M. Long, chairman of the Republican executive committee in Walker County, explained that after Negro enfranchisement, many white Republicans refused to support or even associate with blacks. The demoralization of the party could be traced to that fact. "Race prejudice must be wiped out. Justice must be done. When we have a good officer like Rapier, he should be retained."

Even conservative Republicans came to his defense. Judge Lewis Parsons, Jr., and congressional candidate G. R. Miller praised him as the ablest and foremost representative of his race in Alabama. Socially, he was the peer of any man; he exercised a wide and wholesome influence over blacks. Even a few Democrats defended him. If the feelings of the fifteen thousand Negroes in his congressional district were any indication, an ex-Confederate candidate for Congress said, no politician in America was more universally esteemed. And the president of Lehman and Durr and Company, Meyer Lehman, acknowledged that among the several thousand of his customers over nearly a decade, not one had been more prompt or reliable.

From the highest levels of government as well as from various groups of Negroes came support for the beleaguered black official. Commissioner Raum praised the collector for performing the duties of his office in an excellent manner; Revenue Agent Jacob Wagner extolled his good judgment and efficient managerial skills; United States Senator Henry W. Blair of New Hampshire lauded him as one of the most outstanding Negro leaders in the South; and Senator Windom of Minnesota commended him as a man of wisdom, worth, influence, and integrity. Blacks were particularly upset over the attack on their champion. In behalf of all Negroes who were striving to elevate themselves and lead honest, industrious, and virtuous lives, a presiding elder in the African Methodist Church pleaded that Rapier not be removed; he was the foremost representative black man in Alabama. Montgomery Negro J. N. Fitzpatrick also commended him as a most prominent Negro, a staunch defender of equal rights, and a dedicated Republican. And black tenant farmer Jack Daw poignantly asked: Why had this ungrateful and unkind blow been struck at Rapier? Was his office not clean? Had he not made a faithful and honest officer? Was his Republicanism not good? Was it not patent to every thinking mind that it was only because of his color?

In the midst of the controversy, Rapier opened the campaign of 1882. Though not a candidate himself, and though in failing health, he used the political rostrum once again to attack Conservatism. In speeches at Hayneville, Lowndesboro, Burkeville, and Fort Depost, in Lowndes County, he assailed the sunrise-sunset laws (which prohibited the selling of goods during the evening hours) and blasted the pending county prohibition law. "That is [he] favors stealing and drunkenness," the Hayneville *Examiner* opprobriously commented, "and wants the deadfalls set up again so our farmers can have their crops carried off in the night and sold for whiskey."[12] He attended the state Republican convention in Montgomery (July), and, along with other pro-Spencer Republicans, demanded reforms in the convict lease system, a more liberal state expenditure for public schools, and an amendment to the Alabama election law that would assure every qualified voter that his ballot would be faithfully counted. Serving as permanent chairman of the Fourth District nominating convention in Selma a few weeks later, he supported former circuit judge George Craig and a Negro former state legislator John W. Jones for the two vacancies in Congress (one for the second session of the Forty-seventh Congress created when Charles Shelley was expelled for voting irregularities during his election and the other for a seat in the Forty-eighth Congress). Once their nominations were secured, he asked all Republicans to support them as the regular nominees. But a group of dissidents, led by Lowndes County politicians Benjamin DeLomas and John McDuffie, bolted, held a separate convention in Greensboro, and nominated Hale County Negro Merritt Howze for the latter term. Exhausted by the canvass and suffering from shortness of breath, Rapier could only send a letter to the convention in an attempt to dissuade the members from putting an additional candidate in the field. He failed. Though a Democratic paper predicted that the chances were excellent that the district would have a Negro representative in Congress, the Conservative candidate Shelley defeated Jones, Craig, and Howze, the latter receiving only 157 votes, compared to Craig's 4435, Jones' 4811, and Shelley's 7159.

Although Rapier's physical condition deteriorated rapidly in the months following the election, he continued his fight to retain his post as collector. Dictating another letter to the president early in 1883, he asked that several more letters of recommendation be added to those on file, but when he finally received notification in March that he would be kept on, it was too late. Completely debilitated by a deepening cough and a continuous fever, he wrote in a weak and trembling hand, thanking the president for past favors, but tendering his resignation as collector in the Second District. That such a long struggle would end in a Pyrrhic victory was perhaps symbolic of all his efforts during the post–Civil War era. Subsequently, he received notice that he had been selected as a federal disbursing officer for a new government building in Montgomery, and though he accepted the position (posting a ten-thousand-dollar bond), his condition had worsened by the time construction began, and on May 31, 1883, at the age of forty-five, he died of pulmonary tuberculosis. At the request of his uncle James P. Thomas, his remains were transported to St. Louis, where he was buried, unceremoniously, in an unmarked grave.

Obituary notices appeared in numerous newspapers. The Huntsville *Gazette* said that he left his people a priceless heritage of honesty and integrity. Ironically, the highest tribute came not from a Negro newspaper but from the Conservative journal that had most consistently assailed him during his career in Alabama politics. During the trial of United States Marshal Paul Strobach, accused of making false claims against the government, the Montgomery *Daily Advertiser* editorialized that while the air was thick with rumors of indictments against United States officials for malfeasance in office, the death of James Rapier directed public attention to him as a conspicuous example of official integrity and blameless private life in the community. There had never been a breath of suspicion, the *Advertiser* exulted, nor a syllable of accusation against his fidelity, uprightness, or efficiency in the discharge of his public duties.

Most Alabamians, however, refused to accept the accomplishments of men like Rapier. Instead, they agreed with an editorial appearing in the Marion County *True Democrat* at the time of his death. The Negro, it read, had no appreciation for Christianity, his religious worship being idolatry; he had no moral or social status, his nature being emotional and irrational; and he could not recognize his obligations to society, away from manual labor, his natural sphere. It was self-evident that the Negro should be disfranchised, and that the obnoxious amendments granting him the vote should be repealed. Alabama was a white man's land; the sooner that fact was recognized by the American people, the better it would be for everyone.

Rapier's life made a mockery of such contentions. He not only understood his obligations to society, but threw himself into the crusade to assist freedmen in their struggle for political rights, economic opportunity, and social dignity. He worked for peaceful relations between whites and blacks, and most importantly, he realized, perhaps better than any of his contemporaries, that the final reconstruction of Alabama would depend on racial equality.

Epilogue

The life of James Thomas Rapier poignantly illustrates the inadequacy of conservative sterotypes in recounting the era of reconstruction and the Negro in American history. Dignified, intelligent, principled, and fully aware of his heritage in slavery and freedom, Rapier spent his life trying to improve the social, political, and economic condition of blacks in Alabama and the South. He urged freedmen to accept the responsibilities of citizenship and use the ballot to express their wishes; he organized a Negro labor union in Alabama and helped establish a national association of black workingmen to assist freedmen in obtaining land as well as to ease the plight of black tenant farmers. He personally advanced the interests of numerous sharecroppers and day laborers in his home state. As a congressman, he was a leading spokesman for the 1875 civil rights law, suggested a plan for a national system of public education, and urged Negroes to save their money and educate their children. Throughout his career, despite political pressures, personal attacks, and attempts to bribe him, he clung steadfastly to the principles of political and economic equality for blacks. And his determined, dedicated, and persistent efforts in behalf of his brethren refute the contention of some historians that Negroes in reconstruction (and afterward) were ignorant dupes, unequal to the challenge of nineteenth-century American life.

At the same time, always respectful of the attitudes of white Southerners, he never demanded social equality, mixed schools, or the amalgamation of the races. At the constitutional convention of 1867, he supported a mild disfranchisement clause and a lenient oath of office; in 1868 he favored amnesty for all former Confederates who accepted Negro suffrage and the citizenship clause of the

Fourteenth Amendment. While in Congress he submitted a river
improvement bill to aid the white counties in his district. In his
numerous campaign speeches, convention resolutions, public talks,
and congressional proposals, he never incited racial animosities,
nor did he ever use race as a campaign issue. He so dreaded
violence that on one occasion he placed his political future in
jeopardy by signing a pledge to avert an impending riot. Yet such
an abhorrence to violence and sensitivity to white mores not only
hastened his own political downfall, but caused him great personal
pain. Friendly and outgoing in his private relationships (though
stately, reserved, and dignified in his public appearances), he
anguished over his exclusion from Southern society.

Some historians have asserted that carpetbaggers, scalawags,
and Negroes deviously conspired to subjugate "the intelligence of
Alabama and the south," while Conservative whites, disunited
throughout the period, finally banded together (1874) to rescue the
state from the rule of Africans. This study suggests a contrary
view. From the first Republican nominating convention in 1867
until some time after the Robinson-Strobach fight in 1874, the state
Republican party was torn by internal feuds and disputes over the
very nature of black citizenship. Conservative Republicans, including William Smith, Willard Warner, Arthur Bingham, J. Caleb
Wiley, William Buckley, Robert Knox, and others, all, at one time
or another, opposed Rapier, and on occasion denounced him as
"nothing but a nigger." One of the many ironies of Alabama
reconstruction is the fact that these Republicans, made up mainly
of so-called scalawags, joined the party to guide Negroes in their
new freedom, but were unwilling to accept blacks once they had
attained that freedom.

On the other hand, the Democracy was united against blacks
from the outset. Though Walter Lynwood Fleming, who is still
revered for his thoroughness and informativeness by some scholars,
contended that the disparate factions within the White Man's Party
were forced to come together in order to save the white race from
humiliation and degradation, Fleming himself unwittingly admitted
the cohesiveness of the Democracy by using the term *White Man's
Party*. A close examination of Rapier's career indicates the con-
tinuity of this Conservative anti-Negro feeling. In every political
campaign of the period, except in 1872, when federal courts were
indicting hundreds on Klan charges, the Democrats attacked Rapier

on racial grounds: in 1868 they accused him of trying to "Africanize
Alabama," forcing him to flee from Florence; in 1870 they expressed
great humiliation that a Negro might achieve a high state office;
and in 1874 they promised to win the state or "exterminate the
niggers." Such hostility, indicative of whites in both parties,
suggests that reconstruction was doomed to failure from the outset.

Following reconstruction Rapier counseled his Negro followers
to leave the South. Disillusioned, and, to some extent, embittered,
he advised black tenant farmers that the only way to earn a living
wage, get an adequate education, and secure equal political rights
was to emigrate. Indeed, at the time Rapier testified before the
Senate Exodus Committee, few Southern blacks owned land, most
paid exorbitant rents and interest, and none could send their
children to public schools for more than a few months a year. The
Alabama Negro Labor Union, like its national counterpart, had
made no practical gains for black laborers, and the national civil
rights law had become a dead letter everywhere in the states of the
old Confederacy, as blacks were unable to serve on juries, enter
public places, ride in public conveyances, or (because of a system
of voter fraud, discriminatory local laws, and Democratic gerrymandering) participate meaningfully in politics.

The stigma of color confronted Rapier in all his efforts to better
the condition of his race. With few exceptions, whites believed that
black people belonged to an unalterably lower caste in the social,
political, and economic scale, that the most educated and cultured
black person was beneath the most ignorant and depraved white.
In the atmosphere of reconstruction and post-reconstruction Alabama, it is not surprising that Rapier failed to solve the problems of
hunger, ignorance, and individual dignity. It is surprising, however,
that he never gave up the struggle.

Chronology: James T. Rapier

1837	Born in Florence, Alabama, the son of John H. Rapier, Sr., a free Negro barber, and Susan Rapier, also a free Negro.
1844–1850	Lived with his slave grandmother, Sally, and slave uncle, James P. Thomas, while attending school in Nashville, Tennessee.
1854–1856	Went on the river gambling.
1856–1864	Attended school in Buxton, Canada West, and Toronto, living with his fugitive slave uncle, Henry K. Thomas.
1864	Received a teaching certificate and taught school at Buxton.
1864–1865	Returned to the South, working for a time as a correspondent for a northern newspaper, and later, delivering a keynote address at the Tennessee Negro Suffrage Convention in Nashville.
1866	Returned to Florence, Alabama, rented several hundred acres of land, and became a successful cotton planter.
1867	Organized Negroes in northwest Alabama under the congressional reconstruction acts, attended the first state Republican convention, and won a seat at the Alabama constitutional convention.
1868	Campaigned in behalf of Ulysses Grant, but was driven from Lauderdale County by the Ku Klux Klan.

1869	Attended the first National Negro Labor Convention in Washington, D.C.
1870	Became the first Negro in Alabama history to run for state office (secretary of state), but was defeated.
1871	Received an appointment as Assessor of Internal Revenue and organized the Alabama Negro Labor Union.
1872–1873	Presided over the first meeting of the Alabama Negro Labor Union, defeated William C. Oates for a seat in the Forty-third Congress, and accepted an appointment as state commissioner to the Fifth World Exposition in Vienna, Austria, visiting Europe for five months.
1874–1876	Spoke in favor of the national civil rights bill in Congress, introduced legislation to improve America's commercial water lanes, and voted to regulate railroad rates, but was defeated in both of his bids for reelection in 1874 and 1876.
1878–1883	Appointed Collector of Internal Revenue for the Second District of Alabama, and became an active emigrationist.

Primary Source Material and Nineteenth-Century Black Biography

Historians have long lamented the dearth of primary sources concerning blacks in the nineteenth century. Writing forty years ago, a frustrated W. E. B. DuBois charged that Alabama officials had wantonly destroyed trunks of important documents relating to Negroes in reconstruction. More recently, a discouraged Robin W. Winks anguished that he had uncovered only a handful of middle-period Negro letters and writings during his ten-year research project on blacks in Canada. As a consequence, scholars, including DuBois and Winks, have been forced to rely on the testimony of white observers, despite the obvious (and readily admitted) biases and deficiences of such material in recounting the black experience. Authorities on Negro slavery, for example, have used such primary sources as local newspapers, plantation records, and travelers' accounts; writers concerned with free Negroes have depended on state statutes, petitions to various legislatures, and the accounts of contemporary whites; and researchers of black reconstruction have quoted extensively from white newspapers, the memoirs of white politicians, and again, the observations of white landowners, travelers, and public officials. Perhaps no aspect of black history has suffered more from this scarcity of Negro primary sources, or the biases and inadequacy of white testimony, than black biography.

This study is not free from either of these deficiencies. Though Rapier corresponded often with labor union organizers, internal revenue officials, fellow Republicans, and members of the Rapier-Thomas family, though he probably composed several thousand letters during his life, and though the *Daily State Sentinel* in 1867 said: "He keeps up an extensive correspondence writing late into the night," only seventy of these letters have been preserved for posterity. And among them, embarrassing gaps exist; between 1862 and 1869, for instance, there is no extant Rapier correspondence. In addition, though black newspapers thrived during the era, though at least twelve black-owned, black-edited, and black-published Alabama papers were printed for a year or more, and though the Huntsville *Gazette* said in 1880: "We have four colored newspapers in Alabama, two in Huntsville, one in Montgomery, and one in Marion," only a scattering of issues have been placed in repositories. One number of Rapier's *Republican Sentinel*, and one of his *Republican Sentinel and Hayneville Times*, for example, have been preserved, while only one issue of the Montgomery *Advance*, a Conservative journal edited by James Scott, and two numbers of the *Alabama Republican*, edited by Rapier's friend and political ally, Charles Harris, have been saved. The situation is even worse for the Mobile *Watchman* (edited by Philip Joseph), the *Republican Banner* (published by the Negro Republican Association of Montgomery), the Huntsville *Herald* (edited by Negro educator William Councill), and the Montgomery *Watchman* (owned by another of Rapier's cohorts, A. E. Williams). There are no extant issues.

In contrast, white Republican newspapers have been meticulously preserved for future reference, but, unfortunately, they often exclude material about blacks. The single most important party journal in the state, the *Alabama State Journal*, printed only a few lines about the 1872 Montgomery Negro Labor Union Convention and not a word about Rapier's crucial political campaign in 1874. The administration newspaper in the northern part of the state, the Huntsville *Advocate*, neglected to report a major campaign address by Rapier in that city (1870), though it devoted several pages to a speech of Alabama governor William Smith, who had also made a campaign stop in Huntsville. The *Elmore Republican* not only omitted news items relating to freedmen, but at times opposed black aspirants for political office.

Conservative newspapers ignored the activities of blacks to an even greater extent. In 1870, at the Selma nominating convention, Rapier delivered an hour-long speech concerning "Republicanism and the Negro in Alabama." The Democratic Selma *Times*, after printing lengthy extracts from the speeches of Alabama attorney general Joshua Morse and DeKalb County probate judge Nicholas Davis, concluded an article on the convention by saying: "Rapier, having been called for repeatedly, made a speech, which we cannot

publish, owing that our reporter left the Convention." Likewise, in
1872, at the height of his political power, Rapier spoke to a large
gathering in Barbour County. The Eufaula *Daily Times*, printing
paragraph summaries of speeches by Judge E. M. Keils, County
Solicitor R. D. Locke, and Congressman C. W. Buckley, stated:
"J. R. [*sic*] Rapier of Montgomery also made a speech, but we did
not hear it."

Conservative newspapers that did offer information about Negroes often presented erroneous, highly biased, and disparaging
commentary. The Mobile *Daily Register* called Rapier a "Carpetbagger from Canada," while the Tuskegee *Weekly News* opprobriously termed him a "yellow nigger." The Florence *Journal* said
that Rapier was an ignorant individual, but a very loud talker, a
regular blower, and asserted that he was a subject of Great Britain.
Shortly after he testified at the Senate exodus hearings, the
Montgomery *Daily Advertiser* confessed surprise that Rapier had
been demoralized by Radicalism and his Radical associates.

The evidence, of course, refutes these defamations. Rapier's
schooling in Buxton did not qualify him as a carpetbagger from
Canada. Indeed, he was proud of his birthplace and of the fact that
his parents were buried along the banks of the beautiful Tennessee
River. Further, there is no proof to suggest that he claimed
allegiance to England in 1867, though he was outspoken in his
disapproval of the Republican state ticket. And finally, Rapier had
pressed Negroes to leave Alabama in 1879, having considered
emigration as a possible solution to the problems facing Southern
blacks as early as 1869; to contend that he had been "Radicalized"
at the time of the Senate emigration investigations (1880) is
indicative of the naiveté and nescience of Democratic newspapers
with regard to the attitudes and activities of Negroes.

But despite these vicissitudes—the paucity of personal correspondence, the lack of Negro newspapers, and the obvious
prejudices and predilections of white journals—it is possible, by
closely examining extant Negro letters and newspapers and judi-
ciously using white sources, to fully recount the life of a black
reconstructionist and to do so from a black perspective. This study
has relied on four traditional sources of information: correspondence, county records, newspapers, and printed public documents.
Though scattered in repositories from Ottawa, Ontario, to New
Orleans, Louisiana, letters written by James Rapier contain in-

formation about every phase of his life. Correspondence (twelve letters) concerning his experiences in Canada, his family relationships, and his attitudes during the antebellum period can be found in the Rapier Papers, procured by John Hope Franklin in 1948 for the Moorland-Spingarn Research Center at Howard University in Washington, D.C. The collection also includes seventy-two other letters written by various members of the Rapier family, as well as newspaper clippings, ledgers, a diary, account books, a registry of important events, and the revealing miscellaneous notes and autobiographical reminiscences of James P. Thomas. Letters relating to his Treasury Department appointments and patronage activities (fifteen in number) can be found in the Internal Revenue collections at the National Archives, Washington, D.C., while his political correspondence (twenty letters) can be seen in the John Chandler, Paul Strobach, and John Sherman papers at the Library of Congress as well as in the William Smith, Wager Swayne, Lewis Parsons, and Robert Patton collections at the State Department of Archives and History in Montgomery, Alabama. His work as an educator and labor leader is documented in Rapier letters (six) in the American Missionary Association Papers, Dillard University, New Orleans, and the William King manuscripts, National Archives of Canada, Ottawa, Ontario. Other correspondence concerning various aspects of his career can be found in newspapers, probate court minutes, and the proceedings of Negro conventions.

Newspapers, court records, and printed government documents also provide valuable information about Alabama's leading Negro reconstructionist. His congressional pursuits, Internal Revenue responsibilities, and attitudes on black migration are examined by the Huntsville *Gazette*, edited by Negro Charles Hendley, and the *New National Era*, organized by Frederick Douglass; his political campaigns, labor union involvement, and black convention activities (both state and national) are recounted in the *Daily State Sentinel*, edited by John Hardy, the *Alabama State Journal*, when edited by William Loftin, and (to a lesser extent) in the Conservative Montgomery *Daily Advertiser*, and Union Springs *Times*. His personal financial transactions as a cotton planter, land purchaser, land renter, and moneylender can be traced in the land, mortgage, and will records of Lauderdale, Montgomery, and Loundes counties, Alabama. Also documented in these holdings as well as in court records in Davidson County, Tennessee; St. Louis, Missouri;

and Erie County, New York, are the economic activities of other members of the Rapier-Thomas family. Rapier's congressional career, his work as a labor unionist, educational reformer, and emigrationist are outlined in the *Congressional Record*, *House Journal*, House and Senate *Reports* and *Miscellaneous Documents*. These records also contain testimony on Alabama elections, reports on Negro migration, the Report of the Committee on Education and Labor (Forty-third Congress), minutes of Alabama Negro Labor Union meetings, and proceedings of various other Negro conventions.

Although primary source material concerning blacks is admittedly rare, especially when compared to the voluminous manuscript collections relating to whites, a thorough perusal of traditional sources can produce a surprising amount of valuable and pertinent information. Despite many difficulties, black biography is absolutely necessary if historians are to fully understand the complexities and ambiguities of American society in the mid-nineteenth century.

Abbreviations Used in Notes and Bibliography

AHQ	*Alabama Historical Quarterly*
AHR	*American Historical Review*
AR	*Alabama Review*
CWH	*Civil War History*
JAH	*Journal of American History*
JNH	*Journal of Negro History*
JSH	*Journal of Southern History*
JSocH	*Journal of Social History*
MVHR	*Mississippi Valley Historical Review*
RDJ-LFJ	Records of the Department of Justice, Letters Relating to the Appointment of Federal Judges. RG 60.
RDT-ACC	Records of the Department of the Treasury, Applications for Collectors of Customs. RG 56.
RDT-AIR	Records of the Department of the Treasury, Applications for Assessors of Internal Revenue. RG 56.
RDT-CIR	Records of the Department of the Treasury, Applications for Collectors of Internal Revenue. RG 56.
RG	Record Group

Notes

Prologue

Newspapers consulted include *Alabama State Journal, Colored Tennessean, Daily State Sentinel, New National Era, Southern Republican.* Secondary sources consulted include (for complete bibliographical information see section 8 of the Bibliography) Bennett, Berlin, Blassingame, Bond, Brown, Cash, Christopher, Coulter, Curry ("The Civil War"), DuBois, Dunning, Feldman, Fleming, Fogel and Engerman, Franklin, Genovese, Gutman, Haskins, Kolchin, Lamson, Litwack, Lynch, Meier ("Comment"), Albert Moore, Muller, Owen, Patrick, Rhodes, Robinson, Rogers, Stampp, Stephenson, Sterkx, Taylor ("Historians"), Uya, Vincent, Weisberger, Wharton, Wikramanayake, Williamson, Woolfolk [Wiggins].

1. *Southern Republican*, May 11, 1870.

2. James Ford Rhodes, *History of the United States*, 6 (New York, 1906): 156, 157.

3. Walter Fleming, *The Civil War and Reconstruction in Alabama* (New York, 1905), pp. 403, 537, 553, 772. Fleming erred continually in his factual presentation concerning blacks in reconstruction, describing James Rapier, for instance, as a carpetbagger from Canada, a member of the Forty-Second Congress, and an espouser of "social equality."

4. Quoted in Leon Litwack and Kenneth Stampp, eds., *Reconstruction: An Anthology* (Baton Rouge, 1969), p. 421.

5. *Colored Tennessean*, August 17, 1865.

6. Lerone Bennett, Jr., *Before the Mayflower: A History of the Negro in America* (Chicago, 1962), pp. 202–3.

7. Maurine Christopher, *America's Black Congressmen* (New York, 1971), p. 127.

Chapter 1

Primary sources consulted include (on Sally) Records of the Albemarle [Virginia] Court, Deeds, books 6, 9, 32; Thomas Autobiography (see section 1 of Bibliography); (on riverman Richard Rapier) Records of the Davidson County [Tennessee] Court, Minutes, vol. C, Deeds, vol. M; Records of the Maury County [Tennessee] Court, Wills, vol. 1; Records of the Lauderdale

County [Alabama] Court, Deeds, vol. 1; *Acts of the Alabama General Assembly* (1830) (see section 3 of Bibliography); (on Henry and James Thomas) Thomas Autobiography; Miscellaneous Notes of James Thomas; Rapier Papers; *Buffalo City Directory* (1842) (see section 3 of Bibliography); (on other Negroes) *Nashville Business Directory* (1853); Catherine Avery Papers; Tennessee Legislative Petitions; Records of the Davidson County [Tennessee] Court, Minutes, book E, Wills, vol. 16, Deeds, books 22, 33; *Fourth, Fifth, Sixth, Seventh Census of the United States* (see section 3 of Bibliography); (on legal status) *Acts of the Alabama General Assembly*; *Acts of the Tennessee General Assembly* (see section 3 of Bibliography). Newspapers consulted include *Alabama Republican*, Florence *Enquirer, Gazette, Journal, Republican*, Nashville *Banner, Clarion and Gazette, Daily Gazette, Daily Press and Times, Daily Times and True Union, Republican, Whig, Tennessee Gazette, Impartial Review and Cumberland Repository*. Secondary sources consulted include Blassingame (*Slave Community*), Brewer, Clayton, Fogel and Engerman, Folmsbee, Franklin (*From Slavery*), Freeman, Frederickson, Genovese (*Roll, Jordan, Roll*), Gutman, Hamer, Jordon, Albert Moore, John Moore, Owen Schweninger ("A Slave Family," "Free-Slave Phenomenon"), Stampp (*Peculiar Institution*), Toplin.

1. Thomas Autobiography, chap. 1.

2. Records of the Lauderdale County [Alabama] Court, Wills, vol. 6 (June 3, 1827), p. 117; *Acts of the Eleventh Annual Session of the Alabama General Assembly* (Tuscaloosa, Ala., 1830), p. 36.

3. Thomas Autobiography, pp. 1–6.

4. Ibid., p. 3.

5. Ibid., chaps. 1, 2. In the original manuscript many pages are either unnumbered or numbered two or three times with different numbers; so in some instances I have cited only the chapter. The "Miscellaneous Notes" were written on scraps of paper, backs of envelopes, and even shopping bags, and are not numbered by page. They were composed at various times between 1887 and 1902.

6. John H. Rapier, Sr., to Henry K. Thomas, February 28, 1843, Rapier Papers.

7. John H. Rapier, Sr., to Richard Rapier, April 8, 1845, Rapier Papers.

8. Ellen S. Fogg to E. H. Roster, February 15, 1849, Foster Papers.

9. Thomas Autobiography, chap. 2.

10. Ibid.

11. *Nashville General Business Directory* (Nashville, 1853), p. 68.

12. Thomas Autobiography, p. 64.

13. Ibid., chap. 1; James P. Thomas to John H. Rapier, Jr., March 1, 1856, October 3, 1856, Rapier Papers.

14. John H. Rapier, Sr., to Richard Rapier, April 8, 1845, Rapier Papers.

15. E. H. Foster to Jane Foster, July 30, 1847, Foster Papers; Records of the Davidson County [Tennessee] Court, Minutes, book 1819–1821 (October 1821), p. 208; book E (March 6, 1851), pp. 134, 135.

16. Legislative Papers, Tennessee, Petitions and Memorials, "A Petition to the Constitutional Convention of the State of Tennessee," 1834.
17. Thomas Autobiography, chap. 1.
18. Miscellaneous Notes.
19. Records of the Davidson County [Tennessee] Court, Minutes, book E (March 6, 1851), pp. 134, 135.
20. Ibid.

Chapter 2

Primary sources consulted include (on real estate) Records of the Lee County [Iowa] Court, Deeds, book 19; Records of the St. Louis City Court, Deeds, books 402, 405, 424, 436, 502, 507, 521, 536, 571, 595, 624, 659, 708, 1424, 1519; Records of the Erie County [New York] Court, Deeds, books 99, 167, 132; (on Henry Thomas) Records of the Raleigh Township [Ontario, Canada], Assessment Rolls for 1852, 1865; Rapier Papers; (on Rapier-Thomas family) Foster Papers; *Fifth, Sixth, and Seventh Census of the United States* (see section 3 of Bibliography); Records of the Lauderdale County [Alabama] Court, Wills (1869) vol. B; Records of the Madison County [Illinois] Court, Wills (1898) box 232; (on statutes) *Acts of the Alabama General Assembly* (see section 3 of Bibliography). Newspapers consulted include *Colored Tennessean*, Florence *Gazette*, *Journal*, *Franklin Enquirer*, Nashville *Banner*, *Daily Republican Banner*, St. Louis *Globe*, *Post-Dispatch*, *Southern Advocate*. Secondary sources consulted include Aptheker, Bardolph, Berlin, Brewer, Brown, Clamorgan, Clayton, Dorman, Douglass, England, Fisher, Fitchett, Flomsbee, Franklin (*North Carolina*), Jill Garrett, Genovese (*Roll, Jordan, Roll*), Gutman, Hamer, Imes, Jackson, Rose, Schweninger ("John H. Rapier"), Sterkx, Wikramanayake, Williamson.
1. Records of the Davidson County [Tennessee] Court, Deeds, book 18 (June 1, 1854), pp. 366, 367.
2. Thomas Autobiography, chap. 4.
3. James P. Thomas to John H. Rapier, Jr., October 3, 1856, Rapier Papers.
4. Thomas Autobiography, chap. 4.
5. James P. Thomas to John H. Rapier, Jr., October 3, 1856, Rapier Papers.
6. Ibid.
7. James P. Thomas to John H. Rapier, Jr., November 23, 1856, Rapier Papers.
8. Unlike later historians, Thomas ascribed the cause of the panic to the political involvement of blacks. During the campaign of 1856, he said, Negroes openly discussed the Free Soil movement, the abolitionist crusade, and the platform of the Republican party; they attended political gatherings, listened attentively to the candidates, and generally supported John C. Fremont, who used the slogan: "Free Soil, Free Speech, and Free Men." "At the outdoor meetings, the Negroes would attend and listen to what was said. The Watchmen tried to drive them off, but they would slip around and mix with the crowd somewhere else." According to Thomas, such

activity alarmed whites to the point of violent repression. Thomas Autobiography, p. 110.

9. James P. Thomas to John H. Rapier, Jr., January 21, 1859, Rapier Papers.

10. Thomas Autobiography, chap. 10.

11. James P. Thomas to John H. Rapier, Jr., March 1, 1857, Rapier Papers.

12. Ibid.

13. Ibid.

14. Records of the Lee County [Iowa] Court, Deeds, book 19 (April 10, 1857), p. 456; James P. Thomas to John Rapier, Jr., July 27, 1857, Rapier Papers.

15. Cyprian Claymorgan, *The Colored Aristocracy of St. Louis* (St. Louis, 1858), p. 8.

16. St. Louis *Dispatch*, quoted in the Montgomery [Alabama] *Weekly Advertiser*, February 25, 1868.

17. Records of the St. Louis City Court, Warranty Deeds, book 452 (August 13, 1872), pp. 470, 471; Marriages, vol. 13 (February 12, 1868), p. 243; Deeds, book 402 (February 5, 1870), p. 81; book 486 (January 15, 1874), p. 313; *Tax Book for the Year 1879: State of Missouri* (St. Louis, 1880), pp. 26–29, found in the Records of the St. Louis City Court; St. Louis *Globe*, May 38, 1896; St. Louis *Post-Dispatch*, December 17, 1913.

18. Henry K. Thomas to John H. Rapier, Sr., October 27, 1856, Rapier Papers.

19. There is no record of Thomas's death. The manuscripts, however, are incomplete. He probably died about 1888.

20. The 1830 census takers missed Rapier, but later correspondence indicates that he settled in Florence shortly after his emancipation. Richard Rapier to James P. Thomas, December 14, 1877, Rapier Papers.

21. Quoted in Thomas Freeman, "The Life of James T. Rapier," (Master's thesis, Auburn University, 1959), p. 2.

22. James Rapier to John H. Rapier, Jr., September 27, 1858, Rapier Papers.

23. John H. Rapier, Sr., to John H. Rapier, Jr., September 16, 1857, Rapier Papers.

24. Ibid., August 6, 1857.

25. John H. Rapier, Sr., to Henry K. Thomas, February 28, 1843, Rapier Papers. Except when the meaning is obscured, no editorial changes have been made in the correspondence of John Rapier, Sr.; brackets indicate a word or phrase added for clarity. [*Sic*] has not been used.

26. John H. Rapier, Sr., to John H. Rapier, Jr., March 17, 1857, Rapier Papers.

27. John H. Rapier, Sr., to Henry K. Thomas, February 28, 1843, Rapier Papers.

28. John H. Rapier, Sr., to Richard Rapier, April 8, 1845, Rapier Papers.

29. John H. Rapier, Sr., to John H. Rapier, Jr., September 27, 1858, Rapier Papers. By this time the semi-literate Rapier had become almost obsessed with the idea of a good education for his children. "I must try to help James." "He ought to be encourage, as he want to work." "I must press on him the emportance of having an Education." ibid., June 22, 1857; September 16, 1857; September 27, 1858.

30. S. C. Posey to Wager Swayne, April 25, 1867, Swayne Papers.

31. Florence *Journal*, September 23, 1869; Montgomery *Daily Advertiser*, April 7, 1880. The *Advertiser* was contrasting the correct behavior of John H. Rapier, Sr., with the "mean and mendacious behavior" of his son James, who had testified before the Senate Exodus Committee on the deplorable conditions for blacks in Alabama. U.S. Congress, *Senate Reports*, 46th Cong., 1st sess., 8, no. 693 (1880): 465–82.

32. John H. Rapier, Sr., to John H. Rapier, Jr., September 15, 1856, December 13, 1856, June 26, 1857, Rapier Papers.

33. John H. Rapier, Jr., to James P. Thomas, April 30, 1861, Rapier Papers.

34. John H. Rapier, Sr., to William McLain, January 18, 1854, American Colonization Society Papers.

35. John H. Rapier, Sr., to John H. Rapier, Jr., June 26, 1857, Rapier Papers; Notes of John H. Rapier, Jr., October 7, 1857, p. 235, Rapier Papers.

Chapter 3

Primary sources consulted include (on John Rapier, Jr.) Andrew Johnson Papers; Records of the Lauderdale County [Alabama] Court, Wills (1869) vol. 8; Rapier Papers; American Colonization Society Papers; *Students of the University of Michigan* (1864); *Announcement of the State University of Iowa* (1865) (see section 4 of Bibliography); *Records of the Adjutant General's Office* (see section 2 of Bibliography); (on Buxton) *Reports of the Elgin Association* (1849–1866); *The Ecclesiastical and Missionary Record*; "The Buxton Session Book" (1858) (see sections 4 and 5 of Bibliography); Abbott Papers; King Papers; The Autobiography of William King; (on James Rapier) Thomas Autobiography; Rapier Papers. Newspapers consulted include Baltimore *American*, *Sun*, Minnesota *Times*, *National Anti-Slavery Standard*, *Provincial Freedman*, St. Paul *Times*, Toronto *Globe*, *The Voice of the Fugitive*. Secondary sources consulted include A. M. Harris, Jamieson, Landon, Pease, Peckham, Schweninger ("A Fugitive Negro"), Shaw, Simmons, Tanser, Ullman, Wagandt, Ward, Winks.

1. John H. Rapier, Jr., to William McLain, December 28, 1854, American Colonization Society Papers.

2. Ibid., March 5, 1855.

3. "Notebook of John H. Rapier, Jr.," 1857, pp. 135, 136, Rapier Papers.

4. Ibid., pp. 137–39.

5. Ibid.

6. St. Paul *Times*, July 28, 1858.

7. Minnesota *Times*, December 11, 1856, quoted in the *Northern Herald*, December 13, 1856.

8. Notebook of John H. Rapier, Jr., 1858, p. 99, Rapier Papers. Rapier usually signed his articles with a pseudonym. His favorites were *Inquirer*, *Democracy*, and *R*.

9. John H. Rapier, Jr., to James P. Thomas, February 25, 1861, Rapier Papers.

10. Ibid., February 8, 1862.

11. Ibid., July 28, 1861.

12. Ibid., November 12, 1863.

13. John H. Rapier, Jr., to James P. Thomas, August 19, 1864, found in *Records of the Adjutant General's Office*, Medical Officer's File of John Rapier, RG 94.

14. John H. Rapier, Jr., to Andrew Johnson, January 6, 1865, Johnson Papers.

15. John H. Rapier, Sr., to John H. Rapier, Jr., September 15, 1856, Rapier Papers.

16. James Rapier to John H. Rapier, Jr., January 27, 1857, Rapier Papers.

17. Ibid., March 6, 1857.

18. Ibid., March 3, 1857. The leading Tory, or Loyalist, in the Western District was Edwin Larwill, who had stated that blacks depressed property values, caused warlike tensions between the United States and Canada, and were "indolent, vicious, and ungovernable." Jane and William Pease, *Black Utopia* (Madison, Wis., 1963), p. 105.

19. James Rapier to John H. Rapier, Jr., April 21, 1857, Rapier Papers.

20. Ibid.

21. Ibid.

22. Ibid.

23. Notes of John H. Rapier, Jr., April 21, 1857, Rapier Papers.

24. John H. Rapier, Jr., to James Rapier, September 18, 1857, Rapier Papers.

25. James Rapier to John H. Rapier, Jr., June 26, 1857, Rapier Papers.

26. Ibid., July 19, 1858.

27. Ibid.

28. Ibid.

29. Ibid., February 28, 1858.

30. Ibid., September 27, 1857.

31. Ibid., January 27, 1857.

32. Ibid.

33. Quoted in the Autobiography of William King, p. 555. Though the evidence strongly suggests that Rapier addressed the future monarch, and though, with the possible exception of John Riley, he would have been the logical choice, neither the newspaper accounts (Montreal *Gazette* [August 2, 3, 1860]) nor *The Visit of his Royal Highness, the Prince of Wales to America* (Montreal, 1860) nor William King, who was in London at the time, specifically mentioned who gave the address. See A. A. Taylor, "Negro Congressmen, a Generation After," *JNH* 7 (1922): 134.

34. Autobiography of William King, p. 555.

35. James Rapier to John H. Rapier, Jr., March 17, 1862, Rapier Papers.

36. Ibid. Unfortunately the "Register of Students for the Toronto Normal School, 1860–1863," is not extant. Though it cannot be specifically documented that Rapier graduated from normal school, the evidence suggests that he did. Early in 1862, for example, John Rapier, Jr., who was traveling in the Caribbean, wrote: "I shall probably sail for Canada in September to be in Toronto for October commencement." John H. Rapier, Jr., to James P. Thomas, February 8, 1862, Rapier Papers.

37. James Rapier to John Rapier, Jr., June 26, 1857, Rapier Papers; Records of the Kent County [Ontario] Court, Assessment Roll, Raleigh Township (1864), p. 24.

38. Quoted in A. M. Harris, *A Sketch of the Buxton Mission* (Birmingham, 1866), pp. 7–14.

39. He made the statement at the celebration for the passage of the Fifteenth Amendment, in Montgomery, Alabama, April 26, 1870. *Alabama State Journal*, April 29, 1870.

Chapter 4

Primary sources consulted include (on Nashville Negro Convention) *Annual Cyclopedia of Important Events* (1865) (see section 4 of Bibliography); (on Rapier's land transactions) Records of the Lauderdale [Alabama] Court, Deeds, vol. 18; (on congressional reconstruction) *House Executive Documents*, 39th Cong., 2d sess., vol. 3; 40th Cong., 2d sess., vol. 1 (see section 3 of Bibliography); (on conditions in Alabama) *Acts of the Alabama General Assembly* (1865–1868); *Penal Code of Alabama* (1866); *Records of the Bureau of Refugees, Freedmen and Abandoned Lands* (see section 2 of Bibliography); Bromberg, Chase, Patton, Swayne Papers. Newspapers consulted include *Alabama State Journal*, Athens *Post*, Barbour *Times and News*, *Choctaw Herald*, Cincinnati *Daily Commercial*, *Colored Tennessean*, *Daily Missouri Democrat*, *Daily Picayune*, *Daily State Sentinel*, Florence *Journal*, Huntsville *Advocate*, *Literary Index*, Mobile *Nationalist*, *Daily Register*, Montgomery *Daily Advertiser*, *Daily Mail*, *Moulton Advertiser*, *Union*, Nashville *Daily Gazette*, *Daily Press and Times*, *True Union*, *Dispatch*, *Republican Banner*, *Union and American*, New York *Times*, *North Alabamian and Times*, *Reconstructionist*, Selma Weekly *Times*, *Southern Advertiser*, Union Springs *Herald and Times*. Secondary sources consulted include Alexander, Benedict, Berry, Bethel, Bond, Bromberg, Cash, Cobb, Cook, Cox, Curry (*Radicalism*), Dorris, DuBois, Feldman, Fleming (*Civil War*), Franklin (*Reconstruction*), William Garrett, Gillette, James Green, Harlan, Abram Harris, Hesseltine, Kolchin, Lewis, McFeely, McKitrick, McMillan, McPherson (*Struggle for Equality*), Perman, Rabinowitz ("From Exclusion"), Robert Rhodes, Rogers (*One-Gallused Rebellion*), Schweninger ("Black Citizenship"), Alrutheus Taylor, Thomas, Thornbrough, Trelease.

1. Nashville *Dispatch*, August 12, 1865.

2. Ibid., July 29, 1865.

3. Ibid., October 12, 1865.

4. *Colored Tennessean*, August 17, 1865.

5. Nashville *Daily Press and Times*, August 14, 1865.

6. Ibid.

7. *Daily State Sentinel*, November 25, 1867.

8. *Alabama State Journal*, April 26, 1870.

9. Mobile *Nationalist*, March 15, 1866.

10. *Acts of the General Assembly of Alabama* (Montgomery, 1866), pp. 128, 129.

11. Mobile *Nationalist*, March 15, 1866.

12. Florence *Journal*, December 13, 1865.
13. Ibid., May 9, 1866.
14. George D. Robinson to Colonal Cadel, January 17, 1866, printed in the Mobile *Nationalist*, February 1, 1866.
15. Records of the Bureau of Refugees, Freedmen, and Abandoned Lands, "Register of Complaints, Greenville, Alabama, 1867," pp. 17, 18; "Complaint Book for Selma, Alabama, 1865–1868," pp. 174–76.
16. James Sawyer to J. Giers, May 30, 1866, American Missionary Association Papers.
17. John B. Callis to Wager Swayne, June 7, 1866, Swayne Papers.
18. "Proceedings of the Meeting of Colored People at Florence, Alabama, April 24, 1867," p. 2, Swayne Papers.
19. Florence *Journal*, May 2, 1867.
20. John W. McAlester to Robert Patton, May 30, 1867, Patton Papers.
21. James Stewart to Robert Patton, March 17, 1867, Patton Papers.
22. Florence *Journal*, May 23, 1867.
23. Ibid.
24. Mobile *Nationalist*, March 28, 1867.
25. Ibid., April 25, 1867.
26. Ibid., May 9, 1867.
27. *Daily State Sentinel*, May 21, 1867.
28. Ibid.
29. Montgomery *Weekly Mail*, June 6, 1867.
30. Mobile *Nationalist*, June 27, 1867.
31. Huntsville *Democrat*, quoted in the Montgomery *Weekly Advertiser*, June 18, 1867.
32. Montgomery *Weekly Mail*, April 4, 1867.
33. Mobile *Daily Register*, March 19, 1867.
34. Montgomery *Weekly Advertiser*, May 14, 1867.
35. Florence *Journal*, June 13, 1867.
36. Wager Swayne to Salmon P. Chase, June 28, 1867, Chase Papers.
37. James Rapier to Robert M. Patton, August 28, 1867, Patton Papers. Posey wrote concerning the judgeship: "I have thought S. C. Posey as the most suitable appointee." Sidney Posey to Robert Patton, August 15, 1867, Patton Papers.
38. Neander H. Rice to Robert Patton, August 30, 1867, Patton Papers.
39. J. T. Tanner to Robert Patton, August 15, 1867, Patton Papers.
40. C. W. Wesson to William Smith, October 4, 1867, Swayne Papers.
41. Ibid.
42. Mobile *Nationalist*, October 10, 1867.

Chapter 5

Primary sources consulted include (on convention) *Official Journal of the Alabama Constitutional Convention* (1868) (see section 3 of Bibliography); (on elections) *Alabama Statistical Registers* (1869, 1903) (see section 4 of Bibliography); *Official Returns of Alabama Elections* (1867, 1868); *House Executive Documents*, 40th Cong., 3d sess., vol. 1 (see section 3 of Bibliography). Newspapers consulted are the same as those cited in chapter 4. Secondary sources consulted include Alexander, Bond, Cash, Cobb, Cook, Cox, Cruden, Current, DuBois (*Black Reconstruction*), Fleming (*Documentary History*), Franklin ("Reconstruction and the Negro"), William Garrett, Haskins, Hesseltine, Klingman, Kolchin, Lamson, Litwack, Lynch (*Reminiscences*), McMillan, Edward McPherson, Meier ("Comment"), Albert Moore, Patrick, Perman, Robert Rhodes, Stampp (*The Era of Reconstruction*), Thomas, Trelease ("Who Were the Scalawags"), Uya, Vincent, Wharton, Woolfolk ("The Role of the Scalawag"), Work.

1. *Daily State Sentinel*, November 25, 1867.

2. *Florence Journal*, November 7, 1867.

3. *Official Journal of the Constitutional Convention of Alabama* (Montgomery, 1868), p. 57, hereafter *Official Journal*.

4. Mobile *Nationalist*, November 12, 1867.

5. Montgomery *Daily Advertiser*, November 19, 1867.

6. Mobile *Daily Register*, November 27, 1867.

7. Ibid., November 30, 1867; *Official Journal*, pp. 144–49.

8. *Daily State Sentinel*, December 4, 1867. The Negro convention members included Benjamin Alexander (Greene), Samuel Blandon (Lee), John Carraway (Mobile), Thomas Diggs (Barbour), Peyton Finley (Montgomery), James K. Greene (Hale), Ovid Gregory (Mobile), Jordan Hatcher (Dallas), Benjamin Inge (Sumter), Washington Johnson (Russell), Columbus Jones (Madison), Thomas Lee (Perry), J. Wright McLeod (Marengo), Lafayette Robinson (Madison), Benjamin Royal (Bullock), Alfred Strother and Henry Stokes (Dallas), and Rapier. United States Congress, *House Reports*, 43d Cong., 2d sess., vol. 6, no. 262 (1875): 274–76; Montgomery *Weekly Advertiser*, March 3, 1868; *Daily State Sentinel*, September 25, 1867, November 22, 25, 27, 1867, February 28, 1868; Florence *Journal*, November 7, 1867; *The Alabama Official and Statistical Register* (Montgomery, 1903), p. 125; Monroe Work, "Some Negro Members of Reconstruction Conventions, and Legislatures and Congresses," *Journal of Negro History* 5 (January, 1920): 64–67.

9. Montgomery *Weekly Advertiser*, December 3, 1867.

10. Mobile *Daily Register*, December 10, 1867.

11. Ibid.

12. Ibid., December 7, 1867.

13. Montgomery *Daily Advertiser*, December 7, 1867.

14. Montgomery *Weekly Advertiser*, January 14, 1868.

15. Athens *Post*, January 9, 1868.

Chapter 6

Primary sources consulted include (on the Klan) *American Missionary Magazine* (1869–1872); *Senate Reports*, 42d Cong., 2d sess., vol. 2 (see section 3 of Bibliography), Rapier File in *Records of the United States Treasury Department*, RG 56; *Records of the United States Justice Department* (see section 2 of Bibliography); (on election returns) *Senate Reports*, 42d Cong., 2d sess., vol. 2; *House Miscellaneous Documents*, 43d Cong., 2d sess., vol. 6; Parson Papers; Smith Papers; *Official Returns for the State of Alabama* (see section 3 of Bibliography). Newspapers consulted include the Montgomery *Advance*, *Alabama Beacon*, *Alabama State Journal*, Athens *Post*, *Autauga Citizen*, Barbour *Times and News*, Bluff City *Times*, *Choctaw Herald*, *Elmore Republican*, Florence *Journal*, Huntsville *Advocate*, Mobile *Daily Register*, *Republican*, Monroe *Journal*, Montgomery *Daily Advertiser*, *Daily Mail*, Mouton *Advertiser*, *Union*, *New National Era*, *North Alabamian and Times*, Selma *Weekly Times*, Shelby County *Guide*, *Southern Argus*, *Southern Republican*, Talladega *Sun*, *Watch Tower*, *Tri-Weekly Era and Whig*, Troy *Messenger*, Union Springs *Herald and Times*, Washington *Chronicle*, *Evening Star*, *West Alabamian*. Secondary sources consulted include Bond, Brittain, Cash, Feldman, Gillette, Kolchin, Lewis, Maddex, Rogers, Swinney, Trelease.

1. James Rapier to Chester Arthur, May 31, 1882, Rapier File.

2. Miscellaneous Notes, Rapier Papers.

3. James Rapier to Chester Arthur, May 31, 1882, Rapier File. Rapier told of this incident some years after the event.

4. *North Alabamian and Times*, September 15, 1868.

5. James Rapier to Chester Arthur, May 31, 1882, Rapier File.

6. United States, Congress, 46th Cong., 2d sess., *Senate Reports* 8 (1880): 470, 471.

7. Ibid., 42d Cong., 2d sess., vol. 2, no. 41 (1872): 159, 160. As Rapier was not the only politically prominent black accused in the academy burning, there is some likelihood that the incendiarism was staged to rid the area of leading Negroes.

8. Neander Rice to William Smith, August 18, 1868, Smith Papers.

9. Ibid.

10. United States, Congress, *Senate Reports*, 42d Cong., 2d sess., vol. 2, no. 41 (1872): 11–16.

11. William B. Figures to William Smith, October 20, 1868, Smith Papers.

12. Montgomery *Weekly Advertiser*, March 24, 1868. The seven counties were Greene, Marengo, Montgomery, Perry, Pickens, Sumter, and Wilcox.

13. Quoted in Allen W. Trelease, *White Terror* (New York, 1971), pp. 84, 85.

14. *North Alabamian and Times*, November 17, 1868.

15. United States, Congress, *Senate Reports*, 42d Cong., 2d sess., vol. 2, no. 41 (1872): 227.

16. James Rapier to Henry K. Thomas, September 8, 1869, Rapier Papers.

17. Ibid.

18. James Rapier to George L. White, November 22, 1869, American Missionary Association Papers.

19. George L. White to James Rapier, March 30, 1870, American Missionary Association Papers.

20. *Alabama State Journal*, April 29, 1870.

21. *Southern Republican*, May 11, 1870.

22. *New National Era*, May 26, 1870.

23. *Elmore Republican*, May 13, 1870.

24. Ibid.

25. Huntsville *Advocate*, quoted in the *Alabama State Journal*, July 30, 1870.

26. *Alabama State Journal*, September 2, 1870.

27. Selma *Weekly Times*, September 3, 1870.

28. Ibid., September 10, 1870.

29. *Alabama State Journal*, September 2, 1870.

30. Montgomery *Daily Mail*, September 4, 1870.

31. Union Springs *Times*, September 14, 1870.

32. *Alabama State Journal*, October 7, 1870.

33. *Southern Republican*, September 12, 1870.

34. Huntsville *Advocate*, October 21, 1870.

35. Opelika *Recorder*, quoted in the Montgomery *Daily Advertiser*, October 9, 1870.

36. Moulton *Advertiser*, September 23, 1870.

37. Alabama *Beacon*, September 10, 1870.

38. Ibid., September 24, 1870.

39. William L. Caine to William Smith, October 8, 1870, Smith Papers.

40. Montgomery *Daily Advertiser*, October 4, 1870.

41. J. M. Caleb Wiley to William Smith, September 27, 1870, Smith Papers.

42. Ibid.

43. Ibid.

44. *Alabama State Journal*, October 21, 1870; Montgomery *Daily Mail*, September 8, 1870.

45. Montgomery *Weekly Mail*, September 7, 1870.

46. Troy *Messenger*, October 20, 1870.

47. Florence *Journal*, September 28, 1870.

48. *American Missionary Magazine* (October, 1870), pp. 236, 237.

Chapter 7

Primary sources consulted include (on education for Negroes) *Annual Report of the American Missionary Association* (1865–1874); *John Alvord's Semi-Annual Report on Schools* (1865–1870); *Proceedings of the National Negro Labor Convention* (1869); *Report of the Joint Committee on Reconstruction*,

39th Cong., 2d sess., vol. 3 (see section 3 of Bibliography); American Missionary Association Papers, Windom Papers; (on economic conditions) *House Miscellaneous Documents*, 44th Cong., 1st sess., vol. 1; *House Reports*, 44th Cong., 1st sess., vol. 1; (on Rapier and Freedmen's Bank) *Records of the Bureau of the Comptroller of the Currency* (see section 2 of Bibliography); *Records of the Bureau of Refugees, Freedmen, and Abandoned Lands* (see section 2 of Bibliography); (on Negro labor union movement) *Senate Miscellenous Documents*, 41st Cong., 2d sess., vol. 1 (see section 3 of Bibliography). Newspapers consulted include *Alabama State Journal, Daily Globe, Daily Critic, Daily Intelligencer, Daily State Sentinel*, Mobile *Daily Register*, Montgomery *Daily Advertiser, Daily Mail, New National Era, Our Mountain Home, Southern Republican*, Union Springs *Times and Herald*. Secondary sources consulted include Bethel, Bond, Cruden, DuBois, Fleming (*Freedman's Bank*), James Green, Harlan, Kolchin, Logan, McFeely, Meier (*Negro Thought*), Osthaus, Rabinowitz ("Half a Loaf"), Rogers, Schweninger ("James Rapier," "American Missionary"), Stampp (*The Era of Reconstruction*), Joseph Taylor.

1. James Rapier to John H. Rapier, Jr., March 6, 1857, Rapier Papers.

2. Ibid., February 28, 1858.

3. Quoted in Richard N. Current, ed., *Reconstruction* (Englewood Cliffs, N.J., 1965), p. 50.

4. W. G. Kephart to George Tappan, May 9, 1864, American Missionary Association Papers.

5. *Alabama State Journal*, July 30, 1871.

6. J. N. Fitzpatrick to the Secretary of the Treasury, May 3, 1882, Rapier File.

7. *Proceedings of the Colored National Labor Convention* (Washington, D.C., 1869), p. 3; Washington *Star*, December 6, 1869; *National Anti-Slavery Standard*, December 11, 1869.

8. Washington *Evening Star*, December 7, 1869.

9. United States, Congress, *House Miscellaneous Documents*, 41st Cong., 2d sess., vol. 1, no. 8 (1870): 2, 3.

10. Washington *Star*, December 13, 1869. The other memorialists included John Harris and J. Mackay (North Carolina and South Carolina, respectively), Sella Martin (Massachusetts), John Sampson (Ohio), W. T. J. Hayes (North Carolina), William Wilson (New Jersey), M. VanHorn (Rhode Island), Charles H. Peters (Washington, D.C.), William Perkins (Maryland), J. W. Loguen (New York), Caleb Milburn (Delaware), and Joseph Rainey (South Carolina). *Proceedings of the Colored National Convention*, pp. 30, 31.

11. *Southern Republican*, January 11, 1871.

12. Bluff City *Times*, January 12, 1871.

13. *New National Era*, January 19, 1871.

14. Ibid.

15. United States, Congress, *Senate Reports*, 46th Cong., 2d sess., vol. 8, no. 693 (1880): 136, 137.

16. *Alabama State Journal*, January 3, 1872.

Chapter 8

Primary sources consulted include (on assessorship) *Treasury Department Applications for Assessors and Collectors of Internal Revenue and Customs* (see section 2 of Bibliography); Chandler, Lewis, Sherman, Trumbull, Wade, Wilson, Windom Papers; (on the Klan) *House Reports*, 43rd Cong., 2d sess., vol. 6; *Senate Reports*, 42d Cong., 2d sess., vol. 1–4 (see section 3 of Bibliography); Correspondence to the attorney general in the *Records of the Justice Department*; *Records of the Bureau of Refugees, Freedmen, and Abandoned Lands* (see section 2 of Bibliography); (on conditions in Alabama) Chandler, Parsons, Patton, Rapier, Semple, Sherman, Strobach Papers. Newspapers consulted include *Alabama State Journal*, Bluff City *Times*, *Marion Commonwealth*, Montgomery *Daily Advertiser*, Selma *Times*. Secondary sources consulted include Blaine, Bond, Cash, Gillette, Kolchin, Lewis, Sherman, Somers, Swinney, Trelease.

1. Charles Hays to George Boutwell, March 14, 1871, RDT-AIR.
2. George Spencer, Benjamin Turner, Charles Buckley, to Ulysses Grant, March 7, 1871, RDT-AIR.
3. Montgomery *Daily Advertiser*, April 20, 1871.
4. James Rapier to George S. Boutwell, June 25, 1871, RDT-ACC.
5. Ibid.
6. Ibid.
7. Ibid.
8. *Address to the President of the United States, Mobile, Alabama*, August 19, 1871, RDT-ACC.
9. Q. P. Sibley to George Boutwell, June 25, 1871, RDT-ACC.
10. James Rapier to George Spencer, December 9, 1871, RDT-ACC.
11. John Minnis to A. Akerman, August 21, 1871, RDJ-LFJ.
12. *Proceedings of the Southern States Convention of Colored Men* (Columbia, S.C., 1871), pp. 3, 9.
13. Ibid., pp. 51, 52.
14. *Appendix to the Proceedings of the Southern States Convention of Colored Men* (Columbia, S.C., 1871), p. 93.
15. "Testimony of the Inquiry into the Affairs of the Office of Assessor of Internal Revenue for the Second District of Alabama, Montgomery, Alabama, November 2–4, 1871," pp. 2–5, RDT-AIR.
16. Quoted in Allen W. Trelease, *White Terror* (New York, 1971), p. 304.
17. *Marion Commonwealth*, October 19, 1871.
18. Quoted in Richard Busteed to George Williams, March 29, 1872, RDJ-LFJ.
19. Robert Healy to William E. Chandler, March 15, 1872, Chandler Papers.
20. James Rapier to William Chandler, May 16, 1872, Chandler Papers.

Chapter 9

Primary sources consulted include (on national politics) *Proceedings of the Liberal Republican Convention* (see section 4 of Bibliography); *Congressional*

Globe; Blaine, Bromberg, Chandler, Sherman, Trumbull Papers; (on election returns) *Official Returns of the State of Alabama* (see section 3 of Bibliography); Newspapers consulted include *Alabama State Journal,* Barbour County *Times and News,* Bluff City *Times, Elmore Republican,* Huntsville *Advocate, Marion Commonwealth,* Mobile *Daily Register, Republican,* Montgomery *Daily Advertiser, Moulton Union, National Republican, New National Era,* New York *Times, Republican Sentinel,* Selma *Weekly Times, Southern Argus,* Troy *Messenger,* Union Springs *Herald and Times,* Washington *Evening Star, West Alabamian.* Secondary sources consulted include Blaine, Bond, Brittain, Cash, Douglass, Lewis, Sloan, Swinney, Thornbrough, Van Deusen.

1. Robert Healy to William E. Chandler, March 15, 1872, Chandler Papers.

2. *New National Era,* March 14, 1872.

3. Ibid., April 8, 1872.

4. Ibid., June 20, 1872.

5. Ibid.

6. Ibid.

7. Ibid.

8. Union Springs *Herald and Times,* May 22, 1872.

9. James Rapier to William King, July 7, 1872, King Papers.

10. Ibid.

11. Union Springs *Herald and Times,* July 24, 1872.

12. *Alabama State Journal,* August 13, 1872.

14. Montgomery *Weekly Advertiser,* July 31, 1872.

15. *Alabama State Journal,* August 15, 1872.

16. Only one number of the *Sentinel* is extant, but it was often quoted in other papers. Quoted in the Montgomery *Daily Advertiser,* July 9, 1872; *Alabama State Journal,* June 28, 1872.

17. James Rapier to William E. Chandler, August 30, 1872, Chandler Papers.

18. *Daily State Sentinel,* November 25, 1827.

19. James Rapier to Sarah Thomas, July 10, 1872, Rapier Papers.

20. Ibid.

21. Eufaula *Daily Times,* June 14, 1872.

22. Montgomery *Daily Advertiser,* October 30, 1872; Union Springs *Herald and Times,* October 30, 1872.

23. *Alabama State Journal,* August 30, 1872. Bingham also assailed incumbent Negro congressman Benjamin Turner, who was running for re-election in the First District, claiming that he, too, was illiterate. Such was not the case. Though born a slave (of Mrs. Elizabeth Turner of Selma, Dallas County), Turner had managed a livery stable, acquired real estate, and secured a rudimentary education while still in bondage. Later, he expanded his education by extensive reading. "Mr Turner is a man of color," one observer noted, "self-made in every sense of the word, fully efficient and qualified." Paul Strobach to Secretary of the Treasury, March 10, 1882; George Duskin to George Turner, March 7, 1882, RDT-CIR; *New National*

Era, May 9, 1872. As for Rapier's learning, one historian of Alabama reconstruction correctly suggests that he was perhaps the best educated politician in the entire state—black or white. Horace Mann Bond, *Negro Education in Alabama: A Study in Cotton and Steel* (Washington, D.C., 1939), pp. 17, 26, 27, 308.

24. *Alabama State Journal,* August 21, 1872.

25. James Rapier to William Chandler, August 30, 1872, September 19, 1872, Chandler Papers.

26. Union Springs *Herald and Times,* November 6, 1872.

27. Montgomery *Advance,* November 11, 1872.

Chapter 10

Primary sources consulted include (for trip abroad) *Report of the Commissioners Representing the United States at Vienna* (see section 4 of Bibliography); Records of Commissioners at the Vienna Exposition (see section 2 of Bibliography); *Congressional Record;* (for congressional career) *Biographical Dictionary of American Congresses; Congressional Directory,* 43rd Cong., 1st-2d sess., vol. 1; *House Journal,* 43rd Cong., 1st-2d sess., vol. 1; Desk copies of House bills, 43rd Cong., 1st-2d sess. (see section 3 of Bibliography); (on Congress) Blaine, Bromberg, Chandler, Colfax, Dawes, Schurtz, Sherman, Stephens, Trumbull, Wade, Wilson, Windom Papers. Newspapers consulted include *Alabama State Journal, Daily Critic, Daily Globe, Daily Intelligencer,* Georgetown *Courier,* Mobile *Register, National Republican, New National Era,* New York *Times,* St. Louis *Dispatch, Sunday Herald and Weekly National Intelligencer,* Washington *Chronicle, Evening Star.* Secondary sources consulted include Barns, Blaine, Bromberg, Christopher, Donald (*Charles Sumner*), Douglass, Going, Haskins, Klingman, Lamson, Lewis, Lynch, Edward McPherson, Meier (*Negro Thought*), Nugent, Sharkey, Sherman, Smith, Unger.

1. *Congressional Record,* 43d Cong., 1st sess., (1874), p. 4784, hereafter *Congressional Record.*

2. *New National Era,* October 9, 1873.

3. Birmingham *News,* quoted in the *Alabama State Journal,* August 22, 1873.

4. Eufaula *Times,* June 6, 1873.

5. *National Republican,* April 26, 1874. As there is no reliable study of Negroes in Congress, there are many unanswered questions about black voting records, committee assignments, relationships with one another and with white members, as well as their activities outside Congress. Consequently, the following pages will attempt to do three things: (1) examine as closely as possible every phase of Rapier's career in Washington; (2) investigate the voting records and activities of other black reconstructionists in the Forty-third Congress; and (3) analyze the sectional voting patterns. To accomplish this, it is necessary, at times, to relate incidents that are less important to the Congress as a whole, than to its black membership.

6. *New National Era,* March 13, 1873.

7. *Daily Critic*, December 11, 1873.

8. Washington *Sentinel*, December 13, 1873; *National Republican*, November 29, 30, 1873, December 10, 1873; Washington *Evening Star*, December 9, 1873; *New National Era*, December 18, 25, 1873.

9. *Congressional Record*, p. 53.

10. Edward Atkinson to Henry L. Dawes, February 21, 1874, Dawes Papers.

11. James Rapier to Arthur Bingham, January 22, 1874, printed in the *Alabama State Journal*, February 1, 1874.

12. Montgomery *Daily Advertiser*, February 6, 1874.

13. *Congressional Record*, p. 381.

14. Ibid., pp. 408, 409.

15. United States Congress, *Appendix to the Congressional Record*, 43d Cong., 1st sess. (1874), p. 3.

16. *Congressional Record*, p. 4785.

17. Ibid.

18. *National Republican*, April 26, 1874.

19. "Speeches of Henry Dawes," vol. 46, chap. 8, pp. 5–7, Dawes Papers.

20. J. Medill to James G. Blaine, February 14, 1875, Blaine Papers.

Chapter 11

Primary sources consulted include (on violence in Alabama) Lewis Papers; *Records of the Justice Department* (see section 2 of Bibliography); *House Reports*, 43d Cong., 2d sess., vol. 6; *Senate Reports*, 44th Cong., 2d sess., vol. 1; *House Miscellaneous Documents*, 43d Cong., 1st sess., vol. 1; *Congressional Record; House Executive Documents*, 43d Cong., 2d sess., vol. 15 (see section 3 of Bibliography); Blaine, Chandler, Dawes, Sherman Papers; (on contested election) *Records for the Committee on Elections*, H.R. 45A–F10.4 and H.R. 44A–F8.13 (see section 2 of Bibliography); (on election) *House Reports*, 43d Cong., 2d sess., vol. 6; *Senate Reports*, 44th Cong., 2d sess., vol. 1; *Official Returns for the State of Alabama* (see section 3 of Bibliography). Newspapers consulted include *Alabama State Journal*, Blanton Springs *Herald*, *Clark County Democrat*, *Elmore Republican*, Mobile Daily *Register*, Montgomery Daily *Advertiser*, *National Republican*, *New National Era*, *Republican Union Advocate*, Selma *Republican*, *The Sentinel*, *Southern Argus*, *Sunday Herald and Weekly National Intelligencer*, Tuskegee Weekly *News*, Union Springs *Herald and Times*, Washington *Chronicle*, *Evening Star*. Secondary sources consulted include Barns, Bond, Cox, Going, Haskins, Kolchin, Lewis, Logan, Lynch (*Reminiscences*), Sherman, Smith, Swinney, Trelease, Wharton, Woolfolk [Wiggins].

1. Montgomery *Ledger*, quoted in the *Alabama State Journal*, July 1, 1874.

2. United States Congress, *House Reports*, 43d Cong., 2d sess., 6, no. 262 (1875): 702.

3. *Alabama State Journal*, July 24, 1874.

4. *House Reports*, p. vii.

5. Thomas Ivey to David Lewis, August 5, 1874, Lewis Papers.

6. Ibid.

7. E. M. Keils to David Lewis, August 25, 1874, Lewis Papers.

8. Ibid.

9. *Alabama State Journal*, August 28, 1874.

10. Union Springs *Herald and Times*, August 25, 1874.

11. Ibid., August 26, 1874.

12. *Southern Argus*, September 4, 1874.

13. Union Springs *Herald and Times*, August 26, 1874.

14. Mobile *Daily Register*, April 25, 1874.

15. *House Reports*, p. 293.

16. Tuskegee *Weekly News*, September 17, 1874.

17. *Alabama State Journal*, October 25, 1874.

18. *House Reports*, p. xxiii.

19. Montgomery *Daily Advertiser*, November 7, 1874. With either incredible naiveté or outright mendaciousness, Walter Fleming asserted that the 1874 election was the most peaceful of the reconstruction era. Negroes voted in full strength, he explained, and the campaign was the "fairest" since freedmen gained the franchise. Fleming, *Civil War and Reconstruction in Alabama* (New York, 1905), p. 793.

20. United States, Congress, 44th Cong., 1st sess., *Committee on Elections*, James T. Rapier vs. Jeremiah Williams, Second District, Alabama, December 31, 1874 (H. R. 44A–F8.13); Jeremiah Williams to James Rapier, December 31, 1874, ibid. There is no extant copy of the charges Rapier filed.

21. Montgomery *Daily Advertiser*, December 11, 1874.

22. *House Reports*, p. liv.

23. *Congressional Record*, 2d sess., p. 1001.

24. *Sunday Herald and Weekly National Intelligencer*, February 15, 1875.

25. Ibid.

26. Samuel Smith in *The Negro in Congress* (Chapel Hill, N.C., 1940) concludes that the black reconstructionists failed to accomplish much worthwhile in Congress, as they were all race conscious, supersensitive, and neglected their white constituents.

Chapter 12

Primary sources consulted include (on Democratic return to power) *Journal of the Constitutional Convention of Alabama* (1875); *Acts of the Alabama General Asembly* (1875–1880), (see section 3 of Bibliography); (on Rapier's economic activities) Records of the Lowndes County [Alabama] Court, Mortgages, vols. 5, 10, BB, CC; Records of the Montgomery County [Alabama] Court, Mortgages, vol. 13; (on 1876 election and Republican factionalism) Sherman Papers; *House Reports*, 43d Cong., 2d sess., vol. 2; *Senate Reports*, 46th Cong., 2d sess., vol. 1 (see section 4 of Bibliography); *Records of the Treasury Department for Assessors and Collectors of Internal*

Revenue (see section 2 of Bibliography); (on emigration) *Proceedings of the Nashville Negro Convention* (1879) (see section 4 of Bibliography); *Senate Reports*, 46th Cong., 1st sess., vols. 7–8 (section 4 of Bibliography). Newspapers consulted *Alabama Beacon, Alabama State Journal, Colored Citizen, Henry County Register,* Marengo *News Journal, Marion Commonwealth,* Mobile Daily *Register,* Montgomery *Daily Advertiser, Republican Sentinel and Hayneville Times,* Union Springs *Herald, Wilcox Vindicator.* Secondary sources consulted include Bardolph, Bond, Cash, DeSantis, Douglass, Godkin, Guernsey, Haskins, King, Litwack, Logan, Lynch (*The Facts*), McMillan, McPherson (*The Abolitionist*), Meier (*Negro Thought*), Painter, Rabinowitz ("Half a Loaf"), Sherman, Smith, Swinney, Trelease, Woolfolk ("The Role").

1. That so-called Negro rule was a myth is indicated by the small number of Negro officeholders in Alabama during reconstruction, perhaps fewer than any other Southern state. Besides Rapier, only two blacks: Benjamin Turner and Jeremiah Haralson, ever served in Congress; only six Negroes: Haralson, J. W. Jones, Lloyd Leftwich, Benjamin Royal, A. H. Curtis and Jack Greene, served in the state Senate; and fewer than twenty-eight (of one hundred) ever served in a single session of the general assembly. No Negro ever served in a state office, and only a few, like Montgomery city councilman Lazarus Williams, ever became city or county officials. The strong strain of conservativism among white Republicans, perhaps stronger than in any other state in the deep South, was in part responsible for this. See: Montgomery *Daily Advertiser,* December 3, 1873; Monroe N. Work, "Some Negro Members of Reconstruction Conventions and Legislatures and of Congress," *JNH* 5 (January, 1920): 64; Peter Kolchin, *First Freedom: The Responses of Alabama's Blacks to Emancipation and Reconstruction* (Westport, Conn., 1972), p. 175; Alrutheus A. Taylor, "Negro Congressmen, A Generation After," *JNH* 7 (1922): 127–71.
2. Mobile *Daily Register,* May 28, 1876.
3. Willard Warner to Carl Schurz, May 1, 1876, Schurz Papers.
4. *Marion Commonwealth,* August 3, 1876.
5. Montgomery *Daily Advertiser,* September 16, 1876.
6. *Alabama State Journal,* September 21, 1876.
7. Ibid., September 19, 1876.
8. Ibid., October 8, 1876.
9. *Wilcox Vindicator,* November 1, 1876.
10. United States, Congress, *Senate Reports,* 45th Cong., 2d sess., vol. 1, no. 714 (1877): 161, 256.
11. Haralson testified before the Senate concerning the incident. Ibid., pp. 169, 170.
12. *Republican Sentinel and Hayneville Times,* October 5, 1878.
13. John Sherman to Rutherford B. Hayes, May 15, 1878, RDT-CIR.
14. William C. Bradley to Rutherford Hayes, May 21, 1878, RDT-CIR.
15. R. H. Powell to Rutherford B. Hayes, October 12, 1877, RDT-CIR.
16. Rutherford Hayes to John Sherman, May 22, 1878, RDT-CIR.

17. Henry King, "A Year of the Exodus in Kansas," *Scribner's Monthly* 20 (June 1880): 11–20, 217. There is no adequate study of the 1879 exodus. A recent book on the subject castigates so-called representative colored men (including a fictitious Alabama Congressman "John H. Rainey") as "unswervingly conservative and often anti-Black," but fails even to mention many leading blacks, like Rapier, who vigorously supported emigration. Nell Painter, *Exodusters* (New York, 1977), pp. 26, 27.

18. *Proceedings of the National Conference of Colored Men of the United States Held in Nashville* (Washington, D.C., 1879), p. 21.

19. Ibid., pp. 100, 101.

20. Quoted in the Union Springs *Herald*, May 12, 1879.

21. Montgomery *Daily Advertiser*, August 28, 1879.

22. Hayneville *Examiner*, n.d., quoted in ibid., September 30, 1879.

23. United States, Congress, *Senate Reports*, 46th Cong., 1st sess., vol. 8, no. 693 (1880): 466.

24. Ibid.

25. Ibid., pp. 468, 469.

26. Ibid., p. 782. He also testified that the public schools remained open only three months a year, concluding: "It is my opinion that you can not develop mentally or morally the colored children of the State, for at every branch and crossroads, he will find something to remind him [that] he is a negro." Ibid., p. 471.

27. Montgomery *Daily Advertiser*, April 7, 1880.

28. Ibid.

Chapter 13

Primary sources consulted (on politics) Sherman Papers; Rapier File (see section 2 of Bibliography); *Proceedings of the National Republican Convention* (1880) (see section 4 of Bibliography); (on Rapier's economic activities) Records of the Lowndes County [Alabama] Court, Mortgages, vols. XX, LL, QQ, 44, 48, 3D, VV, YY, ZZ; Records of the Wabaunsee County [Kansas] Court, Deeds, n.v. (1880); Records of the Montgomery County [Alabama] Court, Estates, vol. 5; (on patronage) *Records of the Department of the Treasury for Assessors and Collectors of Internal Revenue* (see section 2 of Bibliography); (on elections) *Official Returns for the State of Alabama* (see section 3 of Bibliography). Newspapers consulted include *The Advance, Alabama Beacon, Alabama Guide, Alabama Republican,* Chicago *Daily News, Times, Tribune, Choctaw Herald, Colored Citizen, Evening Mail,* Hayneville *Examiner, Home Ruler,* Huntsville *Gazette,* Mobile *Daily Register,* Montgomery *Daily Advertiser, National Union, People's Advocate,* Selma *Times, State Index,* Topeka *Tribune,* Washington *Bee.* Secondary sources consulted include De Santis, Going, Harris, Lewis, Meier (*Negro Thought*), Painter, Sherman, Wharton.

1. James Rapier to John Sherman, October 19, 1879, Sherman Papers.

2. Ibid.

3. Ibid.

4. Willard Warner to John Sherman, May 5, 1880, Sherman Papers.

5. Ibid.

6. Ibid.

7. Ibid., May 23, 1880.

8. George Cottin to George Tichenor, May 25, 1880, Sherman Papers.

9. Green B. Raum to James Rapier, May 4, 1882, printed in the Huntsville *Gazette*, May 20, 1882.

10. Willard Warner to John Sherman, July 26, 1880, February 1, 1881, Sherman Papers.

11. James Rapier to Green Raum, March 9, 1881; Rapier to Chester Arthur, May 31, 1882, Rapier File.

12. Hayneville *Examiner*, June 21, 1882.

Bibliography

1. Personal Papers

Abbott, Anderson. Papers. Metropolitan Central Library, Toronto, Ontario.

American Missionary Association. Papers. Amistad Research Center, Dillard University, New Orleans, Louisiana.

Avery, Catherine Pilcher. Papers. State Library and Archives, Nashville, Tennessee.

Blaine, James G. Papers. Library of Congress, Washington, D.C.

Bromberg, Frederick G. Papers. Library of Congress, Washington, D.C.

Chandler, William Eaton. Papers. Library of Congress, Washington, D.C.

Coffee, John. Papers. State Department of Archives and History, Montgomery, Alabama.

Colfax, Schuyler. Papers. Library of Congress, Washington, D.C.

Dawes, Henry. Papers. Library of Congress, Washington, D.C.

Foster, Ephriam. Papers. State Library and Archives, Nashville, Tennessee.

Houston, George Smith. Papers. State Department of Archives and History, Montgomery, Alabama.

Johnson, Andrew. Papers. Library of Congress, Washington, D.C.

King, William. Papers. Public Archives of Canada, Ottawa, Ontario.

Legislative Papers. Petitions. State Library and Archives, Nashville, Tennessee.

Lewis, David Peter. Papers. State Department of Archives and History, Montgomery, Alabama.

Lindsey, Robert. Papers. State Department of Archives and History, Montgomery, Alabama.

Napier, James. Papers. Fisk University, Nashville, Tennessee.

Parsons, Lewis E. Manuscripts. State Department of Archives and History, Montgomery, Alabama.

Parsons, Lewis E., Jr. Papers. State Department of Archives and History, Montgomery, Alabama.

Patton, Robert. Papers. State Department of Archives and History, Montgomery, Alabama.

Public Schools. Letters. Series E. Z. Public Archives of Ontario, Toronto, Ontario.

Rapier Family, Papers. Moorland-Spingarn Research Center, Howard University, Washington, D.C.

Rapier, James. Papers. Moorland-Spingarn Research Center, Howard University, Washington, D.C.

Rapier, John, Jr. Diary, 1856–1860. Moorland-Spingarn Research Center, Howard University, Washington, D.C.

Rapier, John, Jr. Notebook, 1856–1859. Moorland-Spingarn Research Center, Howard University, Washington, D.C.

Rapier, John, Jr. Autobiographical Notes. Moorland-Spingarn Research Center, Howard University, Washington, D.C.

Rutgers, Arend. Journal. In Arthur Garesche Francis Collection. Missouri State Historical Society, St. Louis, Missouri.

Schurz, Carl. Papers. Library of Congress, Washington, D.C.

Semple, Henry C. Papers. State Department of Archives and History, Montgomery, Alabama.

Sherman, John. Papers. Library of Congress, Washington, D.C.

Smith, William H. Papers. State Department of Archives and History, Montgomery, Alabama.

Stephens, Alexander. Papers. Library of Congress, Washington, D.C.

Strobach, Paul. Papers. Library of Congress, Washington, D.C.

Swayne, Wager. Papers. State Department of Archives and History, Montgomery, Alabama.

Thomas, James P. Autobiographical Reminiscences. Moorland-Spingarn Research Center, Howard University, Washington, D.C.

Thomas, James P. Miscellaneous Notes. Moorland-Spingarn Research Center, Howard University, Washington, D.C.

Thomas, James P. Letters. Moorland-Spingarn Research Center, Howard University, Washington, D.C.

Trumbull, Lyman. Papers. Library of Congress, Washington, D.C.

Wade, Benjamin. Papers. Library of Congress, Washington, D.C.
Wilson, Henry. Papers. Library of Congress, Washington, D.C.
Windom, William. Papers. Minnesota Historical Society, St. Paul, Minnesota.
Woodson, Carter. Papers. Library of Congress, Washington, D.C.

2. Government (in the National Archives, Washington, D.C.)

U.S. Attorney General. *Letters Received from United States Attorneys, District Judges, and other Federal Officials, Alabama, 1865-70*. RG 60.

U.S. Bureau of the Census. *Census of the United States: Population Schedules for Lauderdale County, Alabama, 1830-1880*.

U.S. Comptroller of the Currency. Commissioner's Correspondence. Freedmen's Savings and Trust Bank. RG 101.

U.S. Congress. House. "Contested Election: Jeremiah Haralson vs. Charles M. Shelley, 4th District, Alabama." *Committee on Elections*. H.R. 45A-F 10.4, 45th Cong., 1st sess., 1876.

————. "Contested Election: James T. Rapier vs. Jeremiah N. Williams, 2nd District, Alabama." *Committee on Elections*. H.R. 44A-F8.13, 44th Cong., 1st sess., December 31, 1874.

————. *Desk Copies of House Bills*. H.R. 43A-B5, 43d Cong., 1st sess., 1873-1875.

————. *Original House Bills*. H.R. 43A-B1, 43d Cong., 1st sess., 1873-1875.

U.S. Congress. Senate. *Papers Relating to Nominations to Civil and Military Positions in the United States Government by the Senate*. S. 43B-A5, 43d Cong., 2d sess., 1875.

U.S. Department of Justice. *Letters Received from United States Attorneys, District Judges, and other Federal Officials, Middle District of Alabama, 1870-1883*. RG 60.

————. *Southern District of Alabama, 1870-1883*. RG 60.

————. *Northern District of Alabama, 1870-1883*. RG 60.

————. *Letters Sent by U.S. Attorneys, District Judges and Other Federal Officials, Alabama, 1870-1873*. RG 60.

————. *Records Relating to the Appointment of Federal Judges, Marshalls and Attorneys, Alabama, 1873-77*. RG 60.

————. *Records Relating to the Appointment of Federal Judges, Marshalls and Attorneys, Alabama, 1877-81*. RG 60.

————. *Report of Criminal Prosecutions under the Enforcement Acts in Alabama, 1871-72*. RG 60.

U.S. Department of State. "Exhibition Register, 1873." In *Records of the Commissioners Representing the United States at the International Exposition at Vienna,* RG 43. *Liste der in Wien Anwesen den Mitglidieder und Fuction are der Auslandishen Regierungs-Commissionen.* Wien, 1873.

U.S. Department of the Treasury. *Applications for Assessors of Internal Revenue, Alabama, 2d District, 1865-1873.* RG 56.

U.S. Department of the Treasury. *Applications for Collectors.* Mobile, Alabama, 1843-1903. RG 56.

————. *Applications for Collectors of Internal Revenue. Alabama.* RG 56.

————. "Internal Revenue Application File of James T. Rapier." *General Records,* RG 56.

————. "Testimony of the Inquiry into the Affairs of the Office of Internal Revenue for the Second District of Alabama." November 2-4, 1871. Montgomery, Alabama. RG 56.

U.S. Department of War. *Records of the Bureau of Refugees, Freedmen, and Abandoned Lands, Complaint Book. Demopolis, Alabama.* 1866-68. RG 105.

————. *Complaint Book, Huntsville, Alabama, 1865-1868.* RG 105.

————. *Complaint Book, Mobile, Alabama, 1865-1868.* RG 105.

————. *Complaint Book, Montgomery, Alabama, 1866-67.* RG 105.

————. *Complaint Book, Selma, Alabama, 1865-68.* RG 105.

————. *Records of the Bureau of Refugees, Freedmen, and Abandoned Lands, Register of Complaints, Greenville, Alabama, 1867.* RG 105.

U.S. Surgeon General. "Medical Officers' File of John H. Rapier, Jr." *Records of the Adjutant General's Office,* RG 94.

3. Documents: State and National Government

Acts of the Eleventh Annual Session of the General Assembly of the State of Alabama. Tuscaloosa, 1830.

Acts of the First Biennial Session of the General Assembly of Alabama for 1848. Montgomery, 1848.

Acts of the General Assembly of Alabama Passed at the Session of 1874-75. Montgomery, 1875.

Acts of the General Assembly of Alabama Passed at the Session of 1876-77. Montgomery, 1877.

Acts of the General Assembly of Alabama Passed at the Session of 1878–79. Montgomery, 1879.

Acts of the Sixth Biennial Session of the General Assembly of Alabama. Montgomery, 1858.

Acts of the Seventh Biennial Session of the General Assembly of Alabama. Montgomery, 1860.

Acts Passed at the First Session of the Fourteenth General Assembly of the State of Tennessee. Knoxville, 1821.

Acts Passed at the Second Session of the Fourteenth General Assembly of the State of Tennessee. Knoxville, 1822.

Acts Passed at the First Session of the Fifteenth General Assembly of the State of Tennessee. Murfreesborough, 1823.

Acts Passed at the Extra Session of the Sixteenth General Assembly of the State of Tennessee. Knoxville, 1827.

Acts Passed at the First and Second Session of the Nineteenth General Assembly of the State of Tennessee. Nashville, 1832.

Acts Passed by the First Session of the Twenty-fourth General Assembly of the State of Tennessee. Murfreesborough, 1842.

Acts of the State of Tennessee Passed at the First Session of the Twenty-sixth General Assembly. Knoxville, 1846.

Acts of the State of Tennessee Passed at the First Session of the Twenty-eighth General Assembly. Nashville, 1850.

Acts Passed at the First Session of the Twenty-ninth General Assembly. Nashville, 1852.

Acts of the State of Tennessee Passed at the First Session of the Thirtieth General Assembly. Nashville, 1854.

Acts of the State of Tennessee Passed at the First Session of the Thirty-first General Assembly. Nashville, 1856.

Biographical Dictionary of the American Congress 1774–1927. Washington, D.C.: Government Printing Office. 1928.

Canada Board of Registration and Statistics. *Census of the Canadas, 1851–52.* 2 vols. Quebec, 1855.

———. *Census of the Canadas, 1860–61.* Vols. 1 and 2. Quebec, 1864.

Canadian Department of Agriculture, *Census of Canada, 1870–71.* Vols. 1–5. Ottawa, 1873.

Code of Alabama. Compiled by Henry C. Semple. Montgomery, 1852.

Congressional Directory. Compiled by Ben Perley Poore. Washington, D.C.: Government Printing Office, 1873.

Digest of the Laws of the State of Alabama. Compiled by Harry Toulmin. New York, 1823.

Digest of the Laws of the State of Alabama Containing All the Statutes. Philadelphia, 1833.

Davidson County, Tennessee, 1850 Census. Transcribed by Deane Porch. Fort Worth: American Reference Publishers, 1969.

Journal of the Constitutional Convention of the State of Alabama. Montgomery, 1875.

Journal of the House of Representatives of the State of Alabama. Montgomery, 1865–1875.

Journal of the Senate of the State of Alabama. Montgomery, 1865–1875.

Official Journal of the Constitutional Convention of the State of Alabama. Montgomery, 1868.

Private Acts Passed at the Called Session of the Nineteenth General Assembly of the State of Tennessee. Nashville, 1832.

Public Acts Passed at the First Session of the Twentieth General Assembly of the State of Tennessee. Nashville, 1833.

Public Acts Passed at the First Session of the Twenty-first Session of the General Assembly of the State of Tennessee. Nashville, 1840.

State of Alabama. Office of Secretary of State. *Lauderdale County Census, 1866.* Schedule No. 2, *Colored Population.* State Department of Archives and History, Montgomery, Alabama.

State of Alabama. Office of Secretary of State. *Official Returns of Election of Delegates of Constitutional Convention, 1867.* State Department of Archives and History, Montgomery, Alabama.

State of Alabama. Office of Secretary of State. *Official Returns of Elections of State Officers and Congressional Election Returns 1868–1882.* State Department of Archives and History, Montgomery, Alabama.

United States Census Office. *Aggregate Amount of Persons within the United States in 1810.* Washington, D.C.: Government Printing Office, 1811.

United States Census Office. *Census for 1820.* Washington, D.C., 1821.

United States Census Office. *Abstract of the Returns of the Fifth Census.* Washington, D.C., 1832.

United States Census Office. *Compendium of the Enumeration of*

the Inhabitants and Statistics of the United States. Washington,
D.C., 1841.

United States Census Office. *Fifth Census or Enumeration of the
Inhabitants of the United States.* Washington, D.C., 1832.

United States Census Office. *Sixth Census or Enumeration of the
Inhabitants of the United States.* Washington, D.C., 1841.

United States Census Office. *Sixth Census of the United States,*
vol. 4. Population Schedules for Lauderdale County, Alabama.
1840.

United States Census Office. *Seventh Census of the United States.*
Washington, D.C.: Government Printing Office, 1853.

United States Census Office. *The Eighth Census of the United
States.* Washington, D.C.: Government Printing Office, 1864.

United States Census Office. *Free Inhabitants of the City of
Nashville, 1840, 1850, 1860.* Microfilm. State Library and Archives, Nashville, Tennessee.

U.S. Congress. Affairs in Alabama. *House Reports.* 43d Cong.,
2d sess., vol. 6, no. 262, 1875.

———. Alabama Elections of 1874–76. *Senate Reports.* 44th
Cong., 2d sess., vol. 1, no. 704, 1877.

———. Annual Report for the Assistant Commissioners of Freedmen's Bureau for Alabama. *Senate Executive Documents.* 39th
Cong., 2d sess., vol. 1, no. 6, October 31, 1866.

———. Articles of Impeachment against the Honorable Richard
Busteed, Judge of the District Court of the United States, Alabama. *House Miscellaneous Documents.* 43d Cong., 1st sess.,
vol. 1, no. 109, February 2, 1874.

———. *Congressional Record.* 43d Cong., 1st and 2d sess.,
1874–75.

———. *House Executive Documents,* 40th Cong., 2d sess., vol. 1,
no. 1, 1868.

———. *House Journal.* 43d Cong., 1st and 2d sess., 1874–75.

———. Impeachment of Judge Busteed. *House Reports.* 43d Cong.,
1st sess., vol. 1, no. 773, June 20, 1874.

———. Joint Select Committee to Inquire into the Conditions of
Affairs in the Late Insurrectionary States. *Senate Reports.* 42d
Cong., 2d sess., vols. 1–4, 1872.

———. Letter from Clifton B. Fisk to War Department. *House
Executive Documents.* 39th Cong., 1st sess., no. 69, July 24, 1865.

———. Memorial from Negro National Labor Union. *Senate*

Miscellaneous Documents. 41st Cong., 2d sess., vol. 1, no. 8, December 6, 1869.

———. Memorial of a Committee of the National Labor Convention. *Senate Miscellaneous Documents.* 41st Cong., 3d sess., vol. 1, no. 25, January 19, 1871.

———. A Memorial of a Convention of Colored Citizens Assembled in the City of Montgomery, Alabama. *House Executive Documents.* 43d Cong., 2d sess., vol. 1, no. 46, December 2, 1874.

———. Negro Exodus from the Southern States. *Senate Reports.* 46th Cong., 1st–2d sess., vols. 7–9, no. 693, 1879–80.

———. *Report of the Joint Committee on Reconstruction.* 39th Cong., 2d sess., Part 3, 1866.

———. U.S. Troops in Alabama. *House Executive Documents.* 43d Cong., 2d sess., vol. 15, no. 110, January 19, 1875.

U.S. Dept. of Commerce. Bureau of the Census. *Heads of Families at the First Census of the United States Taken in the Year 1790.* Washington, D.C.: Government Printing Office, 1908.

———. Bureau of the Census. *Negro Population 1790–1915.* Washington, D.C.: Government Printing Office, 1910.

———. Bureau of Foreign and Domestic Commerce. International Fairs and Expositions. Washington, D.C.: Government Printing Office, 1929.

4. Proceedings and Reports

Alabama Official and Statistical Register. Montgomery, 1903.

Alvord, John. *Semi-Annual Reports on Schools and Finances of Freedmen.* Vols. 1–10. Washington, D.C., 1866–70.

The American Annual Cyclopedia and Register of Important Events for 1865. Vol. 18. New York: D. Appleton and Co., 1866.

Annual Report of the American Missionary Association. New York, 1865–75.

"Buxton Session Book, 1850–80." Kent Museum, Chatham, Ontario.

Catalogue of Officers and Students of the University of Michigan with a Statement of the Course of Instruction in Various Departments for 1864. Ann Arbor: University of Michigan, 1864.

Circular and Announcement of the Seventeenth Session of the Medical Department of the Iowa State University. Keokuk: Iowa University, 1864.

on (Selma, Dallas Co.). 1883.
ist (Negro. Mobile, Alabama). 1865–69.
tional Era (Negro. Washington, D.C.). 1870–74.
uskegee, Macon Co.). 1873–74.
ge. 1894.
Times. 1863–83.
amian and Times (Tuscumbia, Colbert Co.). 1867–7...
Herald (St. Paul, Minnesota). 1857.
tain Home (Talladega, Talladega Co.). 1872, 1874.
e's Advocate (Negro. Alexandria, Virginia). 1880–83...
Freedman (Chatham, Ontario). 1855.
nstructionist (Tuscaloosa, Tuscaloosa Co.). 1868.
an Sentinel (Negro. Montgomery, Alabama). 1872.
an Sentinel and Hayneville Times (Negro. Montgomery, *ma*). 1878.
an Union Advocate (Selma, Dallas Co.). 1874.
Record. 1873–74.
is Globe-Democrat. 1895–1913.
is Post-Dispatch. 1879.
l Times. 1858.
Republican. 1874.
Weekly Messenger. 1867.
Weekly Times. 1869–72, 1880.
entinel (Washington, D.C.). 1873–75.
y County Guide. 1870–74.
hern Advertiser (Troy, Pike Co.). 1867–68.
hern Advocate (Huntsville, Madison Co.). 1825–26.
hern Aegis (Ashville, St. Clair Co.). 1874.
hern Argus (Selma, Dallas Co.). 1869–74.
thern Republican (Demopolis, Marengo Co.). 1869–71.
e Spectator (Northport, Tuscaloosa Co.). 1872.
e State Index (Selma, Dallas Co.). 1880–83.
e Sun (Talladega, Talladega Co.). 1869–71.
nday Herald and Weekly National Intelligencer (Washington, D.C.) 1873–75.
alladega Watch-Tower. 1870, 1872.
ennessee Gazette (Nashville, Tennessee). 1815–21.
opeka Tribune. 1880–85.
oronto Globe. 1855.
The Tri-Weekly Era and Whig (Opelika, Lee Co.). 1870.

Fourth Annual Report of the Directors of the Elgin Association. Toronto, 1853.

Hodgson, Joseph, ed. *The Alabama Manual and Statistical Register.* Montgomery, 1869.

List of Southern Union Loyalists 1861–1865. Washington, D.C.: Government Printing Office, 1873.

Minutes and Proceedings of the General Convention for the Improvement of the Colored Inhabitants of Canada, June 16, 17, 1853. Windsor C. W., 1853.

Officers and Students of the University of Michigan with a Statement of the Course of Instruction in the Various Departments for 1864. Ann Arbor, 1864.

Proceedings of the Colored National Labor Convention Held in Washington, D.C., December 6–10, 1869. Washington, D.C., 1869.

Proceedings of the Liberal Republican Convention in Cincinnati, May 1st, 2d, 3d, 1872. New York, 1872.

Proceedings of the National Convention of the Colored Men of America Held in Washington, D.C., January 13–16, 1869. Washington, D.C., 1869.

Proceedings of the National Conference of Colored Men of the United States Held in Nashville, Tennessee, May 6–9, 1879. Washington, D.C., 1879.

Proceedings of the Republican National Convention Held at Chicago, Illinois, June 3–9, 1880. Chicago, 1881.

Proceedings of the Republican State Convention Held in Montgomery, July 4, 1878. Montgomery, Ala., 1878.

Republican Campaign Text Book for 1878. Washington, D.C.: Republican Congressional Committee, 1878.

Speech of Governor Lewis P. Parsons to Citizens of Mobile, January 30, 1868. State Department of Archives and History, Montgomery, Alabama.

Thurston, Robert., ed. *Reports of the Commissioner of the United States to the Vienna International Exhibition in 1873.* 4 vols. Washington, D.C.: Government Printing Office, 1876.

5. Newspapers and Magazines

The Advance (Negro. Montgomery). 1880, 1881.
The Advance (Montgomery). 1870–72.
Alabama Beacon (Greensboro, Hale, Co.). 1870, 1874–76, 1880–84.
Alabama Guide (Negro. Montgomery). 1884.

Alabama Republican (Huntsville, Madison, Co.). 1818–22.
Alabama Republican (Negro. Montgomery). 1880.
Alabama State Journal (Montgomery). 1868, 1869–76.
American Missionary Magazine. 1866–75.
The Anti-Slavery Reporter (London, England). 1852–62.
Athens *Post.* 1865–68.
Autauga *Citizen.* 1869–70.
Baltimore *American.* 1864.
Baltimore *Sun.* 1864.
Barbour County *Times and News.* 1868–73.
Blanton Springs *Herald.* 1871–74.
Bluff City *Times* (Eufaula, Barbour Co.). 1869–72.
The Capitol (Washington, D.C.). 1874.
Charleston *News and Courier.* 1884.
Chicago *Daily News.* 1880.
Chicago *Times.* 1880.
Chicago *Tribune.* 1880.
Choctaw Herald. 1868–83.
The Cincinnati *Daily Commercial,* 1865.
Clark County Democrat. 1874–75.
The Colored Citizen (Negro. Washington, D.C.). 1871.
The Colored Citizen (Negro. Fort Scott, Topeka, Kansas). 1878–
    80.
Colored Tennessean (Negro. Nashville, Tenn.). 1865–66.
The Daily Critic (Washington, D.C.). 1873–74.
The Daily Globe (Washington, D.C.). 1873.
The Daily Intelligencer (Washington, D.C.). 1869.
The Daily Missouri Democrat. 1868.
The Daily Picayune (Montgomery). 1868.
The Daily State Sentinel (Montgomery). 1867–68.
Detroit *Tribune.* 1892.
Ecclesiastical and Missionary Record. 1849–62.
Elmore Republican. 1870–74.
Eufaula *Daily News.* 1872–73.
The Evening Mail (Selma, Dallas Co.). 1882.
Florence *Enquirer.* 1840.
Florence *Gazette.* 1825, 1827, 1846, 1858–60.
Florence *Journal.* 1865–70, 1871.
Florence *Register.* 1826, 1827.
Florence *Republican.* 1874.

Florence *Times-Journal.*
Forney's Sunday Chronic
The Franklin Enquirer. 18.
Georgetown *Courier.* 1874
Hayneville *Examiner.* 1880,
Henry County Register, 187
The Home Ruler (Camden,
Huntsville *Advocate.* 1866–74
Huntsville *Gazette* (Negro). 18.
The Impartial Review and C
    Tennessee). 1805–8.
The Iron Age (Birmingham, Ala
Jacksonville *Republican.* 1874.
The Literary Index (Florence, Lau
Marengo News-Journal. 1874–75.
Marion *Commonwealth.* 1871–74.
Minnesota Times (St. Paul, Minnes
Mobile *Daily Register.* 1865–80.
Mobile *Daily Tribune.* 1874.
Mobile *Republican.* 1870, 1872.
Monroe *Journal.* 1870.
Montgomery *Daily Advertiser.* 1865–8
Montgomery *Daily Mail.* 1865–69, 187(
Moulton *Advertiser.* 1867–70.
Moulton *Union.* 1867–68, 1870, 1872.
Nashville *Banner.* 1858.
Nashville *Clarion and Gazette.* 1800–22, 1
Nashville *Daily Gazette.* 1862, 1864–65.
Nashville *Daily Press and Times.* 1863–64,
Nashville *Daily Republican Banner.* 1841.
Nashville *Daily Times and True Union.* 1864
Nashville *Daily Union.* 1847.
Nashville *Dispatch.* 1864–65.
Nashville *Republican.* 1825, 1836.
Nashville *Republican Banner.* 1865–67.
Nashville *Union and America.* 1865–66.
Nashville *Whig.* 1812–26.
National Anti-Slavery Standard. 1852, 1856–62,
National Banner (Nashville, Tennessee). 1826.
National Republican (Washington, D.C.) 1872–75.

National Uni
The Nationa
The New N
The News (
New York *A*
New York *
North Alab*
Northern F
Our Moun
The Peop
Provincia
The Reco
Republic
Republic
Alaba
Republi
Russell
St. Lou
St. Lou
St. Pa
Selma
Selma
Selma
The S
Shelb
Sout
Sou
Sou
Sou
Sor
Th
Th
Tl
'S

Troy *Messenger*. 1869–74.
Tuscaloosa *Blade*. 1872–75.
Tuskegee *Weekly News*. 1874.
Union Springs *Herald and Times*. 1866–75.
The Voice of the Fugitive (Negro. Chatham, Ontario), 1852.
Washington *Bee*. 1882, 1883.
Washington *Chronicle*. 1869. 1870, 1871, 1874, 1875.
Washington *Evening Star*. 1869, 1871–75.
West Alabamian (Carrolton, Pickens Co.). 1870, 1872, 1874–75.
Wilcox Vindicator. 1876, 1877.
Working Man's Advocate (Montgomery, Alabama). 1877.

6. County Court Records

Assessment Books. Erie County, Buffalo, New York.
Assessment Rolls. Raleigh Township. Kent County, Ontario.
Land Deed Records. Albemarle County, Charlottesville, Virginia.
Land Deed Records. Davidson County, Nashville, Tennessee.
Land Deed Records. Erie County, Buffalo, New York.
Land Deed Records. Lauderdale County, Florence, Alabama.
Land Deed Records. St. Louis, Missouri.
Land Deed Records. Wabaunsee County, Alma, Kansas.
Marriage Records. St. Louis, Missouri.
Minute Books, Davidson County, Nashville, Tennessee.
Minutes of the Probate Court. Davidson County, Nashville, Tennessee.
Minutes of the Probate Court. Lauderdale County, Florence, Alabama.
Minutes of the Probate Court. Maury County, Columbia, Tennessee.
Minutes of the Probate Court. St. Louis, Missouri.
Mortgage Records. Montgomery County, Montgomery, Alabama.
Mortgage Records. Lowndes County, Hayneville, Alabama.
Tax Books. St. Louis, Missouri.
Tax Lists. Davidson County, State Library and Archives, Nashville, Tennessee.
Vital Statistics. Raleigh Township, Kent County, Ontario.
Will Books. Albemarle County, Charlottesville, Virginia.
Will Books. Lauderdale County, Florence, Alabama.
Wills and Inventories. Davidson County, Nashville, Tennessee.
Wills and Settlements. Maury County, Columbia, Tennessee.

7. City Statutes and Directories

Buffalo City Directory. Buffalo, N.Y., 1844.

Buffalo City Directory. Buffalo, N.Y., 1847–48.

Cambell and Richardson's St. Louis Business Directory. St. Louis, 1862–1874.

Edwards Annual Directory of the Inhabitants of St. Louis. St. Louis, 1859–1865.

Gould's St. Louis Directory. St. Louis, 1875–1913.

King's Nashville City Directory. Nashville, 1866.

Montgomery City Directory. Montgomery, Ala., 1880.

Nashville General Business Directory. Nashville, 1853.

Nashville Business Directory. Nashville, 1855.

Revised Laws of the City of Nashville. Nashville, 1850.

Revised Laws of the City of Nashville. Nashville, 1854.

Singleton's Nashville Business Directory for 1865. Nashville, 1865.

8. Secondary Sources

Alexander, Thomas. B. "Persistant Whiggery in the Confederate South, 1860–1877." *JSH* 27 (1961): 305–29.

———. "Persistent Whiggery in Alabama and the Lower South, 1860–1867." *AR* 12 (1959): 35–52.

Aptheker, Herbert. *A Documentary History of the Negro in the United States.* 2 vols. New York: Citadel Press, 1956.

———. *American Negro Slave Revolts.* New York: Columbia University Press, 1943.

Bardolph, Richard. *The Negro Vanguard.* New York: Vintage, 1958.

———. ed. *The Civil Rights Record: Black Americans and the Law, 1849–1970.* New York: Crowell Publishers, 1970.

Barnes, William H. *The American Government: History of the Forty-Third Congress.* Washington, D.C.: W. H. Barns, 1875.

Benedict, Michael Les. *The Impeachment Trial of Andrew Johnson.* New York: Norton and Co., 1973.

Bennett, Lerone Jr. *Before the Mayflower: A History of the Negro in America, 1619–1964.* Chicago: Johnson Publishing Co., 1966.

———. *Black Power U.S.A.: The Human Side of Reconstruction.* Chicago: Johnson Publishing Co., 1967.

Berlin, Ira. "The Structure of the Free Negro Cast in the Antebellum United States." *JSocH* 9 (1976): 297–318.

———. *Slaves Without Masters: The Free Negro in the Antebellum South.* New York: Pantheon Books, 1974.

Berry, Mary Frances. *Military Necessity and the Civil Rights Policy: Black Citizenship and the Constitution, 1861-1868.* Port Washington, New York: Kennikat Press, 1977.

Bethel, Elizabeth. "The Freedmen's Bureau in Alabama." *JSH* 14 (1948): 49–92.

Blaine, James G. *Twenty Years of Congress.* Norwich, Conn.: Henry Bill Publishing Co., 1893.

Blassingame, J. W. *Black New Orleans, 1860-1880.* Chicago: University of Chicago Press, 1973.

———. *The Slave Community: Plantation Life in the Ante-Bellum South.* New York: Oxford University Press, 1972.

Bond, Horace Mann. *Negro Education in Alabama: A Study in Cotton and Steel.* Washington, D.C.: Associated Publishers, 1939.

———. "Social and Economic Forces in Alabama Reconstruction." *JNH* 22 (1938): 290–348.

Brewer, Willis. *Alabama: Her History, Resources, War Record and Public Men, 1540-1872.* Montgomery: Barret and Brown, 1872.

Brittain, Joseph M. "Negro Suffrage and Politics in Alabama Since 1870." Ph.D. dissertation, University of Indiana, 1958.

Bromberg, Frederick G. "The Reconstruction Period in Alabama." Iberville Historical Society Papers. Nos. 3 and 4, 1905.

Brown, Letitia Woods. *Free Negroes in the District of Columbia: 1790-1846.* New York: Oxford University Press, 1972.

Cash, William M. "Alabama Republicans during Reconstruction: Personal Characteristics, Motivations, and Political Activity of Party Activists, 1867-1880." Ph.D. dissertation, University of Alabama, 1973.

Christopher, Maurine. *America's Black Congressmen.* New York: Thomas Crowell Co., 1971.

Clarmorgan, Cyprian. *The Colored Aristocracy of St. Louis.* St. Louis: n.p., 1858.

Clayton, W. W. *History of Davidson County, Tennessee.* Philadelphia: J. W. Lewis and Co., 1880.

Cobb, Henry E. "Negroes in Alabama during the Reconstruction Period, 1865-1875." Ph.D. dissertation, Temple University, 1952.

Cook, Marjorie H. "Restoration and Innovation: Alabamians Adjust to Defeat, 1865-1867." Ph.D. dissertation, University of Alabama, 1968.

Coulter, E. Merton. *The South During Reconstruction, 1865-1877.* Baton Rouge: Louisiana State University Press, 1947.

Cox, LaWanda and Cox, John. *Politics, Principle, and Prejudice, 1865-1866: Dilemma of Reconstruction America.* Glencoe, Ill.: Quadrangle Press, 1963.

Cruden, Robert. *The Negro in Reconstruction.* Englewood Cliffs, N. J.: Prentice Hall, 1969.

Current, Richard N., ed. *Reconstruction, 1865-1877.* Englewood Cliffs, N.J.: Prentice Hall, 1965.

Curry, Richard O. "The Civil War and Reconstruction, 1861-1877: A Critical Overview of Recent Trends and Interpretations." *CWH* 20 (1974): 215-38.

————, ed. *Radicalism, Racism, and Party Realignment: The Border States During Reconstruction.* Baltimore: Johns Hopkins University Press, 1969.

DeSantis, Vincent. *Republicans Face the Southern Question.* Baltimore: Johns Hopkins University Press, 1959.

Donald, David. *Charles Sumner and the Rights of Man.* New York: Alfred Knopf, 1970.

————. "The Scalawag in Mississippi Reconstruction." *JSH* 10 (1944): 447-60.

Dorman, Lewy. "The Free Negro in Alabama from 1819-1861." Master's thesis, University of Alabama, 1916.

Dorris, Jonathan T. *Pardon and Amnesty under Lincoln and Johnson.* Chapel Hill: University of North Carolina Press, 1953.

Douglass, Frederick. *Life and Times of Frederick Douglass.* Hartford, Conn.: Park Publishing Co., 1882.

DuBois, William E. B. *Black Reconstruction.* 1935. Reprint New York: Russell and Russell, 1962.

————. "Reconstruction and Its Benefits." *AHR* 15 (1910): 781-99.

DuBose, John W. *Alabama's Tragic Decade: 1865-1874.* Birmingham: Webb Book Co., 1940.

Dunning, William A. *Essays on the Civil War and Reconstruction.* New York: Macmillan Co., 1897.

————. *Reconstruction: Political and Economic, 1865-1877.* New York: Harper and Brothers, 1907.

England, J. Merton. "The Free Negro in Ante-Bellum Tennessee." *JSH* 9 (1943): 37-58.

————. "The Free Negro in Ante-Bellum Tennessee." Ph.D. dissertation, Vanderbilt University, 1941.

Enzor, Frankie C. "Walter Lynwood Fleming." *AHQ* 20 (1958): 636-46.

Fourth Annual Report of the Directors of the Elgin Association. Toronto, 1853.

Hodgson, Joseph, ed. *The Alabama Manual and Statistical Register.* Montgomery, 1869.

List of Southern Union Loyalists 1861-1865. Washington, D.C.: Government Printing Office, 1873.

Minutes and Proceedings of the General Convention for the Improvement of the Colored Inhabitants of Canada, June 16, 17, 1853. Windsor C. W., 1853.

Officers and Students of the University of Michigan with a Statement of the Course of Instruction in the Various Departments for 1864. Ann Arbor, 1864.

Proceedings of the Colored National Labor Convention Held in Washington, D.C., December 6-10, 1869. Washington, D.C., 1869.

Proceedings of the Liberal Republican Convention in Cincinnati, May 1st, 2d, 3d, 1872. New York, 1872.

Proceedings of the National Convention of the Colored Men of America Held in Washington, D.C., January 13-16, 1869. Washington, D.C., 1869.

Proceedings of the National Conference of Colored Men of the United States Held in Nashville, Tennessee, May 6-9, 1879. Washington, D.C., 1879.

Proceedings of the Republican National Convention Held at Chicago, Illinois, June 3-9, 1880. Chicago, 1881.

Proceedings of the Republican State Convention Held in Montgomery, July 4, 1878. Montgomery, Ala., 1878.

Republican Campaign Text Book for 1878. Washington, D.C.: Republican Congressional Committee, 1878.

Speech of Governor Lewis P. Parsons to Citizens of Mobile, January 30, 1868. State Department of Archives and History, Montgomery, Alabama.

Thurston, Robert., ed. *Reports of the Commissioner of the United States to the Vienna International Exhibition in 1873.* 4 vols. Washington, D.C.: Government Printing Office, 1876.

5. Newspapers and Magazines

The Advance (Negro. Montgomery). 1880, 1881.

The Advance (Montgomery). 1870-72.

Alabama Beacon (Greensboro, Hale, Co.). 1870, 1874-76, 1880-84.

Alabama Guide (Negro. Montgomery). 1884.

Alabama Republican (Huntsville, Madison, Co.). 1818–22.

Alabama Republican (Negro. Montgomery). 1880.

Alabama State Journal (Montgomery). 1868, 1869–76.

American Missionary Magazine. 1866–75.

The Anti-Slavery Reporter (London, England). 1852–62.

Athens *Post.* 1865–68.

Autauga *Citizen.* 1869–70.

Baltimore *American.* 1864.

Baltimore *Sun.* 1864.

Barbour County *Times and News.* 1868–73.

Blanton Springs *Herald.* 1871–74.

Bluff City *Times* (Eufaula, Barbour Co.). 1869–72.

The Capitol (Washington, D.C.). 1874.

Charleston *News and Courier.* 1884.

Chicago *Daily News.* 1880.

Chicago *Times.* 1880.

Chicago *Tribune.* 1880.

Choctaw Herald. 1868–83.

The Cincinnati *Daily Commercial,* 1865.

Clark County Democrat. 1874–75.

The Colored Citizen (Negro. Washington, D.C.). 1871.

The Colored Citizen (Negro. Fort Scott, Topeka, Kansas). 1878–80.

Colored Tennessean (Negro. Nashville, Tenn.). 1865–66.

The Daily Critic (Washington, D.C.). 1873–74.

The Daily Globe (Washington, D.C.). 1873.

The Daily Intelligencer (Washington, D.C.). 1869.

The Daily Missouri Democrat. 1868.

The Daily Picayune (Montgomery). 1868.

The Daily State Sentinel (Montgomery). 1867–68.

Detroit *Tribune.* 1892.

Ecclesiastical and Missionary Record. 1849–62.

Elmore Republican. 1870–74.

Eufaula *Daily News.* 1872–73.

The Evening Mail (Selma, Dallas Co.). 1882.

Florence *Enquirer.* 1840.

Florence *Gazette.* 1825, 1827, 1846, 1858–60.

Florence *Journal.* 1865–70, 1871.

Florence *Register.* 1826, 1827.

Florence *Republican.* 1874.

Florence *Times-Journal*. 1873–74.
Forney's Sunday Chronicle (Washington, D.C.). 1874.
The Franklin Enquirer. 1825.
Georgetown *Courier*. 1874.
Hayneville *Examiner*. 1880, 1883.
Henry County Register, 1873–78.
The Home Ruler (Camden, Wilcox Co.). 1881–84.
Huntsville *Advocate*. 1866–74.
Huntsville *Gazette* (Negro). 1879–85.
The Impartial Review and Cumberland Repository (Nashville, Tennessee). 1805–8.
The Iron Age (Birmingham, Alabama). 1874.
Jacksonville *Republican*. 1874.
The Literary Index (Florence, Lauderdale Co.). 1867–68.
Marengo News-Journal. 1874–75.
Marion *Commonwealth*. 1871–74.
Minnesota *Times* (St. Paul, Minnesota). 1856–57.
Mobile *Daily Register*. 1865–80.
Mobile *Daily Tribune*. 1874.
Mobile *Republican*. 1870, 1872.
Monroe Journal. 1870.
Montgomery *Daily Advertiser*. 1865–84.
Montgomery *Daily Mail*. 1865–69, 1870.
Moulton *Advertiser*. 1867–70.
Moulton *Union*. 1867–68, 1870, 1872.
Nashville *Banner*. 1858.
Nashville *Clarion and Gazette*. 1800–22, 1823–27.
Nashville *Daily Gazette*. 1862, 1864–65.
Nashville *Daily Press and Times*. 1863–64, 1868.
Nashville *Daily Republican Banner*. 1841.
Nashville *Daily Times and True Union*. 1864–65.
Nashville *Daily Union*. 1847.
Nashville *Dispatch*. 1864–65.
Nashville *Republican*. 1825, 1836.
Nashville *Republican Banner*. 1865–67.
Nashville *Union and America*. 1865–66.
Nashville *Whig*. 1812–26.
National Anti-Slavery Standard. 1852, 1856–62, 1869–70.
National Banner (Nashville, Tennessee). 1826.
National Republican (Washington, D.C.) 1872–75.

National Union (Selma, Dallas Co.). 1883.
The Nationalist (Negro. Mobile, Alabama). 1865–69.
The New National Era (Negro. Washington, D.C.). 1870–74.
The News (Tuskegee, Macon Co.). 1873–74.
New York *Age*. 1894.
New York *Times*. 1863–83.
North Alabamian and Times (Tuscumbia, Colbert Co.). 1867–72.
Northern Herald (St. Paul, Minnesota). 1857.
Our Mountain Home (Talladega, Talladega Co.). 1872, 1874.
The People's Advocate (Negro. Alexandria, Virginia). 1880–83.
Provincial Freedman (Chatham, Ontario). 1855.
The Reconstructionist (Tuscaloosa, Tuscaloosa Co.). 1868.
Republican Sentinel (Negro. Montgomery, Alabama). 1872.
Republican Sentinel and Hayneville Times (Negro. Montgomery, Alabama). 1878.
Republican Union Advocate (Selma, Dallas Co.). 1874.
Russell Record. 1873–74.
St. Louis Globe-Democrat. 1895–1913.
St. Louis *Post-Dispatch*. 1879.
St. Paul *Times*. 1858.
Selma *Republican*. 1874.
Selma *Weekly Messenger*. 1867.
Selma *Weekly Times*. 1869–72, 1880.
The Sentinel (Washington, D.C.). 1873–75.
Shelby County Guide. 1870–74.
Southern Advertiser (Troy, Pike Co.). 1867–68.
Southern Advocate (Huntsville, Madison Co.). 1825–26.
Southern Aegis (Ashville, St. Clair Co.). 1874.
Southern Argus (Selma, Dallas Co.). 1869–74.
Southern Republican (Demopolis, Marengo Co.). 1869–71.
The Spectator (Northport, Tuscaloosa Co.). 1872.
The State Index (Selma, Dallas Co.). 1880–83.
The Sun (Talladega, Talladega Co.). 1869–71.
Sunday Herald and Weekly National Intelligencer (Washington, D.C.) 1873–75.
Talladega *Watch-Tower*. 1870, 1872.
Tennessee Gazette (Nashville, Tennessee). 1815–21.
Topeka *Tribune*. 1880–85.
Toronto *Globe*. 1855.
The Tri-Weekly Era and Whig (Opelika, Lee Co.). 1870.

Troy *Messenger*. 1869–74.
Tuscaloosa *Blade*. 1872–75.
Tuskegee *Weekly News*. 1874.
Union Springs *Herald and Times*. 1866–75.
The Voice of the Fugitive (Negro. Chatham, Ontario), 1852.
Washington *Bee*. 1882, 1883.
Washington *Chronicle*. 1869. 1870, 1871, 1874, 1875.
Washington *Evening Star*. 1869, 1871–75.
West Alabamian (Carrolton, Pickens Co.). 1870, 1872, 1874–75.
Wilcox Vindicator. 1876, 1877.
Working Man's Advocate (Montgomery, Alabama). 1877.

6. County Court Records

Assessment Books. Erie County, Buffalo, New York.
Assessment Rolls. Raleigh Township. Kent County, Ontario.
Land Deed Records. Albemarle County, Charlottesville, Virginia.
Land Deed Records. Davidson County, Nashville, Tennessee.
Land Deed Records. Erie County, Buffalo, New York.
Land Deed Records. Lauderdale County, Florence, Alabama.
Land Deed Records. St. Louis, Missouri.
Land Deed Records. Wabaunsee County, Alma, Kansas.
Marriage Records. St. Louis, Missouri.
Minute Books, Davidson County, Nashville, Tennessee.
Minutes of the Probate Court. Davidson County, Nashville, Tennessee.
Minutes of the Probate Court. Lauderdale County, Florence, Alabama.
Minutes of the Probate Court. Maury County, Columbia, Tennessee.
Minutes of the Probate Court. St. Louis, Missouri.
Mortgage Records. Montgomery County, Montgomery, Alabama.
Mortgage Records. Lowndes County, Hayneville, Alabama.
Tax Books. St. Louis, Missouri.
Tax Lists. Davidson County, State Library and Archives, Nashville, Tennessee.
Vital Statistics. Raleigh Township, Kent County, Ontario.
Will Books. Albemarle County, Charlottesville, Virginia.
Will Books. Lauderdale County, Florence, Alabama.
Wills and Inventories. Davidson County, Nashville, Tennessee.
Wills and Settlements. Maury County, Columbia, Tennessee.

7. City Statutes and Directories

Buffalo City Directory. Buffalo, N.Y., 1844.

Buffalo City Directory. Buffalo, N.Y., 1847–48.

Cambell and Richardson's St. Louis Business Directory. St. Louis, 1862–1874.

Edwards Annual Directory of the Inhabitants of St. Louis. St. Louis, 1859–1865.

Gould's St. Louis Directory. St. Louis, 1875–1913.

King's Nashville City Directory. Nashville, 1866.

Montgomery City Directory. Montgomery, Ala., 1880.

Nashville General Business Directory. Nashville, 1853.

Nashville Business Directory. Nashville, 1855.

Revised Laws of the City of Nashville. Nashville, 1850.

Revised Laws of the City of Nashville. Nashville, 1854.

Singleton's Nashville Business Directory for 1865. Nashville, 1865.

8. Secondary Sources

Alexander, Thomas. B. "Persistant Whiggery in the Confederate South, 1860–1877." *JSH* 27 (1961): 305–29.

———. "Persistent Whiggery in Alabama and the Lower South, 1860–1867." *AR* 12 (1959): 35–52.

Aptheker, Herbert. *A Documentary History of the Negro in the United States.* 2 vols. New York: Citadel Press, 1956.

———. *American Negro Slave Revolts.* New York: Columbia University Press, 1943.

Bardolph, Richard. *The Negro Vanguard.* New York: Vintage, 1958.

———. ed. *The Civil Rights Record: Black Americans and the Law, 1849–1970.* New York: Crowell Publishers, 1970.

Barnes, William H. *The American Government: History of the Forty-Third Congress.* Washington, D.C.: W. H. Barns, 1875.

Benedict, Michael Les. *The Impeachment Trial of Andrew Johnson.* New York: Norton and Co., 1973.

Bennett, Lerone Jr. *Before the Mayflower: A History of the Negro in America, 1619–1964.* Chicago: Johnson Publishing Co., 1966.

———. *Black Power U.S.A.: The Human Side of Reconstruction.* Chicago: Johnson Publishing Co., 1967.

Berlin, Ira. "The Structure of the Free Negro Cast in the Antebellum United States." *JSocH* 9 (1976): 297–318.

———. *Slaves Without Masters: The Free Negro in the Antebellum South.* New York: Pantheon Books, 1974.

Berry, Mary Frances. *Military Necessity and the Civil Rights Policy: Black Citizenship and the Constitution, 1861-1868.* Port Washington, New York: Kennikat Press, 1977.

Bethel, Elizabeth. "The Freedmen's Bureau in Alabama." *JSH* 14 (1948): 49–92.

Blaine, James G. *Twenty Years of Congress.* Norwich, Conn.: Henry Bill Publishing Co., 1893.

Blassingame, J. W. *Black New Orleans, 1860-1880.* Chicago: University of Chicago Press, 1973.

————. *The Slave Community: Plantation Life in the Ante-Bellum South.* New York: Oxford University Press, 1972.

Bond, Horace Mann. *Negro Education in Alabama: A Study in Cotton and Steel.* Washington, D.C.: Associated Publishers, 1939.

————. "Social and Economic Forces in Alabama Reconstruction." *JNH* 22 (1938): 290–348.

Brewer, Willis. *Alabama: Her History, Resources, War Record and Public Men, 1540-1872.* Montgomery: Barret and Brown, 1872.

Brittain, Joseph M. "Negro Suffrage and Politics in Alabama Since 1870." Ph.D. dissertation, University of Indiana, 1958.

Bromberg, Frederick G. "The Reconstruction Period in Alabama." Iberville Historical Society Papers. Nos. 3 and 4, 1905.

Brown, Letitia Woods. *Free Negroes in the District of Columbia: 1790-1846.* New York: Oxford University Press, 1972.

Cash, William M. "Alabama Republicans during Reconstruction: Personal Characteristics, Motivations, and Political Activity of Party Activists, 1867-1880." Ph.D. dissertation, University of Alabama, 1973.

Christopher, Maurine. *America's Black Congressmen.* New York: Thomas Crowell Co., 1971.

Clarmorgan, Cyprian. *The Colored Aristocracy of St. Louis.* St. Louis: n.p., 1858.

Clayton, W. W. *History of Davidson County, Tennessee.* Philadelphia: J. W. Lewis and Co., 1880.

Cobb, Henry E. "Negroes in Alabama during the Reconstruction Period, 1865-1875." Ph.D. dissertation, Temple University, 1952.

Cook, Marjorie H. "Restoration and Innovation: Alabamians Adjust to Defeat, 1865-1867." Ph.D. dissertation, University of Alabama, 1968.

Coulter, E. Merton. *The South During Reconstruction, 1865-1877.* Baton Rouge: Louisiana State University Press, 1947.

Cox, LaWanda and Cox, John. *Politics, Principle, and Prejudice,
1865-1866: Dilemma of Reconstruction America*. Glencoe, Ill.:
Quadrangle Press, 1963.

Cruden, Robert. *The Negro in Reconstruction*. Englewood Cliffs,
N. J.: Prentice Hall, 1969.

Current, Richard N., ed. *Reconstruction, 1865-1877*. Englewood
Cliffs, N.J.: Prentice Hall, 1965.

Curry, Richard O. "The Civil War and Reconstruction, 1861–
1877: A Critical Overview of Recent Trends and Interpretations."
CWH 20 (1974): 215–38.

———, ed. *Radicalism, Racism, and Party Realignment: The
Border States During Reconstruction*. Baltimore: Johns Hopkins
University Press, 1969.

DeSantis, Vincent. *Republicans Face the Southern Question*. Baltimore: Johns Hopkins University Press, 1959.

Donald, David. *Charles Sumner and the Rights of Man*. New York:
Alfred Knopf, 1970.

———. "The Scalawag in Mississippi Reconstruction." *JSH* 10
(1944): 447–60.

Dorman, Lewy. "The Free Negro in Alabama from 1819–1861."
Master's thesis, University of Alabama, 1916.

Dorris, Jonathan T. *Pardon and Amnesty under Lincoln and
Johnson*. Chapel Hill: University of North Carolina Press, 1953.

Douglass, Frederick. *Life and Times of Frederick Douglass*. Hartford, Conn.: Park Publishing Co., 1882.

DuBois, William E. B. *Black Reconstruction*. 1935. Reprint New
York: Russell and Russell, 1962.

———. "Reconstruction and Its Benefits." *AHR* 15 (1910): 781–99.

DuBose, John W. *Alabama's Tragic Decade: 1865-1874*. Birmingham: Webb Book Co., 1940.

Dunning, William A. *Essays on the Civil War and Reconstruction*.
New York: Macmillan Co., 1897.

———. *Reconstruction: Political and Economic, 1865-1877*. New
York: Harper and Brothers, 1907.

England, J. Merton. "The Free Negro in Ante-Bellum Tennessee."
JSH 9 (1943): 37–58.

———. "The Free Negro in Ante-Bellum Tennessee." Ph.D. dissertation, Vanderbilt University, 1941.

Enzor, Frankie C. "Walter Lynwood Fleming." *AHQ* 20 (1958):
636–46.

Feldman, Eugene. *Black Power in Old Alabama: The Life and Stir-ring Times of James Rapier, Black Congressman from Alabama.* Chicago: Museum of African-American History, 1968.

———. "James T. Rapier, Negro Congressman from Alabama." *Phylon,* 19 (1958): 417–23.

Feldstein, Stanley, ed. *The Poisoned Tongue: A Documentary History of American Racism and Prejudice.* New York: Morrow and Co., 1972.

Fisher, Roger A. "Racial Segregation in Ante-Bellum New Orleans." *AHR* 64 (1969): 926–37.

Fitchett, Horace E. "The Origin and Growth of the Free Negro Population of Charleston, South Carolina." *JNH* 26 (1941): 421–37.

Fleming, Walter L. *The Civil War and Reconstruction in Alabama.* New York: Columbia University Press, 1905.

———. *Documentary History of Reconstruction.* 2 vols. Cleveland: A. H. Clark, 1906.

———. *The Sequel of Appomattox.* New Haven: Yale University Press, 1919.

———. *The Freedman's Savings Bank: A Chapter in the Economic History of the Negro Race.* Chapel Hill: University of North Carolina Press, 1927.

Fogel, Robert W. and Stanley Engerman. *Time on the Cross: The Economics of American Negro Slavery.* Boston: Little Brown and Co., 1974.

Folmsbee, Stanley and Robert E. Corlew, Enoch Mitchell. *Tennessee: A Short History.* Knoxville: University of Tennessee Press, 1969.

———. *History of Tennessee.* 4 vols. New York: Lewis Publishing Co., 1960.

Franklin, John Hope. *The Free Negro in North Carolina, 1790–1860.* Chapel Hill: University of North Carolina Press, 1943.

———. *From Slavery to Freedom.* 4th ed. New York: Alfred Knopf, 1974.

———. *Reconstruction After the Civil War.* Chicago: University of Chicago Press, 1961.

———. "Reconstruction and the Negro." In *New Frontiers of the American Reconstruction,* edited by Harold Hyman. Urbana, Ill.: University of Illinois Press, 1966.

Freeman, Thomas J. "The Life of James T. Rapier." Master's thesis,

Auburn University, 1959.

Frederickson, George M. *The Black Image in the White Mind.* New York: Harper and Row, 1971.

Garrett, Jill Knight. *A History of Florence, Alabama.* Columbia, Tenn.: Jill Knight Garrett, 1968.

———. *A History of Lauderdale County, Alabama.* Columbia, Tenn.: Jill Knight Garrett, 1964.

Garrett, William. *Reminiscences of Public Men in Alabama for Thirty Years.* Atlanta: Plantation Publishing Co., 1872.

Genovese, Eugene. *The Political Economy of Slavery.* New York: Vintage, 1967.

———. *Roll, Jordan, Roll: The World the Slaves Made.* New York: Pantheon Books, 1974.

Gillette, William. *The Right to Vote: Politics and the Passage of the Fifteenth Amendment.* Baltimore: Johns Hopkins University Press, 1965.

Godkin, E. L. "The Flight of Negroes." *Nation* 28 (1879): 242.

Going, Allen. *Bourbon Democracy in Alabama, 1874-1890.* University, Ala.: University of Alabama Press, 1951.

Green, Fletcher. "Walter Lynwood Fleming: Historian of Reconstruction." *JSH* 2 (1936): 497-521.

Green, James and Paul Worthman. "Black Workers in the New South, 1865-1896." In *Key Issues in the Afro-American Experience,* edited by Nathan Huggins, et al. New York: Harcourt Brace, 1971.

Guernsey, F. R. "The Negro Exodus." *International Review* 7 (1879): 373-90.

Gutman, Herbert. *The Black Family in Slavery and Freedom, 1750-1925.* New York: Alfred Knopf, 1976.

———. *Slavery and the Numbers Game: A Critique of Time on the Cross.* Urbana, Ill.: University of Illinois Press, 1975.

Hamer, Philip. *Tennessee: A History, 1673-1932.* 4 vols. New York: American Historical Society, 1933.

Harlan, Louis R. "Desegragation in New Orleans Public Schools During Reconstruction." *AHR* 67 (1962): 663-75.

Harris, Abram and Sterling Spero. *The Black Worker: The Negro and the Labor Movement.* New York: Columbia University Press, 1931.

Harris, A. M. *A Sketch of the Buxton Mission and the Elgin Settlement.* Raleigh, Canada: J. S. Wilson, 1866.

Haskins, James. *Pinckney Benton Steward Pinchback*. New York: Macmillan Co., 1973.

Hesseltine, W. B. "Confederate Leaders in Postwar Alabama." *AR* 4 (1951): 5–21.

Imes, William. "The Legal Status of Free Negroes and Slaves in Tennessee." *JNH* 4 (1919): 254–72.

Jackson, Luther Porter. *Free Negro Labor and Property Holding in Virginia, 1830–1860*. Washington, D.C.: Associated Publishers, 1942.

Jamieson, Annie Straith. *William King: Friend and Champion of Slaves*. Toronto: n.p., 1925.

Jordon, Winthrop. *White Over Black: American Attitudes Toward the Negro, 1550–1812*. Chapel Hill: University of North Carolina Press, 1968.

King, Henry. "A Year of the Exodus in Kansas." *Scribner's Monthly* 20 (1880): 211–18.

Klingman, Peter. *Josiah Walls: Florida's Black Congressman of Reconstruction*. Gainsville, Fla.: University of Florida Press, 1976.

Kolchin, Peter. *First Freedom: The Responses of Alabama Blacks to Emancipation and Reconstruction*. Westport, Conn.: Greenwood Press, 1972.

Lamson, Peggy. *The Glorious Failure: Black Congressman Robert Brown Elliott and the Reconstruction of South Carolina*. New York: W. W. Norton and Co., 1973.

Landon, Fred. "The Buxton Settlement in Canada." *JNH* 3 (1918): 360–68.

———. "Negro Colonization Schemes in Upper Canada Before 1860." *Transactions* (Royal Society of Canada) 23 (1929): 73–80.

———. "Social Conditions Among Negroes in Upper Canada." *Ontario Historical Society Papers* 22 (1925): 144–61.

Lewis, Elsie M. "The Political Mind of the Negro, 1865–1900." *JSH* 21 (1955): 189–202.

Litwack, Leon and Kenneth Stampp, editors. *Reconstruction: An Anthology of Revisionist Writings*. Baton Rouge: Louisiana State University Press, 1969.

Logan, Rayford. *The Betrayal of the Negro*. 1954. Reprint New York: Macmillan, 1965.

Lynch, John Roy. *The Facts of Reconstruction*. New York: Neale Publishing Co., 1913.

————. *Reminiscences of an Active Life*. Edited by John Hope Franklin. Chicago: University of Chicago Press, 1970.

McFeely, William. "Unfinished Business: The Freedmen's Bureau and Federal Action in Race Relations." In *Key Issues in the Afro-American Experience*, edited by Nathan Huggins et al, vol. 2. New York: Harcourt, 1971.

————. *Yankee Stepfather: General O. O. Howard and the Freedmen*. New Haven: Yale University Press, 1968.

McKitrick, Eric. *Andrew Johnson and Reconstruction*. Chicago: University of Chicago Press, 1960.

McMillan, Malcolm. *Constitutional Development in Alabama, 1798-1901*. Chapel Hill: University of North Carolina Press, 1955.

McPherson, Edward. *The Political History of the United States of America During the Period of Reconstruction*. Washington, D.C.: Philip and Solomons, 1871.

McPherson, James. *The Abolitionist Legacy: From Reconstruction to the NAACP*. Princeton: Princeton University Press, 1975.

————. *The Struggle for Equality*. Princeton: Princeton University Press, 1964.

Maddex, Jack Jr. *Virginia Conservatives, 1867-1879: A Study of Reconstruction Politics*. Chapel Hill: University of North Carolina Press, 1970.

Meier, August. "Comment on John Hope Franklin's Paper." In *New Frontiers of the American Reconstruction*, edited by Harold Hyman. Urbana, Ill.: University of Illinois Press, 1966.

————. *Negro Thought in America, 1880-1915*. Ann Arbor: University of Michigan Press, 1963.

Moore, Albert Burton. *History of Alabama and Her People*. Chicago: American Historical Society, 1927.

Moore, John Hebron. "Simon Gray, Riverman: A Slave Who Was Almost Free." *MVHR* 49 (1962): 472–84.

Muller, Philip. "Look Back Without Anger: A Reappraisal of William A. Dunning." *JAH* 61 (1974): 325–38.

Nugent, Walter T. K. *Money and American Society, 1865-1880*. New York: Free Press, 1968.

Osthaus, Carl. *Freedmen, Philanthropy, and Fraud: A History of the Freedmen's Savings Bank*. Urbana, Ill.: University of Illinois Press, 1976.

Owen, Thomas McAdory. *History of Alabama and Dictionary of*

Alabama Biography. 4 vols. Chicago: S. J. Clark Publishing Co., 1921.

Painter, Nell Irvin. *Exodusters: Black Migration to Kansas After Reconstruction.* New York: Alfred Knopf, 1977.

Patrick, Rembert. *The Reconstruction of the Nation.* New York: Oxford University Press, 1967.

Pease, Jane and William H. *Black Utopia: Negro Communal Experiments in America.* Madison: State Historical Society, 1963.

Peckham, Howard H. *The Making of the University of Michigan, 1817-1967.* Ann Arbor: University of Michigan Press, 1967.

Perman, Michael. *Reunion Without Compromise: The South and Reconstruction, 1865-1868.* London: Cambridge Press, 1973.

Rabinowitz, Howard N. "From Exclusion to Segregation: Southern Race Relations, 1865-1890." *JAH* 63 (1976): 325-50.

———. "Half a Loaf: The Shift from White to Black Teachers in the Negro Schools of the Urban South, 1865-1890." *JSH* 40 (1974): 565-94.

Rankin, David C. "The Origins of Black Leadership in New Orleans During Reconstruction." *JSH* 40 (1974): 417-40.

Rhodes, James Ford. *History of the United States from the Compromise of 1850.* 8 vols. New York: Macmillan Co., 1907.

Rhodes, Robert S. "The Registration of Voters and the Election of Delegates to the Reconstruction Convention in Alabama." *AR* 8 (1955): 119-42.

Robinson, Wilhelmena. *Historical Negro Biographies.* New York: Publishers Co., 1967.

Rogers, William Warren. *The One-Gallused Rebellion: Agrarianism in Alabama, 1865-1896.* Baton Rouge: Louisiana State University Press, 1970.

Rogers, William Warren and Robert David Ward. *August Reckoning: Jack Turner and Racism in Post-Civil War Alabama.* Baton Rouge: Louisiana State University Press, 1973.

Rose Willie Lee. *Rehearsal for Reconstruction: The Port Royal Experiment.* New York: Bobbs-Merrill, 1964.

Schweninger, Loren. "A Fugitive Negro in the Promised Land: James Rapier in Canada, 1856-1864." *Ontario History* 67 (1975): 91-104.

———. "A Slave Family in the Antebellum South." *JNH* 60 (1975): 29-44.

———. "The American Missionary Association and Northern

Philanthropy in Reconstruction Alabama." *AHQ* 32 (1970):
129–56.

––––––. "Black Citizenship and the Republican Party in Reconstruction Alabama." *AR* 29 (1976):83–103.

––––––. "Document: The Dilemma of a Free Negro in the Ante-
Bellum South." *JNH* 62 (1977): 283–88.

––––––. "The Free-Slave Phenomenon: James P. Thomas and the
Black Community in Ante-Bellum Nashville." *CWH* 22 (1976):
293–307.

––––––. "James Rapier and the Negro Labor Movement, 1869–
1872." *AR* 28 (1975): 185–201.

––––––. "John H. Rapier, Sr.: A Slave and Freedman in the Antebellum South." *CWH* 20 (1974): 23–34.

Sharkey, Robert. *Money, Class, and Party: An Economic Study of
the Civil War and Reconstruction.* Baltimore: Johns Hopkins
University Press, 1959.

Shaw, Wilfred, ed. *The University of Michigan: An Encyclopedic
Survey.* 2 vols. Ann Arbor: University of Michigan Press, 1951.

Sherman, John. *John Sherman's Recollections of Forty Years in the
House, Senate and Cabinet: An Autobiography.* 2 vols. Chicago:
Werner Co., 1895.

Simmons, Donald. "Negroes in Ontario from Early Times to 1970."
Ph.D. dissertation, University of Western Ontario, 1971.

Sloan, John. "The Ku Klux Klan and the Alabama Election of
1872." *AR* 18 (1965): 113–23.

Smith, Samuel. *The Negro in Congress, 1870–1901.* Chapel Hill:
University of North Carolina Press, 1940.

Somers, Robert. *The Southern States Since the War, 1870–71.*
Edited by Malcolm McMillan. 1871. Reprint University, Ala.:
University of Alabama Press, 1965.

Stampp, Kenneth. *The Era of Reconstruction, 1865–1877.* New
York: Vintage, 1965.

––––––. *The Peculiar Institution: Slavery in the Ante-Bellum South.*
New York: Vintage, 1956.

Stephenson, Wendell. "Some Pioneer Alabama Historians: Walter L. Fleming." *AR* 1 (1948): 261–78.

Sterkx, H. E. *The Free Negro in Antebellum Louisiana.* Rutherford,
N.J.: Fairleigh Dickinson University Press, 1972.

Swinney, E. "Enforcing the Fifteenth Amendment, 1870–1877."
JSH 28 (1962): 202–18.

Tanser, Henry. *The Settlement of Negroes in Kent County, On-*

tario. Chatham: A. Tanser, 1939.

Taylor, Alrutheus A. "Historians and Reconstruction." *JNH* 23 (1938): 16–34.

———. "Negro Congressmen a Generation After." *JNH* 7 (1922): 127–76.

———. *The Negro in Tennessee, 1865-1880*. Washington, D.C.: Associated Publishers, 1938.

Taylor, Joseph E. "The Colored National Labor Union, Its Birth and Demise, 1869–1872." Master's thesis, Howard University, 1959.

Thomas, James D., Jr. "The Alabama Constitutional Convention of 1867." Master's thesis, Auburn University, 1947.

Thornbrough, Emma Lou, ed. *Black Reconstructionists*. Englewood Cliffs, N.J.: Prentice Hall, 1972.

Toplin, Robert Brent. "Peter Still versus the Peculiar Institution." *CWH* 13 (1967): 340–49.

Trelease, Allen. *White Terror: The Ku Klux Klan Conspiracy and Southern Reconstruction*. New York: Harper and Row, 1971.

———. "Who Were the Scalawags?" *JSH* 29 (1963): 445–68.

Ullman, Victor. *Look to the North Star: A Life of William King*. Boston: Beacon Press, 1969.

Unger, Irwin. *The Greenback Era: A Social and Political History of American Finance, 1865-1879*. Princeton: Princeton University Press, 1964.

Uya, Okon Edet. *From Slavery to Public Service: Robert Smalls, 1839-1915*. New York: Oxford University Press, 1971.

Van Deusen, Glyndon. *Horace Greeley: Nineteenth-Century Crusader*. Philadelphia: University of Pennsylvania Press, 1953.

Vincent, Charles. *Black Legislators in Louisiana During Reconstruction*. Baton Rouge: Louisiana State University Press, 1976.

Wagandt, Charles. *The Mighty Revolution: Negro Emancipation in Maryland, 1862-1864*. Baltimore: Johns Hopkins University Press, 1964.

Ward, Samuel Ringgold. *Autobiography of a Fugitive Negro: His Anti-Slavery Labours in the United States, Canada, and England*. London: John Snow, 1855.

Weisberger, Bernard. "The Dark and Bloody Ground of Reconstruction Historiography." *JSH* 25 (1959): 427–47.

Wharton, Vernon. *The Negro in Mississippi, 1865-1890*. Chapel Hill: University of North Carolina Press, 1947.

Wikramanayake, Marina. *A World in Shadow: The Free Black in*

Antebellum South Carolina. Columbia, S.C.: University of South Carolina Press, 1973.

Williamson, Joel. *After Slavery: The Negro in South Carolina During Reconstruction, 1861-1877*. Chapel Hill: University of North Carolina Press, 1965.

Winks, Robin. *The Blacks in Canada: A History*. New Haven: Yale University Press, 1971.

Wish, Harvey. "Slave Insurrection Panic of 1856." *JSH* 5 (1939): 206-22.

Woodward, C. Vann. *The Burden of Southern History*. Baton Rouge: Louisiana State University Press, 1960.

Woolfolk [Wiggins], Sarah. "Five Men Called Scalawags." *AR* 17 (1964): 45-55.

———. "The Role of the Scalawag in Alabama Reconstruction." Ph.D. dissertation, Louisiana State University, 1965.

Work, Monroe N. "Some Negro Members of Reconstruction Conventions and Legislatures and of Congress." *JNH* 5 (1920): 63-119.

Index

Abbott, Dr. Anderson, 29
Africa, 22, 24, 73
Alabama: laws of, 15, 19–20, 42, 151;
court system of, 43; readmittance
to Union of, 67; constitution of
1865, 58, 85; constitution of 1868,
56–67; elections in, 66, 81–83, 106–
16, 146–47, 153–57, 166–71, 177;
violence in, 68–83, 133–50; Equal
Rights Association in, 133–34;
Republican factionalism in (see
Republican factionalism)
Alabama and Chattanooga Railroad,
76
Alabama State Journal, xix, 76
Alexander, Charles, 173
Alexander, John, 48
Alexander, Nathan, 158
Alvord, John, 85
American Colonization Society, 22,
24
American Missionary Association, 29
Applegate, Andrew, 57, 59, 60, 63
Apprenticeship, 42
Archduke Carl Hotel (Vienna,
Austria), 118
Arthur, Chester, 175, 178
Ash, William, 171, 172
Athens, Alabama, 54
Atkinson, Edward, 123
Auburn Agricultural and Mechanical
College, 149

Barber, Asa, 136
Barber: James P. Thomas as, 5, 6;

Henry K. Thomas as, 15; duties of,
16; income of, 16; John H. Rapier,
Sr., as, 16–18
Barnard, T. U., 48
Bates, W. B. Y., 97
Beckett, Dr. William, 28
Beecher, Henry Ward, 25
Bell, Hiram, 126
Bell, Jake, 69
Benham, V. M., 52
Berry, Lawrence, 48
Betts, H. W., 139, 140
Bibb, W. J., 79
Billings, Walter, 137
Bingham, Arthur: discounts impor-
tance of Alabama Labor Union, 92;
supports Charles Buckley for Con-
gress, 106; campaigns with Rapier,
115; attacks Rapier, 125, 204 n; in
Montgomery County politics, 138;
opposes Rapier, 144
Bingham, Daniel, 53, 58, 60–63
Black Belt, 48, 125; Rapier tours, 73;
snows in, 107; gerrymandering of
congressional districts in, 151
Black citizenship, 51, 98
Black codes, 41
Black enterprise, 4, 6–8, 14, 15, 21,
173
Black leaders: at Nashville Negro
Suffrage Convention, 38–39; at
Alabama constitutional conven-
tion, 56; in South, 57; at Columbia,
South Carolina, convention, 99; at
New Orleans convention, 107–8;

Specie payments, 122, 152
Speed, Joseph, 58, 61, 167
Spencer, George: opposition to
   William Smith, 75; supports Rapier
   for Assessor of Internal Revenue,
   94; opposes Willard Warner, 97;
   and Republican factionalism, 98;
   supports Rapier for Congress, 107;
   backs Rapier's Montgomery Port
   Bill, 125; as leader of Republican
   faction, 152
Spring Hill, Alabama, 145
Stanton, John C., 76
Stanwood, M. D., 101-3
States' rights, 126; and Liberal Re-
   publican party, 108, 111
Steele, Charles, 138
Stephens, Alexander, 125-26
Stevens, Thaddeus: views on Negro
   suffrage of, 38; Rapier's opinion of,
   42
Steward, Dr. James: against Negro
   suffrage, 46; represents Lauderdale
   County at Republican convention,
   53
Strange, Littleberry, 63
Stribling, Lewis, 48
Strobach, Paul: brings Klan under
   control, 105; campaigns with
   Rapier, 115; as leader of party
   faction, 138; mentioned, 178
Sumner, Charles, 73; views on Negro
   suffrage, 38; Rapier's view of, 42;
   death of, 128; memorial ceremony
   for, 129; Lamar's eulogy of, 129
Sumner civil rights bill, 130; dis-
   cussed by Alabama blacks, 133;
   Rapier's position on, 134
Sumter County, Alabama, 103
Sunrise-sunset laws, 168, 177
Swayne, Wager, 52

Taney, Chief Justice Robert B., 51
Tanner, J. T., 53
Taylor, Alrutheus A., xv
Tenant farmers: on Rapier's planta-
   tions, 41, 157, 173; condition of,
   84, 164-65

Tennessee laws governing emancipation of slaves, 4; circumvention of
   by Rapier-Thomas family, 4, 7;
   Nashville blacks' attitude toward,
   7-8; and white Tennesseans, 8;
   requiring free blacks to leave state,
   9; and status of Negro children at
   birth, 15
Tennessee Negro Suffrage Convention, 18-19, 38-39
Tennessee River, 2, 3, 29, 41
Tennessee Valley, 41; activities of
   Klan in, 70; newspapers of, 70
Thomas, Charles S. (white plantation
   owner), 1
Thomas, Henry K. (James Rapier's
   uncle): birth of, 1; youth of, 3;
   flees from the South, 4; settles in
   Buffalo, 4; as family man, 34;
   Rapier corresponds with, 72
Thomas, Henry (Limestone County
   Negro), 65
Thomas, James P. (James Rapier's
   uncle): birth of, 3; youth of, 4-5; as
   quasi-free slave, 4; education of, 5;
   hires out to Frank Parish, 5; estab-
   lishes barbershop, 5-6, 11; economic independence of, 8; views
   toward poor whites of, 9; emancipation of, 9; trip to New Orleans
   of, 11; visits Central America, 11-
   12; flees from South, 13; settles in
   Saint Louis, 14; amasses fortune,
   14; marries Antoinette Rutgers, 14;
   corresponds with John Rapier, Jr.,
   27; hears Rapier's political speech,
   68; transports Rapier's remains to
   Saint Louis, 178; death of, 14
Thomas, John (Charles S. Thomas's
   son), 1, 2
Thomas, Maria (James Rapier's aunt),
   34, 72
Thomas, O. O., 157, 173
Thomas, Sarah (James Rapier's
   cousin), 15, 29, 113
Thompson, Holland: as party leader,
   49; seeks Congressional nomination, 110, 113